# ADVENTURES IN
# REPUTATION

# ADVENTURES IN REPUTATION

*With an Essay on Some "New"*
*History and Historians*

BY

## WILBUR C. ABBOTT

FRANCIS LEE HIGGINSON PROFESSOR OF HISTORY IN
HARVARD UNIVERSITY

KENNIKAT PRESS/Port Washington, N.Y.

*In memory of*

W. W. G.

# PREFACE

THE success of an earlier volume, *Conflicts with Oblivion*, the correspondence to which it has given rise, and the demand for more such essays, has encouraged, perhaps unwarrantably, the publication of another series of like sort. As in the case of the former volume, some of these essays in reputation have appeared before, though for the most part in somewhat different form, and for permission to reprint such parts as have already been published, thanks are due to the Harvard University Press, to the Massachusetts Historical Society, the *Yale Review*, and the *Saturday Review of Literature*.

The concluding essay, *Some " New " History and Historians*, is included here for two reasons. The first is that a continuing demand for it from many sources has exhausted the supply of separate copies of it now in print, and the volume of the Reports of the Massachusetts Historical Society, where it appeared in its first form, is not always easily accessible to those who apparently are anxious to read it. The second reason is that history is, after all, not merely in itself a conflict with oblivion but is, in a sense, an adventure in reputation; and the form and spirit in which it is written are, in consequence, of importance to such an adventure.

Finally, the author takes this opportunity to thank not only those under whose auspices the material already published has appeared for their permission to use it here, but to those numerous correspondents, otherwise unknown to him, who have furnished him with information and suggestions in regard to the essays both in the former volume and in this.

W. C. A.

CAMBRIDGE, MASSACHUSETTS
May 9, 1935

# CONTENTS

# ILLUSTRATIONS

ADVENTURES IN
REPUTATION

LORD MACAULAY

*From a photograph*

# THOMAS BABINGTON MACAULAY:
## HISTORIAN

UNLESS all signs fail, the so-called "picturesque" school of historical writing is coming back into favor; and while that news may not cause a universal thrill, it will interest—it does interest—more persons than would have seemed possible twenty years ago. Its earlier manifestations we have seen in the form of "best-selling non-fiction," that ingenious phrase which reveals at once the reading habit of the modern world and the means by which it is tested. These first, but far from shy, harbingers of a new season of historical composition do not, indeed, inspire one with entire confidence in their portrayal of the past, nor with too sanguine hopes for the future of historiography, if it should follow on their lines. In the realm of historical writing they lean too much to the side of imagination, too little to the side of fact; yet to those who have struggled through the deserts of history as it has too often been written in the past half century, even these works offer some hopes of better things. Whatever their improprieties as biography, they are not, of course, properly speaking, history at all. But they recall dimly a day, two generations since, when the muse of history spoke a tongue all men could understand, and told them stories they were glad to read; a day when history was still reckoned a form of literature and still held the mirror up to life.

If this is true, if history is to take her place once more among the muses, without wholly abandoning the scientific society which she has kept so long and from which she has learned so much, we may have a revival of the old favorites. Once more Froude's magic may charm us all; once more Motley may make the heroism of the Netherlands alive; once more Green's pageant may attract spectators; and Parkman — who of them all has best survived the drought — may find new readers of his great epic. If that day comes, we may turn back to him once reckoned the greatest of them all, Thomas Babington Macaulay, the master of that noblest and most difficult of all forms of literary composition, the writing of history.

This is a fitting time. It is now almost precisely three-quarters of a century since Macaulay laid down the pen which brought him fame and fortune. Two generations as men reckon them have passed since his death; and in far truer sense than John Morley wrote, some forty years ago, it is now possible to say that " those of us who never knew him, nor ever saw him, may now think about his work with that perfect detachment which is impossible in the case of contemporaries." In so far he now belongs to the ages as much as Gibbon or Thucydides. It was not easy even for Morley to divest himself of all his prepossessions. It is easier for us, not only because we are farther removed from the controversies of the nineteenth century, but because we have the opinions of two generations of critics as well as of scholars to help us measure his achievement.

Even so, it is not easy to view his work with entire detachment. With his great countryman, Edward Gibbon, Macaulay occupies a place in the first rank of historians; yet between them is a profound difference. Gibbon's

theme is far removed from every-day affairs; its controversial passages are the concern only of scholars like himself, or of theologians; and in those higher altitudes few
men may come to blows. Macaulay's work is concerned
with matters still part of our lives and our opinions. Each
was a timely book; but Gibbon wrote of Rome's decline
and fall for those who saw about them, even as they read,
like symptoms of decay in their own land — popular
tumults, the break-up of old political connections, loss of
prestige and of empire. Macaulay wrote not of decline
and fall but of rise and progress, for an age flushed with
the triumph of parliamentary government and of industry, a new colonial empire and renewed prestige.

Each roused fierce controversy, Gibbon in the field of
faith, Macaulay in that of politics. The fires of religious
controversy which Gibbon fanned to flame have now
somewhat sunk, while those of politics have reached new
intensity; and though some may urge that Gibbon is the
better reading for such an age as ours, the issues which
Macaulay raised are more immediate and more controversial than even Gibbon's wider problem of the break-up
of society. Nor were their books more different than their
lives. Had Gibbon not written *The History of the Decline
and Fall of the Roman Empire*, he would now be forgotten,
or at best recalled as one of the petty placemen who bat-
tened on the state till Burke and his successors lopped off
their sinecures. Had he written nothing, Macaulay's life
would be a part of English history, for he was not merely
a man of letters but a statesman whose legislation is written in the statute-book.

Yet who could have foreseen his rise in politics? The
son of a merchant-philanthropist whose self-sacrificing
share in ending the slave-trade cost him his fortune but
gained him a memorial in Westminster Abbey; brought
up among those shrewd, prosperous friends of humanity
known as " the Clapham sect "; an infant phenomenon

who read at three, who at seven began an outline of world history, at eight wrote hymns, historical poems, and a missionary treatise — does this presage political eminence? Yet after preparation in a private school, and a career at Cambridge, some study of law and some writing, the Tory Lord Lyndhurst made him commissioner in bankruptcy, the Whig Lord Lansdowne gave him a seat in Parliament; and not long thereafter he became a member and presently secretary of the Board of Control of India. At thirty-four he was appointed to the Supreme Council at Calcutta; and he came back, still under forty, to become secretary at war with a seat in the cabinet. Where is there a like case in English history of rise so fast and far with so few advantages of wealth or birth? How did he manage it?

He rose by sheer ability and self-confidence, by his tongue and pen. He made his first speech at twenty-three before the Anti-Slavery Society. His first notable article, an essay on Milton, appeared in the *Edinburgh Review* when he was twenty-five; and the editor's remark, " The more I think, the less I can conceive where you picked up that style," has become the classic comment on the quality to which he owed success. His first speeches in Parliament, especially on Reform, gave him standing in politics, his capacity for business a place in administration.

He did not rise by mere intellectual ability; that is impossible in any form of government. Macaulay had none of Green's desire to " hide in his study and yet gain a quiet name." There was need of a world of men for him; and, from the first, he took the oldest of formulas for attracting attention — he attacked. Before he was thirty he challenged the Utilitarians, and maintained a single-handed conflict, not without success, against such formidable antagonists as John Stuart Mill and even the great Bentham himself. He was daunted by neither age nor reputation; and he possessed the essence of that fine flower of the English universities, the clever insolence which they prize perhaps too much.

He could say of one pamphleteer's lucubrations on the dangers to the church, that such opinions " had been abandoned by statesmen to aldermen, by aldermen to clergymen, by clergymen to old women, and by old women to Sir Harcourt Lees." His review of Croker's edition of Boswell, however well deserved, embittered Croker's life; it is said that the quarrel with Macaulay hastened Croker's death. He never hesitated to assert himself — and when he wrote his *History* its first word was " I." In him the Whigs found a doughty champion; they cheered him on; they gave him place and recognition, for he was worth their while. Yet at the moment when it seemed that, " new man " as he was, without wealth or birth, the highest post was not wholly beyond his grasp, he turned from politics to letters, and so, to many minds, would seem to have forsworn ambition. No one in like position ever made such a choice; even when it came John Morley's turn, he took the other path.

The reasons for that choice, however unusual, are fairly obvious. Macaulay was ambitious not alone for place and power but for immortality. That, he felt, lay not in politics but in literature, and at forty he could do what he liked best. He had come back from India with thirty thousand pounds saved from his salary; his uncle left him ten thousand more. He was thus at the point where, if ever, men write history, for it has been often observed no great history is ever written much before forty, and perhaps none without a competence. Like his first subject, Milton, Macaulay had long contemplated writing something which the world would not willingly let die; he had considered several such subjects; and, in a sense, the one he chose was determined for him by his life and his opinions.

He was a Whig.  He believed firmly in progress and in civil liberty, in parliamentary government, in material welfare, in toleration, in colonial empire and a vigorous foreign policy; and he naturally inclined to chronicle the events which brought those blessings on his countrymen. His long experience in politics confirmed his predilections, and his essays showed his bent — for what are they but an outline of the seventeenth and eighteenth centuries?  To these was added the great stimulus of that mass of notes collected by his friend Sir James Mackintosh, some fifty volumes of them, gathered from newsletters, French archives, the Stuart papers and like sources, which were put into his hands by Mackintosh's family after the death of that Whig oracle.  To them Macaulay owed much, yet to assume, as Croker did, that he owed everything and was ungrateful, does Macaulay double injury.  No one can read his tribute to those documents and their compiler, no one can read his *History* beside Mackintosh's fragment on the Revolution, without perceiving that Macaulay did what the case required, and that between the books is a great gulf fixed, a gulf not to be bridged by any mass of notes.

Nor was he, like many writers, a man of one book. Had he died at forty, he would still have been famous; for, beside a political career which many men might well have thought enough, he had established a new form of literature.  If, as he said, he did not " invent " the historical essay — which was Southey's task — he raised it to greatness and permanence as a literary form; and his " brief lives in the manner of Plutarch," as he called them, have found few rivals in any literature.  Moreover, he presently wrote poetry, and poetry which, if not great, was all but indistinguishable from greatness, and popular even beyond its quality.  " Every schoolboy knows — " No! few or no schoolboys now know what once were on every schoolboy's tongue — those *Lays of Ancient Rome.*

So, on three counts at least, he had some claim to be remembered, apart from his *History*.

What sort of man was this who set out on high adventure in quest of immortality? A short, square, solid man, ungainly in appearance, of great vigor and a strong constitution; " an emphatic, hottish, really forcible person," wrote Carlyle, " with a good, honest, oatmeal face." He had no wife, nor child, nor even a dog; he spent all his affection on his sisters and their families. He did not smoke nor drink — within the earlier meaning of that latter word. He did not hunt, nor shoot, nor fish, nor play any active game. He cared but little for the great outdoors; he was essentially a city man. He knew and cared little about painting or sculpture; and it is recorded that he never recognized but one tune, " The Campbells are coming " — if its stirring sounds may properly be called a tune.

Yet he was neither a recluse nor a misanthrope. He had a passion for his fellow-men; he loved society; he had a gift for friendship; he was almost absurdly charitable. He was lively and full of jokes and good stories, which amused even Queen Victoria; he was a most engaging companion; he enjoyed his food. But most of all he revelled in the now lost art of conversation. In an age when talk is all but confined to such noises as naturalists tell us that the so-called " lower " animals make about their food and shelter, the weather, their ailments and their neighbors, their work and play, or prey, or noise for its own sake, such high debate on the great problems of life and thought as Macaulay and his friends enjoyed seems hardly worth more than passing mention as one of the inexplicable foibles of our ancestors. To some who did not like him he appeared as the " tyrant of the table," or the " troubadour of the dining-rooms." Brougham described him as " absolutely renowned in society as the greatest bore that ever yet appeared " — but that was after Macaulay had achieved the impossible and talked Brougham down. Charles Sumner recognized his " magnificent attainments and power " but regretted that he did not show " some deference to others " — one suspects Charles Sumner among them. Yet though Greville said he " did not usurp conversation and revealed no assumption of superiority," the remark attributed to Sydney Smith perhaps reveals the truth. " Macaulay," he is reported to have said, " some day when I am dead, you will regret that you have never heard me say a word."

Friend and foe admitted his amazing fund of knowledge, his incredible memory — " a book in breeches," Sydney Smith declared, a literary-historical anthology. All agreed that, despite his poor delivery, he was one of the most popular and effective speakers who ever addressed the House of Commons. His transparent honesty, his strength of character, his solid judgment, were as well recognized as his positive opinions and his gift of expression. All respected, most admired, some detested him. Take him for all in all, as Mr. Gladstone said with that impeccable platitudinosity permitted only to great orators, " he was not like other men."

So this extraordinary man set out to write a history; and what did he propose? There are but three beginnings possible for a history — a generalization, a statement of fact, or one of purpose. He chose the last. " I purpose," he began, " to write the history of England from the accession of James the Second down to a time within the memory of men now living," the rise of England " from a state of ignominious vassalage . . . to the place of umpire among European powers."

Nor was this to be a mere paean of rejoicing. He proposed " to record disaster mixed with triumphs, and great national crimes and follies far more humiliating than any disaster " ; how " the system which effectually secured our liberties against kingly power gave birth to a new class of abuses from which absolute monarchies are exempt."

Finally, what should he include?

The history of our country during the past hundred and sixty years [he wrote] is eminently the history of physical, of moral, and of intellectual improvement. . . . It will be my endeavor to relate the history of the people as well as the history of the government, to trace the progress of useful and ornamental arts . . . the rise of religious sects . . . the changes of literary taste . . . to portray the manners of successive generations, and not to pass by . . . even the revolutions which have taken place in dress, furniture, repasts and public amusements.

Thus he stretched his canvas, mixed his colors, and outlined his great historical picture. It would involve, he estimated, between a dozen and twenty volumes in all. And how did he succeed in this large project? Philip Gilbert Hamerton once declared that no man can say how much he can accomplish in ten years. Just ten years from Macaulay's statement of his plan, the first two volumes of his *History* appeared. They covered the period to 1689 and not quite all of that. Six years later, the third and fourth took his story to 1697; and the last volume, issued posthumously and only in part revised, reached 1702. In the course of twenty years, he did a tenth of what he planned to do.

It was not all he did. While it was going on, he sat in Parliament; he held office; he wrote more essays and prepared them for publication; and he wrote the *Lays of Ancient Rome*. His judgment on the path to immortality was correct. On these writings his reputation rests; for who now recalls his speeches or state papers, able as they were; or his political activities? Something more than two thousand pages of his *History*; as many more of essays; a volume of addresses; and one of poetry — such was his life work. Measured by his own standard, it fell far short of his ambitions; measured by the work of others, it is in bulk what we expect of great historians. What of its qual-

ity, and of its reputation? Did it, despite its incomplete-
ness, set him where he hoped to be, among the immortals;
did he gain literary immortality by renunciation of political eminence?

To these questions there has usually been given one
answer, but there are, in fact, two very different replies.
With the public, the success of Macaulay's *History* is a
romance of letters. Edition after edition was hurried from
the press. The famous royalty check of twenty thousand
pounds from his enraptured publishers feebly represents
the popularity of a work which the whole world devoured
with incredible avidity. The story of the Australian squatter's shack which had three books, the Bible, Shakespeare,
and Macaulay, has become the classic anecdote to illustrate how widely he was read. But perhaps a better tale
is that which tells how on one occasion when he was
travelling in France his train was stopped by some con-
struction work being done by an English crew of navvies.
When they learned somehow that Macaulay was among
the passengers, they insisted on seeing him — and even
hearing him — and shaking his hand — and so revealed,
among other things, how far we have progressed since
mid-Victorian days. From every side poured in con-
gratulations and appreciation of his book. During his
lifetime, unquestionably, he felt repaid for all he gave up
for his *History*; it made him the leading literary figure in
the English-speaking world.

Amid this chorus of approval, the voices of his critics
were little heeded by the public in general, and even by
the author and his friends. Yet from the first there was a
strong note of dissatisfaction evident; and of his later volumes, *Blackwood's Magazine* declared that " everybody
reads, everybody admires, nobody believes " his *History*.
The *Athenaeum* remarked his splendid effects of " literary
gold and purple," but added with an acidity incomprehensible to-day, " We do not suppose that these forms of

rhetoric will reascend from the fish-stalls into our draw-
ing-rooms and literature."

What, then, of the fate of his great *History* since his
death? Macaulay's friends speak long and lovingly of
sales and editions, readers and royalties; but these are
no proof even of greatness, much less of immortality.
Macaulay's first essay was about a man who had some
twenty pounds for an immortal epic; and we are told on
good authority that books that live are seldom those one
lives by writing.

There is a better test than numbers of longevity; it is
the test of quality as revealed by taste and knowledge;
and, between these two, historians' reputations are in
parlous state. Macaulay would seem to have chosen the
feeblest of foundations for enduring fame. Half way between a science and an art, history has three potent
enemies — the finding of new facts, a changing taste in
style, and alteration in the spirit of the world. Works of
imagination, poems, novels, plays, suffer no loss by new
discoveries; scientific works have little style to lose; but
history, however great its style, may be displaced by new-
found documents. However unassailable its facts, its
style may make it, in time, all but unreadable; and a
change in men's outlook may make it distasteful to them.
Nevertheless, some histories survive, and must possess
some permanent qualities. What are they; what, in fact,
is history at all; and how did Macaulay meet its requirements?

" What is truth? " asked jesting Pilate, and paused for
an answer, which has not yet been given. " What is history? " asks the German historian, nor jests, nor pauses
for an answer. " History," he says, " is primarily a socio-
psychological science," and so fills many solid pages.
History, said Bolingbroke, is philosophy teaching by example. It is past politics, said Freeman; it is crystallized
rumor, said Carlyle. It is, says Croce, contemporary

thought about the past. It is, says one, a series of incidents or events which cannot be repeated at will; it is,
another says, the narrative of men's behavior, as groups
or individuals, under stress of circumstance. It is, declares a third, the record of human activities, affecting
and affected by environment. It is the " substance of
innumerable biographies " ; it is, says the cynic, " dead
gossip." It is, Macaulay declared, " a compound of
poetry and philosophy." But whatever definition you
may choose, it is apparent that what Macaulay wrote was
history; there only remains the question as to how he
wrote it.

The task of the historian is to make the past alive; to
find truth at the bottom of a thousand wells of documents,
to bring her to the surface, and to clothe her properly; for,
despite the proverb, most naked truth is as unlovely as
most human nakedness. And how shall that be done?
" It is," said Lord Bacon, " the true office of history to
represent events together with counsels, and to leave the
observations and conclusions to the liberty and faculty of
each man's judgment." On the contrary, said Napoleon,
" the historian is a judge who is the organ of posterity."
Upon that issue men still divide, but most of them side
with Napoleon. They read history not merely for a knowledge of the past — and we are all in some sort antiquarians — but for an interpretation of the present and a
guide to the future; and the commonest demand upon
historians is for judgment and for prophecy.

That demand, at least, Macaulay met perhaps almost
too fully. He was far from being what Lord Bacon and
the scientific school would have, a mere court reporter.
He was a judge — his enemies said he was an advocate —
and in this respect, he pleased the multitude. But, once
he had passed the limits of his generation, he faced severer tests; he had to meet the critics — and posterity. The
first reviewers laid down the lines of the assault, chiefly

in the field of style. The later critics' task was to assail his facts, his opinions, and his judgment. It was upon these last their fiercest attack was directed, and not without reason; for, whatever else Macaulay lacked, he was not wanting in the gifts of downright opinion, vigorous character and pungent expression, which make readers and enemies.

It was not with impunity that he could describe the seventeenth-century Highlanders in terms not inappropriate to the North American Indians, not forgetting their dirt, their vermin, and their itch. He could not hope to go scatheless from an account of seventeenth-century chaplains who combined with their religious functions those of a messenger, a gardener, or a groom, and for whom a waiting-woman, not always of spotless reputation, was reckoned a suitable helpmeet. He could expect nothing but abuse from Quakers or Tories in return for his right and left shots which brought down their less admirable qualities. No tribute which he paid to the virtues of these classes could atone for his reflections on their failings. He did not so expect, nor was he disappointed. Nor can one doubt that, as in his famous description of the Puritan ban on bear-baiting, his critics were inspired not merely by the discomfort of those whom he, they said, " maligned," but by the pleasure of his readers in his malignancy.

In consequence, three bodies of detractors have taken the field against him. The first were those who combed his books for small errors of fact — that Magdalen's famous trees were elms, not oaks; that Spencer Cowper had no " bag of gold," only six or eight guineas, more or less; that Talmash did not " claim " that he was led into a snare by Marlborough's treachery. The second group were those who objected to the spirit of his work and its sweeping generalizations. The third were those who resented his treatment of their heroes, based, they claimed,

on insufficient or garbled evidence, and a harsh, unsympa-
thetic judgment of their characters.

The first charge we may well admit at once. Historians, being human if they are true historians, are
liable, like all men, to the making of mistakes. The
second criticism is more difficult to discuss; and one case
may serve for all. Were country clergymen in the seventeenth century worse off than in the mid-nineteenth
century? Macaulay said they were, and backed his statement with the authority of Restoration dramatists and
eighteenth-century satirists and novelists, reinforced by
historians like Clarendon and Echard, and Heylin's *Life
of Laud*. His opponents challenged the testimony of the
imaginative writers as incompetent in history, and ad-
duced church writers, with contrary evidence from his
own authorities, on the other side.

There is no greater problem in our lives than this — to
draw correct conclusions on general conditions from conflicting evidence. We meet it every day. But, reading
the long clerical controversy through, one less concerned
with " the honour of the cloth," or with his own opinion,
is inclined to think that had Macaulay's phrase been less
pungent, had he even omitted that passage which he got
from Swift as to the reputation of the chaplain's wife
being sometimes a bit " blown upon," there is small
ground for such a great to-do; that, after all, he was not
far from right, no farther, at least, than most of his critics.

Within limits the same may be said of nearly every
controversy to which his *History* gave birth, even of that
most hotly contested issue of the case of William Penn.
It is a well-known story — how, after the Monmouth rebellion, various persons, including certain young girls of
Taunton, were condemned to be punished for walking in
a procession to welcome the rebel Duke, and how certain
maids of honour about the court solicited the government
through " Mr. Penne " for the privilege of collecting a

ransom for " the maids of Taunton " from their parents
to keep them out of jail. It is no less well known how
Macaulay identified this agent with the Quaker leader
and how bitterly that was denied by the Quakers. It is
difficult or even impossible to defend the historian's language about the Quaker hero — though it is scarcely less
difficult to justify Penn's course at a crisis of English history. But as to the charge that it was to him that the ransom letter was addressed, neither Macaulay nor his critics
nor any one to-day, without more definite evidence, can
have more than a moral conviction as to whether the
document in the case, the letter addressed to " Mr.
Penne," was intended for the Quaker leader or for his
namesake George. It probably was addressed to George;
it may have been addressed to William; but had George
been the Quaker and William the pardon-monger, who
can doubt the argument would be as vigorous — with the
parts reversed? Nor does the controversy lack a touch of
comedy; for it nowhere appears that anything ever came
of it. So far as we know, neither George nor William ever
moved in the matter; and so far, at least, they are equally
guiltless.

Here, as in virtually every other case, it is Macaulay's
positiveness, his assertiveness, his gift of vituperation,
rather than the evidence, which give rise to most of the
charges against him. He was a hanging judge; he often
weakened his case by over-stating it. He was a good
hater. He hated cant, hypocrisy and sham; he hated
treachery and cruelty and dishonesty; he hated injustice.
But above all, like Mr. F's aunt, he did hate a fool; and
he had a marvellous capacity for expressing his dislikes.
It has been said of him that the Revolution of 1688, sane,
sensible, satisfactory, bloodless, was peculiarly suited to a
genius which, like his, lacked passion. In the face of his
critics, the words seem out of place. " Those who have
lived through historical events as I have," wrote the his-

torian Mommsen, " begin to see that history is neither made nor written without love or hate "; and this, if anything, must be Macaulay's defence. He may have stressed his evidence at times to convict those whom he believed guilty; but he did not lack, nor did he manufacture, evidence. No less a scholar than Mark Pattison observed of his account of the Magdalen College case, with which Penn was also concerned, that Macaulay's " brilliance of style obscures the solid scholarship beneath " — a charge which one might wish were oftener levelled against scholarly historians.

Yet it is not historians proper who have found most fault with Macaulay; it is the men of letters, and the champions of individuals or classes or causes which came off badly at his hands. Bacon's biographer, Spedding, denounced his account of Bacon in terms worthy of Macaulay's own worst efforts. Carlyle joined Boswell's editor, Hill, in assailing him for his treatment of Johnson's biographer. Others have attacked him for his judgment of Horace Walpole and Warren Hastings; and Winston Churchill's genius for vituperation has exhausted itself — one hopes — in denouncing Macaulay's treatment of Marlborough. He voices the commonest grievance of that group which sneers at the historian's " omniscience " — but all of them, even Churchill, find it difficult, and many of them find it impossible, to dispute his facts. One almost suspects that some of his opponents have taken to heart at times that ancient dictum of the law, " If your case is weak abuse your opponent."

For, contrary to a widely accepted but wholly erroneous opinion, Macaulay made few statements without evidence to back them, and the tale of his researches is an amazing chronicle. To enormous reading and an incredible memory, to long experience in letters and affairs, to the tremendous accumulations of the Mackintosh papers, he added extraordinary industry in securing evidence. He visited the places he described; he ransacked libraries; he talked and wrote to antiquarians; he took endless notes. It was said of him, scarcely with exaggeration, that he would read twenty books to write a sentence and travel a hundred miles to write a line of description. Admitting all its faults, admitting that much new material has appeared, after two generations of such critical scrutiny as seldom falls to the lot of any work, his *History* remains astonishingly true, despite the fact that it is readable.

And it is more than readable; many books are that. It is one of the few works of its kind in reading which one may lose count of time. Yet admitting this, agreeing, if in nothing else, in that he was a master of historical narrative, in his lifetime critics pointed out that he wrote for masses caught by resounding phrases and dogmatic utterance; and that, in consequence of the spread of education to the lower classes, his fame would probably increase. It was a well-meant sneer, but not good prophecy; for it is probable that Macaulay's *History* is not as popular now as it was some forty years ago. The change seems to have come about the end of the last century. It was then noted that it was the older generation which appreciated him, the younger which found fault; that Sir James Stephen " could forgive him anything and was violently tempted to admire even his faults," while his son, Leslie, was one of Macaulay's most severe critics.

With this we come to the crux of the whole question, the test of an enduring history; and, more than that, the effect of the " progress of society " upon historical writing. This involves far more than changing taste in style; more than the problem of Macaulay's reputation; more than a reaction against what we call " Victorianism." It is a part of larger things; and these, in general, are three. The first is the changing temper of England.

Macaulay wrote in the full tide of the Victorian suc-

cess, strong, confident, robust, courageous, undisturbed
by doubts or fears. But with the close of the century,
English industrial supremacy declined; the old dominance of the upper and even of the upper middle classes
was challenged. It was not yet necessary for those classes
to fight for existence, but it seemed necessary to justify
that existence. Distrustful, fearful of the future, they
resented the aggressive confidence of the great Victorians; they deprecated the self-satisfaction of a more
assured generation. " Americans," said one of them,
complainingly, " are so self-confident." " Englishmen,"
retorted the American, " used to be." In that era of
doubt and disillusionment only one voice was raised in
the old strain, and that was out of India. When Kipling
came to England, he wrote the " Recessional."

But if all this affected Macaulay's reputation, the
second of these changes affected it still more. As reading
has spread over wider areas, it has, as it were, thinned;
while the pressure of life has been so greatly increased by
labor-saving devices that leisure has disappeared. The
" limit of attention " — that is, the length of time which
people can, or will, devote to anything but pure fiction —
has gone down. In a day when eye and ear do duty for
the mind; when history is told in pictures, and " visual
education " seeks to replace the lore of books; when moving-pictures and vaudeville and radio offer their attrac-
tions; in a world filled with the marvels of science, in
which great disasters and crimes and sporting events fill
the newspapers at the expense of more important things,
for obvious reasons, Macaulay's essays now surpass his
*History* in popularity — and, in America at least, there is
not now an editor who would consider publishing even
essays of such length.

Yet the third count is heaviest of all. Even as he wrote,
Macaulay's muse was changing her garments and language, if not her character. When, striving to rouse the

spirit of their people against Napoleon, German leaders established chairs of history, promoted the printing of the chronicles of the past, and trained youth to carry on historical research, a new age dawned for history. The *Monumenta Historica Germaniae* began to fill the shelves of libraries, and Niebuhr began to overshadow Gibbon. History became a means of educational discipline; archives were " discovered " and explored; and nothing was reckoned truly " historical " unless written from " unpublished materials." The phrase " historical scholar " replaced that of " historical writer," and both were called indiscriminately " historians." History tended to become an esoteric cult, forswore the world in cloistered " seminar," and, as economics was reckoned the " dismal," so history tended to become the dull science.

It was in many ways a salutary change. Rhetoric was replaced by reason; emotion by evidence; the " intuition of genius " by research; and the past was revealed in its true character. But not in its colors, true or false; for the devotees of such history were content with truth not only unadorned, but naked, bald, deprived of flesh and spirit, the very skeleton of truth. The result was beneficial to history as a science; it was all but fatal to history as a form of literature. If it was cleansed, it was also dulled, as the art of synthesis was overwhelmed by the science of analysis. What fate could a man like Macaulay hope for in a world like this? It was inevitable. Men wholly unacquainted with his period spoke of his " errors " and his " ignorance." Men who had never read his *History* were loud in its dispraise; for, obviously, if it were interesting, it could not be true.

The scholars were ably seconded by the philosophers. Men like Emerson and Arnold and Morley resented not only Macaulay's tricks of style, but still more his self-assertiveness, his optimistic realism. They desired more of subtlety, less practical philosophy; more mystery of life, of depths within and forces from without.  In their view, Macaulay's concept of man was too much that of the Happy Warrior.  He reflected too little on the eternities and immensities; he took too little interest in the submerged tenth.  Macaulay had none of the experiences which induce these qualities.  He was not long nor desperately poor; he was never ill.  He had little or no knowledge of German philosophy; he did not have strabismus, nor dyspepsia, nor *Weltschmerz*, nor a wife.  He did not go to Heidelberg or Göttingen, where he might conceivably have acquired some or all of these.  This is not satire; one may read it on the printed page.  And it is true.  Macaulay despised that type of mind enormously concerned with questions about which it is impossible to know anything, much less to do anything; and he has had his reward.

" A man of letters," says Morley, " in an age of battle and transition like our own, fades into an ever-deepening distance unless he has while he writes that touching and impressive quality — the presentiment of the eye, a feeling of the difficulties and interests that will engage and distract man on the morrow."  Beautifully and gracefully expressed, this voice, not of Victorian confidence but of Georgian doubt, is the form of criticism most difficult to meet.  Yet is it the business of history to delineate the shadows of coming events, or to tell sad stories of the deaths of future kings?  All great historians have been chroniclers of conflict — Herodotus with his Greek and Persian war; Thucydides with his Spartans and Athenians; Gibbon with his Romans and Teutons; Clarendon with his Cavaliers and Parliamentarians.  It may be that our history will change.  It may be that it will come to chronicle the struggles of men against nature, or ignorance or space.  It may be that the history of common men by common men for common men, the story of the eternal common things, will triumph over the story of uncommon

men and things, that the littleness of life will overpower
its greatness.   Yet, even so, ought not the trumpet rather
than the lute remain the instrument of historians?  Will
not the call to battle always rouse the spirit more than
the creak of the rocking-chair, or the pleasant sound of
the running water in the bath-room of the writer of
"social history"?

If it comes to that, Macaulay did not lack the sense of
"social history," for he wrote his famous third chapter,
which remains a model for all "social" historians.  But
to that he added another product of the imagination too
rare among social historians, the poetic gift.  He wrote
not merely the *Lays of Ancient Rome*, which his favorite
character "every schoolboy" once knew — and now
knows no more — but less well-known verses like that
haunting *Epitaph to a Jacobite*.

> To my true king I offered free from stain
> Courage and faith; vain faith and courage vain.
> For him I threw lands, honours, wealth, away,
> And one dear hope that was more prized than they.
>
> .    .    .    .    .    .    .    .    .    .
>
> Oh thou, whom chance leads to this nameless stone,
> From that proud country which was once mine own,
> By those white cliffs I never more must see,
> By that dear language which I spake like thee,
> Forget all feuds, and shed one English tear
> O'er English dust.   A broken heart lies here.

Though, doubtless, that will seem to some only another
piece of mawkish "mid-Victorian" sentiment, it still
must touch some hearts.

Each of us gets his effects in his own way, historians not
least.   Who can read unmoved that passage in Froude
which describes the falling fortunes of Wolsey?

If he could only see the divorce arranged, the King remarried, the
succession settled, and the laws and manners of the country reformed,
he would retire from the world and would serve God the remainder of

his days. To these few trifles he would confine himself — only to these; he was past sixty, he was weary of the world, his health was breaking, and he would limit his hopes to the execution of a work for which centuries imperfectly sufficed. It seemed as if he measured his stature by the lengthening shadow, as his sun made haste to its setting.

Who can forget Prescott's magnificent account of the march of Cortez upon Mexico with his little band of conquistadores — and Prescott among them, for who but a member of that company could have so described them, and who among them but Prescott? Who can forget Motley's story of the siege of Leyden, of the sufferings of the beleaguered garrison, of the fears of the besiegers, of the taunts of the royalists, " Go up to the tower, ye Beggars and tell us if ye can see the ocean coming over the dry land to your relief " ? Who can doubt that Motley was there to see the ocean crawling in upon the doomed Spaniards, the wild Zealanders harpooning the wretched fugitives, the quays lined with the famishing population welcoming its deliverers? Who can read that immortal funeral oration of Pericles which begins, " So they gave their bodies to the commonwealth and received, each for his own memory, praise that will never die," and ends, " for the whole earth is the sepulchre of famous men, and their story is not graven only on stone over their native earth, but lives on far away, without visible symbol, woven into the stuff of other men's lives " — who can read that passage and not realize that its author heard it, if not from the lips of its speaker, from the soul of Greece?

It is the same with all of them; with Gibbon who lived with the legions and the senators and the emperors; with Parkman who accompanied the voyageurs, the soldiers and the priests in their conquest of a Continent; with Macaulay, who stood among the crowds at the trial of the bishops, who saw the court and heard the arguments, who, when the acquittal came, shouted with the rest.

He stood among the throng which lined the way to welcome the coming of the Prince of Orange; he saw the army pass, the two hundred English gentlemen, each with his negro servant, the formidable Swedes in their black armor and fur coats, the no less formidable " whiskered infantry of Switzerland," the regiment of Ossory, men who " had repelled the fiery onset of the French on the field of Seneff, crossed swords with the infidels in the cause of Christendom on that great day when the siege of Vienna was raised." He rode by the side of the Prince in battle and sat with him in council; he listened to debates in Parliament, to arguments in the courts; he lived and moved and thought in the days which he described, as all the great historians have done.

And as each got his effects in his own way, so Macaulay achieved his own results in his. As Prescott and Parkman and Motley chronicled and described, as Froude lifted his prose to new heights by figures of speech, as Macaulay's hero Thucydides not merely brought before his readers such episodes as the sufferings of the disastrous expedition to Sicily, but made them see the fatal policy which led to it, and put that policy into the mouths of its framers, so Macaulay shared something of his great model. Yet with a difference, for he had not merely, like Thucydides, experienced something of all these things himself, he had evidence for what he said. He had been a lawyer, and he was able to describe procedure, evidence and argument as few men have done. He had been in Parliaments and councils and he knew what happened there. Many of his great passages read like orations; others like legal arguments; others like debates in the Commons; and still others like inspired journalism — which they were. Through them all run two great qualities and one which underlies them both. The first is eloquence; the second common-sense; the third imagination. But it is not imagination merely, not the free flight of fancy, but an imagination within the limits of the evidence, disciplined, controlled, and buttressed by the facts. This, in the last resolution of the case, is what makes great historians. Without it, history is a dead story of dead men; too much, and it is sounding brass and tinkling cymbal, dying with the last note of melody. It is the combination of the imagination and the evidence, with something of the lofty quality of the mind and soul beyond even these, which makes the great historian; and of this rare combination Macaulay had his share.

Against some of its foes his reputation can contend. But against how many and for how long? One of the latest books reveals the present objections to his work. " It cannot be said," observes this curt survey, " that his work is reliable; and while it has great and undoubted merits, his ' purple patches ' are on the whole rather irritating to the present-day reader."

Macaulay has, in short, suffered something of the fate of the subject of his first essay, John Milton, with whom he has so much in common. No one can read either without perceiving that each owed no small part of his charm to his wide reading, especially of the Bible and the classics from which each drew that depth of suggestion which makes them all but unmatched in English literature. Each elevates the mind; each makes us feel that men are better and nobler than perhaps they are; each rouses to achievement. Like the ballad of Chevy Chase to the Percy, their words stir like a trumpet. Each was a stylist and a moralist — whose style and morals are now out of date. Who now recalls a tithe of Milton's classical, or even Biblical, references? Who speaks of the phlogiston theory with a physicist, or of the philosopher's stone with a chemist? They are echoes of dead and far-off things, as obsolete as the passion for liberty, security of property, and an intelligence or a property test for the franchise. They are as dead as Milton's Puritan theology and Macaulay's Whiggish principles. So Macaulay's history like Milton's epic is little read; it is consigned to the limbo of " courses " in the schools; and the history consumed by the masses is produced by ignorant but entertaining journalists and novelists, or at best by compilers of text-books.

Yet as to every action, we are told, there is a reaction, so there may be reaction against reaction. Submerged beneath the dogmas of a generation which believed that history to be true must of necessity be dull, the suspicion gains ground that dulness is no proof of truth nor bad writing of profundity. Macaulay is undoubtedly coming back. Where Professor Gardiner once wrote that the *History* must all be done over again, Professor Firth observes, in editing it, that while that task " made some defects and omissions more apparent, it has increased, not diminished, my admiration for what Macaulay succeeded in doing," and suggests not re-writing but re-editing. Undergraduates take more pleasure in Macaulay than in their text-books, and his *History*, like his essays, still finds unemotional publishers to reprint it, " sixty years after."

With all the imposing terminology of the " new " history, it comes down to this — we have found new sources of information. All the machinery of " analysis " and " criticism," and even of " social history," was known to earlier historians. The rest is searching out the evidence and using what common-sense God gave us to interpret it, and not making the result a dumpheap of facts. It is only making the past live again in as nearly as possible the form in which it once existed — only that! And when historical " scientists " learn to write — if ever; when journalists and novelists learn some history — again, if ever; we may have history once more a part of literature; and when and if it is, it may be that Macaulay will come into his own again.

# LORD CHESTERFIELD:
## ARISTOCRAT

FAME, like life itself, has in it such great elements of chance that it would be a bold spirit who dared prophesy which of his contemporaries would be remembered, let us say, even a century hence, and for what qualities or achievements. If an Asiatic monarch's name is now preserved only in the word mausoleum, the memory of a French physician in nicotine and that of a French general in martinet; if quassia immortalizes a West Indian negro sorcerer, and poinsettia an American politician, what shall be said of one who was in his lifetime eminent as a privy councillor, ambassador, administrator, wit, statesman and orator, and whose title is now known to millions who never knew his name, and much less who he was, as merely a synonym for good manners, a variety of topcoat, a kind of couch or sofa — and now a cigarette? For such has been the fate of Philip Dormer Stanhope, fourth Earl of Chesterfield, some time a great figure in the world of politics and society, now to most men merely an adjective or at best a proper noun.

Doubtless in his pleasant, cynical way he would not be wholly displeased at even such an immortality, nor is it, all in all, entirely inappropriate. He was of the world, worldly; he was something of a philosopher; he desired,

LORD CHESTERFIELD

*From an early engraving*

like all men, to be remembered when he was gone; and he had a sense of humor. As his age and class recede into the past, his fame has in it, indeed, a touch of obsolescence he would not have liked so much, for in his day Lord Chesterfield was, in a peculiar sense, the glass of fashion, if not the mould of form. He was the incarnation of the eighteenth century. To many minds that period seems as alien and remote as the Middle Ages or the Judea of King Herod's time. With their Yule logs and minstrels, Three Kings and star of Bethlehem, its inns, stage-coaches and hearty gentlemen in riding-coats now share honors on our Christmas cards, as the Age of Enlightenment has grown romantic with the passage of the years. It was observed by a Victorian critic that " there is probably no epoch in our history with which we have so little in common as the first decades of the eighteenth century " — that is to say the era of Lord Chesterfield; and a learned volume has been written to demonstrate that even its philosophers, like Voltaire, Diderot and Hume, " were actually living in a mediaeval world," that their underlying conceptions " were still making allowance for certain alterations in the bias, the same as those of the thirteenth century."

Yet, viewed in the long perspective of human history, it was only yesterday. It was, indeed, akin to earlier ages, as it owed much to them, but with all its superficial differences, with all the changes wrought by science and invention, Lord Chesterfield's century is even more akin to its grandchild, the twentieth. It seems so close to our own day in so many ways that one might almost believe the notion that family characteristics are repeated in alternate generations had some odd counterpart in those artificial generations we call centuries. The building of the Heavenly City was not confined to St. Augustine nor to eighteenth-century philosophers; for our own time is still prolific in visions of the millennium. However anticipated by its predecessors, however it differed from the Victorian era, as we read through the literature of the eighteenth century and reflect upon its interests and its achievements, it seems almost incredible how clever its thinkers and writers were to think and write so much, so many years ago, which has occurred to us so recently. Were there no simpler explanation possible, we might almost suspect that they had read them in the works of our own intelligentsia; for if that age owed much to its predecessors we owe more to it.

In this respect, at least, Lord Chesterfield is typical of his time; and the adventures of his reputation from his day to our own not merely form a curious chapter in the history of our social evolution but seem to bring us closer to his century. The work by which he is now chiefly remembered in the world of literature — his *Letters* to his son and godson — is still reprinted and still read. Despite its brief eclipse in the Victorian age, it is, and it would be in any age, a timely publication, for it is timeless. It belongs to the great ageless literature of the *Comédie humaine*, with Horace and Seneca and de Retz, La Rochefoucauld, Polonius and Poor Richard. It is, as we say patronizingly of so many things, from Aristophanes' comedies to Shakespeare's slang, so " modern."

It is, in part, the eternal, if not immutable, voice of that strange, artificial, selfish, fascinating unreality which men — and more especially women — have created and called Society. It echoes the immemorial strivings of humanity after the pleasant emptinesses of a life at once delightful and barren; its desperate efforts to find substitutes for work and play and danger inaccessible to those who have them as companions of their daily lives; its no less desperate efforts to keep other people out of its charmed circle. But his letters are much more than an echo. They form a manual of the art of life and living with our fellow-men and women, that ancient art which

we call " getting on in the world." Of this Lord Chesterfield has long been popularly regarded as the chief representative among English-speaking peoples; for this condemned — and read; for, as was said of de Retz's work,
if the art of life can be learned from a book, his is that
book.

On these two things — the use of his title as a proper
noun, and these letters — his reputation rests; and that
very fact is at once a commentary on the means by which
human reputation is achieved and the changes which it
undergoes. Judging by what he was and did while he was
alive, few men could have appeared as certain of being
remembered as Lord Chesterfield — but not remembered thus. He was a member of the highest class of
eighteenth-century society, a type and symbol of that
aristocracy which in his day had reached its zenith, its
great age and its last; for, whatever else it was, the eighteenth century was the golden age of aristocracy. More
than a preceptor of manners; more than a man of letters,
in whatever sense; more than a man of fashion; more
even than a statesman and a diplomat; he was an eminent and influential leader of the Whig party. That was
to be at the apex of the social and political pyramid; it
was, as it were, a thing in itself.

If the English aristocracy modelled its manners on
those of its neighbors across the Channel, the French
aristocrats were dependent on the crown; the English
were its masters. They were, for the most part, Whigs;
for your true aristocrat is — or was — a Whig. This
close-knit oligarchy of related families, this " Venetian
system " of " silken barons," had made and unmade
kings; and in his day by virtue of its members' birth,
wealth and abilities, it ruled government and society
alike. It differed from the nobility of a hundred years
before; still more from the mediaeval baronage; most of
all from modern plutocrats. To its members, as to their

like in all ages, wealth was essential; but wealth was not enough. There remained birth, talents, power; wit, if God granted it — though God has seldom granted wit to wealth, or even to birth or power; and, in particular, it possessed a quality now, men say, fast vanishing from the western world, the quality of good manners.

The Whig aristocrats had all the accompaniments of wealth and power. England was studded with their country-seats, their splendid mansions, their wide lawns and parks and fields; London was adorned with their stately town-houses. Great farmers and horticulturists, they turned England into a garden and a granary; great leaders of society, they turned its capital into a city club; great statesmen and politicians, they turned its Parliament into an arbiter of world destinies. Merely to be among that chosen company would seem to be enough to ensure remembrance; and with all of these gifts Fortune endowed Lord Chesterfield. He had birth and wealth and power and wit, and good manners above all; he had estates and a town-house; and, like the rest, he played a part in politics.

For the great Whig aristocrats were not only country gentlemen and leaders of society, much less mere ornaments of a royal court. They were active, hard-working and successful men, statesmen and politicians, financiers, diplomats, administrators, orators, and most of all, parliamentarians. They had their pocket-boroughs and their seats in Parliament, by purchase or inheritance; and to birth and wealth they added talent. What could make head against the eloquence of Halifax and Somers' legal gifts, Montague's financial ability, Wharton's skill in electioneering, the genius of Marlborough both in court and camp, the talents of their successors — Stanhope, Townshend, Walpole, Carteret, Newcastle, the first Pitt? Not the Tories, discredited by impossible loyalty to the Stuart cause; not even Continental autocrats and min-

isters and diplomats and generals. Against all their antagonists at home and oversea the Whig leaders played
the game of politics with courage and success.

Their championship of parliamentary government and
of the public and private rights of Englishmen attracted
to their side all liberal elements. Their tolerant, Protestant policy drew the support of moderate churchmen
and Nonconformists; their encouragement of trade attracted the commercial interests. Their support of the
Hanoverian dynasty bound the crown to them. Their
talent for finance secured the national confidence; their
triumphs in war and in diplomacy contributed to the
people's love of glory and their love of gain. In their
hands trade flourished, the bounds of empire widened,
and England emerged into a European, then into a world
power. Whatever the defects of their system, if to make a
nation rich and powerful and feared, and on the whole
contented, is the business of statesmanship, they governed wisely and they governed well; and they had their
reward. They held the offices. From powder-monkey
to admiral, from lieutenant to commander-in-chief, from
tide-waiter to prime minister and even archbishop, they
held them all. And more — for over fifty years the history of their country is little more than the record of their
names and their activities.

To office, wealth and talents they added birth. Though
the Whig oligarchs of the early eighteenth century had
come to power by way of revolution, they were not such
men as usually rise to eminence by such means. They
were, for the most part, of families which, raising their
fortunes amid the ruins of the church during the sixteenth century, still commemorated the origins of those
fortunes in the names of their country-seats like Welbeck
Abbey and Houghton Priory. Augmenting their pos-
sessions in civil wars and Irish disturbances, by Stuart
generosity or necessities, by hard bargains and shrewd

investments, but most of all by marriage alliances, they had joined estate to estate, title to title in those troubled years. Some, like Lord Chesterfield, traced a long and honorable ancestry as far back as the Middle Ages; some, like the Duke of Grafton, a shorter and less honorable descent from one of Charles II's mistresses; some, like the Duke of Newcastle, whose first eminent forbear was a master-baker under Henry VII, had less eminent antecedents. But from whatever source and by whatever means, they had grown from knights or simple burgesses to viscounts and barons, earls, marquises and dukes.

Merely to be a member of this shining company would seem a recipe for immortality, and into this group and very near its heart Lord Chesterfield was born. Among his kinsmen he counted the Earls of Stanhope, of Strathmore and of Harrington; and, though remotely, many others, including the great Duke of Newcastle. His mother was the daughter of that Earl of Halifax whose eloquence had defeated the Exclusion Bill and whose talents had made him, in some sort, the arbiter of the Revolution period.

As he was born, so was he brought up to play that part in public life and in society which was at once the heritage and the principal pursuit of Whig aristocrats. Unlike most of his fellows he did not, indeed, attend a public school, but under the guidance of his grandmother, Lady Halifax, a French governess and a French tutor, he was prepared for Cambridge. There at Trinity Hall, he became a scholar and threatened to become a pedant. " When I talked my best," he wrote in later years, " I talked Horace; when I aimed at being facetious, I quoted Martial; and when I had a mind to be a fine gentleman, I talked Ovid." He spent an hour a day at civil law with the Whig Dr. Johnson, fellow of Trinity and professor in the university. He spent as much on philosophy, and attended the blind Professor Saunders' lectures on mathematics. He learned to read Lucian and Xenophon in Greek and took a course in anatomy. So, after two years of this, he went on the " grand tour," which led him, as it happened, only to the Hague and Paris. Thence he and many like him hurried home on the death of Anne to take their places in court and Parliament under the new Whig Hanoverian dispensation, which was to rule England for nearly fifty years; and thus the fourth Earl of Chesterfield set out on his adventure in search of a reputation.

For that pursuit he had one further qualification — he lived long — and if each age did not possess its own charm, one might observe that he lived in an interesting period. He was born six years after the Glorious Revolution brought William of Orange to the English throne. He grew to manhood during the reign of Anne and the War of the Spanish Succession. He entered public life with the accession of George I and lived into the reign of George III, through the administrations of Walpole, the Pelhams and their successors, and into that of North. He witnessed two efforts of the Stuart supporters to overthrow the Hanoverian dynasty. He saw the desperate activities of the Emperor Leopold to secure the succession of the Hapsburg lands to his daughter, Maria Theresa, by the so-called Pragmatic Sanction; the breaking of the pledges he secured from other powers; and the wars of the Austrian Succession. He saw the rise of Prussia and of Pitt; the overthrow of France in India and North America and the development of the old British Empire. He saw the fall of the old Whigs under George III; and he died at the moment that the breach between the mother-country and the colonies foreshadowed the American Revolution. Thus his life coincided almost exactly with the Whig ascendancy with which it was bound up.

Nor was he a passive spectator of these great events. On his return from the Continent he had been made a

gentleman of the bedchamber and a member of Parliament. He rose rapidly both in court and public life. He
became successively captain of the gentlemen-pensioners,
a lord of the bedchamber, a member of the House of
Lords, a privy councillor and ambassador at the Hague.
He took a leading part in negotiating the marriage of the
Prince of Orange with the Princess Anne. He was made
knight of the Garter and lord steward of the household,
and, returning to the Hague, he signed the second
Treaty of Vienna, whereby England, Holland and the
Empire sought to preserve the Pragmatic Sanction and
the peace of the Continent.

That was the climax of his diplomatic life. He fell ill;
he fell out with Walpole and turned to opposition in the
House of Lords; he was dismissed from his court offices.
He married George II's illegitimate half-sister, Petronilla
Melusina von der Schulenberg, who brought with her a
fortune of fifty thousand pounds, besides three thousand
pounds a year on the Irish establishment and expectations from her mother. With her he lived long and ami-
cably — in adjoining houses — consoling himself with a
new mistress in addition to Mlle. de Bouchet, whom he
had met at the Hague some years before and by whom he
now had an infant son.

Having fought Walpole and helped to overthrow him,
in the newspapers and in the House of Lords he opposed
the government's Hanoverian policy when the scrap of
paper which was the Pragmatic Sanction was torn up and
the Wars of the Austrian Succession began. He helped
drive Carteret from the direction of foreign affairs; he
advised Newcastle on the choice of ministers; he undertook another diplomatic mission to the Dutch; he spent
nine months as lord lieutenant of Ireland, whence he returned to take a place as secretary of state in the cabinet.
He quarrelled with Newcastle and retired from politics,
refusing a dukedom and putting aside ambitions to be

prime minister which were suggested to him.  Presently he gave up gambling, and when he heard George Selwyn had christened him " Joe Miller " after the great professional humorist, he resigned his membership in White's Club, and, gradually withdrawing from politics and society, he took up the age-old pursuits of old age.  He turned to building Chesterfield House in South Audley Street; to collecting a picture-gallery for it; and, when it was just completed, his brother left him a house and garden at Blackheath to which he then transferred his energies.  He read widely; he rode a little; he wrote for the newspapers and to his friends; he patronized the arts and their professors, especially the men of letters; he went to watering-places in search of health; he nursed his gout; grew deaf; and gradually, as he said, " slid gently to the bottom of the hill of life."

Such was the outline — or the skeleton — of a career peculiarly typical of the age and class to which Lord Chesterfield belonged.  If to contend successfully with one's own generation is a recipe for immortality, he should have been remembered long and honorably, even though he never rose to the heights in politics to which he might have aspired.  What more could Fame demand?  Yet even place and influence, like birth and title, are no recipe for immortality.  In his career was nothing extraordinary or exceptional.  There were a score like it in most of its incidents; there were dozens which had in them something of its activities and achievements.  The lists of their majesties' households, of their diplomatic and administrative services and of their councillors, are full of names almost, if not quite, as eminent as that of Chesterfield — names which this generation has never even heard.  Of them it may be said, as Chesterfield's biographer, the worthy Dr. Maty, with all the good-will possible, observed of Chesterfield's father, " of him we know little more than that he was an Earl of Chesterfield."

Who now recalls, or even can discover without some pains, who preceded or followed the fourth Earl of Chesterfield in most of his offices and employments? Who now recalls the character and career or even the name of that " perfect courtier," Lionel Cranfield Sackville, first Duke of Dorset, whose life almost exactly coincided with that of Chesterfield and whose official activities were so curiously like his as to be all but interchangeable up to a certain point. Each " came into the world with the Whigs "; each became a gentleman of the bedchamber at the accession of George I; each was a privy councillor; a member of the House of Lords; lord steward of the household; knight of the Garter; even lord lieutenant of Ireland, as they wove in and out of office, succeeding and succeeded by the other. Though Dorset was never an ambassador and Chesterfield was never Warden of the Cinque Ports; though the one was known for his wit, the other for his " love of low humour and buffoonery," each was reckoned in his time a man of fashion and of skill in politics and each was praised by Swift for conversation, taste and knowledge. Yet who knows anything of the first Duke of Dorset now? Even to his descendant, the family chronicler, he is " a shadowy figure " — and she a modern novelist! In that respect Lord Chesterfield had the best of it, though that best was poor. We search in vain for even a mention of the first Duke of Dorset's name in eighteenth-century history, where Chesterfield has a line or two, and once a paragraph, though rather for his wit and writings than his public services.

Yet many men of some political eminence are remembered chiefly for what they did outside of politics. What, then, of Chesterfield's private activities? Apart from public life, the Whig aristocrats, and he among them, spent their time and money as men have always spent them since men had time and money to spend. Some, like Walpole, were great hunters with horse or gun; some, like

Walpole's brother-in-law, nicknamed " Turnip " Townshend from his chief hobby, were great farmers; but
Chesterfield, though he had " the most flowery garden in
London," was neither a hunter nor a farmer but an in-
door man. Some were great gamblers; some great readers; some, like Chesterfield, were both. They all drank,
some heavily; and they all had gout, or, like Chesterfield,
gout and rheumatism both. Some married; some kept
mistresses; some, like Chesterfield, did both. Some, like
Walpole, collected pictures; some, like Somers, collected
books — though there the Tory Harley far surpassed
them all — and some, like Chesterfield, collected both.
Many were patrons of men of letters; he was the friend
of Pope and Swift and Addison, of Arbuthnot and Gay,
of obscure poets and a Dublin publisher.

As men of fashion they were as God made them, with
such improvements, or the reverse, as their parents, their
tutors, and their associates could effect; and for the most
part they had good manners of a formal sort; but none of
them had such good manners as Lord Chesterfield. Yet,
when all is said and done, however such private qualities
and practices have contributed to the amenities or the
annoyances of life, they have seldom caused men to be
remembered by succeeding generations. The first Duke
of Dorset had many claims to fame; he had birth and
wealth and place and power; he doubtless had good manners; his " low humour " may even have contributed as
much to the gayety of his generation, on a different
plane, as the witty sallies of Lord Chesterfield. Yet who
recalls the first Duke of Dorset now? Truly all men are
equal till one writes a book!

Yet, in a sense, Lord Chesterfield never wrote a book;
he wrote letters. When his son was five years old he began to write to him, and even when absorbed by cares of
state, he wrote him with amazing frequency. Till his
son's death he maintained that correspondence; and be-

fore that time he had begun to write to his godson in the same fashion. For a third of a century he wrote to those two young men; and when he died they found a long letter addressed to his godson which is among the classics of English epistolary and admonitory literature.

Nor was his letter-writing confined to them. He wrote a multitude of other letters — to George II's mistress, Lady Howard, one to her lap-dog, and two to George II himself. He wrote to nearly every man of prominence in English politics of his time, except Sir Robert Walpole; to Walpole's brother-in-law and rival, Lord Townshend, most of all. He wrote to the Duke of Newcastle frequently for nearly twenty years until they parted political company. He wrote to his kinsman, Lord Harrington; to Bubb Dodington and George Lyttleton; to Sir Thomas Robinson and the Earl of Marchmont; to the first Duke of Dorset and the fourth Earl of Sandwich; to the Duke of Devonshire and Lord Huntingdon; to Lord Hyndford and Sir Charles Hanbury-Williams; to the Duke of Cumberland, the first Baron Eliot and Colonel Guy Dickens; to General — then Colonel — Braddock and the Prince of Orange. He wrote with great frequency to his friend and factotum, Solomon Dayrolles. He wrote to the Bishop of Waterford and Alderman Faulkner of Dublin. He wrote to Baron Torck and to Count Bentinck; to Mesdames de Monconseil and du Boccage; to Mrs. Jean Marishall and Miss Gertrude Hotham. He wrote to Dr. Warburton and Dean Swift; to Voltaire and Montesquieu. But most of all he wrote to his son and godson — more than four hundred of some twenty-seven hundred of these letters which have been preserved to us were addressed to them.

Besides these he wrote a number of the then fashionable "Characters." He contributed to periodicals like that which, first published by a man named Mist, was transformed, as Chesterfield observed, " by a natural progression," into *Fog's Journal*. He wrote for " the only fashionable vehicle in which men of rank and genius choose to convey their sentiments to the public," the *World*, or *Common Sense*, which was, we are informed, " mostly moral and calculated for the improvement of manners and taste." He prepared his speeches in the House of Lords with all the care that men give to work intended for the press. Yet all of this availed nothing, apparently, to assure his fame, for none of it was published under his name while he lived.

What reputation he had then he owed to his public services and to his oratory, but most of all to his conversation. Premeditated or spontaneous, his wit was second to that of none of his generation, perhaps to that of any period in English history; and he paid the penalty. Before he died, though not long before, unauthorized collections of his writings and sayings began to appear as *The Humours of Lord Chesterfield*, *Lord Chesterfield's Witticisms*, and *The New Foundling Hospital for Wit*. So the statesman, ambassador, orator, counsellor and man of fashion of the early Hanoverian period left the stage on which he played such parts in the character of a professional humorist. The *Annual Register* contented itself with a bare statement of his death and dignities, and so far he was at one with the first Duke of Dorset.

Were this not enough for him to contend with in his efforts to achieve a lasting reputation, another element contributed to the injury of that reputation. The publication of his will served as the basis for an attack upon his character; and when his son's widow sold his letters to her husband to the publisher Dodsley and Dodsley printed them, his fate seemed sealed. At once not merely the professional scandal-mongers and moralists but many others fell upon the dead lion; and, as he had written of Pope, Chesterfield suffered the " natural consequence of his shining turn to satire, of which many felt, and all feared, the smart." He had some of the sharpest pens and the worst tempers of the eighteenth century against him, as well as some of its most eminent moralists, and he could no longer defend himself.

Samuel Johnson had long since damned him in the eloquent, if untruthful, dedication to his *Dictionary*, by which Lord Chesterfield is now best recalled by students of English literature. He now described the teachings of the *Letters* as combining the manners of a dancing-master with the morals of a species of female not mentioned in polite society since the accession of Queen Victoria, nor in polite literature for some time before. He sneered that he had thought their author " a lord among wits " but found him only " a wit among lords." John Wesley vigorously denounced his teachings of " deep dissimulation." Cowper pilloried him as a

> . . . polished and high-finished foe to truth,
> Grey-haired corrupter of our listening youth.

George Coleman in his prologue to Garrick's *Bon Ton*, written in bad poetry and worse taste, added his fling at Chesterfield's advice on behavior. " A friend to Religious and Civil Liberty " pictured him as a " harlequin," made up of a " frivolous compound of whim, wickedness, cunning and congee." Thus he who had been the friend of men of letters and their champion in Parliament, had his reputation fixed by them as firmly, and as unfairly, as Shelley's libel was presently to damn Castlereagh.

It was in vain that Burke rallied to his defence, praising the *Letters* in unmeasured terms. It was no less in vain that Lady Chesterfield, angered by these attacks, commissioned the librarian of the British Museum, Dr. Maty, to write a memoir of her husband to be prefixed to his works as a defence of his character. The good Doctor did his best. He enumerated his hero's virtues, his wit, his politeness, his diplomatic skill, his administrative ability,

his eloquence, his public uprightness, his private ami-
ability. " These," he concluded, " were his excellencies
— let those who surpass him speak of his defects." His
challenge was answered. The men of letters determined
the reputation of Lord Chesterfield. It was that of the
hard, cold, worldly, selfish, sneering, cynical voluptuary
by which Charles Dickens personified him as Sir John
Chester in *Barnaby Rudge*. Thus pilloried for his wit and
wickedness by two such powerful groups, what could he
hope for from posterity?

Yet even the diatribes of his enemies bore out Burke's
judgment. Youth and its elders listened to Chesterfield.
His *Letters* were immediately and enormously popular.
The first collection of them ran through five editions in a
year, and through eleven before the close of the century.
They were reprinted in Dublin at least twice; and even in
America, at the height of the Revolutionary War, a Boston
publisher issued an edition. In whole or part they were
translated into French, Spanish, Dutch and German, and
the *Economy of Human Life* attributed to him was done into
Italian and Portuguese. Success drew other letters from
their hiding-places; and nothing better testifies to their
author's gifts than the fact that his correspondence had
been so carefully preserved. Dodsley published a Supplement; Willis, the Faulkner series; Dr. Maty's successor
added a store of writings; and, in view of this retort to his
condemnation of Lord Chesterfield and his writings, Dr.
Johnson might well have recalled his own dictum that
" no man was ever written down but by himself."

Thanks, then, to his pen, by the end of the eighteenth
century Lord Chesterfield's literary fame seemed finally
secure; but this was not all the tale. As the nineteenth
century went on, his letters to his godson and to his godson's father saw the light of print. Lord Mahon, with
family piety, edited the *Letters* and the *Works*. Then, for
some forty years, under Victorian influence, their pub-

lication ceased save for a series of extracts and sayings; but, as that influence waned, since the last years of the Victorian era no less than six editions of the *Letters* have appeared. With these and an uncounted number of books drawn from his writings as manuals of etiquette and principles of politeness, maxims, gems of wit and wisdom, guides to life and conduct, Lord Chesterfield will never lack a monument to his literary gifts. If he has not been canonized as the apostle of good manners to the English, he has, at least, been classicized; so that it will no doubt happen to him, as was once written of Pope, "And dunces edit him whom dunces feared."

Yet, curiously enough, as his literary reputation rose, opinion of his character declined. It was but natural, perhaps, that his personal reputation should not have followed that of his literary skill. In his lifetime he had made enemies. Horace Walpole, though he recanted later, disliked his father's opponent. Hervey hated the man who said that " at the beginning God created three different species, men, women, and Herveys." No Hanoverian king of England cared to be reminded that under that family " the crown of three kingdoms has shrunk into an electoral cap," or that the best way to make the Stuarts unpopular was to make them electors of Hanover. Bubb Dodington could not forgive a character which read: " With submission to my Lord Rochester, God made Dodington the coxcomb that he is; mere human nature could never have brought it about. He is a coxcomb superior to his parts, though his parts are superior to almost anybody's." Still less, perhaps, were the feelings soothed of persons like the unmarried lady who appealed to him for sympathy against the calumnious report that she was the mother of twins. " I make it a rule of life," he answered, " never to believe more than half of what the world says." Such a gift, combined with studied indifference to what was said about him, naturally infuriated some of the most vocal elements of his time; and in the pages of their diaries and memoirs and letters their animosities pursued him beyond the grave, as his wit lived on to answer them.

Thus despite, or, indeed, on account of, his *Letters* and his wit, Chesterfield's conflict with oblivion began inauspiciously enough. He did achieve such immortality as the *Encyclopaedia Britannica* confers; but that was a mixed blessing. To an account of his public career it added that " the high character he had supported through life received no small injury after his death from a fuller display of it by his own hand," that is to say by the *Letters* which every one was then reading. As to their teachings the *Encyclopaedia* contented itself with quoting Dr. Johnson's bitter epigram. It did not give that up for fifty years, and even its latest edition echoes its first judgment of the man. That eighteenth-century guide to taste and literature, the *Gentleman's Magazine*, was scarcely less severe. Had his morals been as unexceptionable as his talents, it concluded, he would have been " the wonder of his age " ; but in view of his *Letters*, and especially his will which left the mother of his son only five hundred pounds, omitted all mention of his wife, and not merely cut his servants off with ten years' wages but called them his " unfortunate friends, equals by nature," the editor, obviously, could not approve of him.

So in the long argument which has raged over his character from the time of Maty and Johnson until now, the first advantage lay with the moralists. They held that advantage for a century. At almost the same moment that Dickens pilloried him as Sir John Chester, Lord Mahon, though admitting his talents, took up Maty's challenge and enumerated his defects. These were — odd and in the main unjust as they may seem to-day — " a want of generosity, dissimulation . . . a passion for play . . . contempt for abstract science and looseness of

religious principles," together with a lack of " the genuine
glow of patriotism and the kindling warmth of private
friendship." It was at about the same time that the
*Encyclopaedia Britannica* added, untruthfully, that " his
lordship's works do not appear to have attracted much
attention."

Such was the hard judgment of the great Age of Victoria. That judgment lasted long. Lecky described Lord
Chesterfield's " delicate but fastidious taste, his low moral
principle, his hard, keen and worldly wisdom." And in
an article attributed to Leslie Stephen we find that
though he " had too much genuine intelligence to be con-
temptible, and certain relics of natural affection and even
of patriotism " to be actually hateful, " on the whole we
must doubt whether familiarity with this high priest of
the Graces . . . will much heighten our regret for their
loss." " Ugh! What a father! " wrote Mr. Birrell, sum-
ming up Chesterfield — and the Victorians — in a phrase.

Yet if he found no champions in the British Isles during
the Reign of Virtue, in other quarters he was more fortunate. In the United States the judicious Channing
took occasion to point out that though Lord Chesterfield's name was connected with hypocrisy, worldliness,
and libertinism, it was a curious fact that this depended
upon letters he had not intended for publication. Moreover he observed, anticipating later judgments, " The
reader who has forbearance enough to discriminate, will
not deny that the *Letters* contain a great amount of practical good sense . . . the reader who can be satisfied with
skilful and perfectly intelligible accounts of man as he is
. . . will discern in these *Letters* as good a summary as he
ever found in a collection of French, or even Roman,
sentences."

He touched there upon the secret of the controversy.
Sixty years earlier, the author of the article in the *Gentleman's Magazine* had noted that " Even the licentiousness

of France," could not excuse Lord Chesterfield's advising his son to break the seventh commandment. Whether moved by the sneer at the morals of his fellow-countrymen, or by the assumption of the slighter validity of that commandment among them, or merely by the desire for a subject for a *causerie de lundi*, Lord Chesterfield found his first and greatest champion in Sainte-Beuve, about the middle of the nineteenth century. That gifted essayist laid down the lines of a defence which became a standard, if debatable, apology for the *Letters*. Denouncing Johnson's epigram as supremely unjust, he observed that the particular youth to whom these letters were addressed needed the advice his father offered him, and that this advice was such as Horace might have given his own son. He welcomed the French verve and vivacity, the *Je ne sais quoi* of the imaginative and colorful style, the " charming course of worldly education " ; and in general confirmed the worst suspicions of Chesterfield's English critics as to French morality.

It is a curious and entertaining paradox brought out by the long controversy that Chesterfield might have sunk into a decent semi-obscurity had it not been for the writings which made his literary reputation at the expense of that of his character. Everything has been said on one side or the other — except two. The first is that his latest editor with an inquiring, even a statistical, mind has taken pains to count how many times Lord Chesterfield's advice concerning mistresses occurs. He finds just eight passages in more than four hundred letters; and it is a tribute to the patience of the readers — if they read for this alone — that they have found it worth their while to endure so much excellent advice for such small return of scandal.

The second observation is related to the first. It is that his advice seems to have had effect proportional to its rarity. When his son died, Lord Chesterfield found that son had been a virtuous husband for some years, with children of his own! It is a fearful thought — can it be possible that all the bad advice now showered on us is having no more weight, that our false prophets are no more heeded, that the world is more moral and more sensible than its self-appointed guides? And it recalls an old and wholly undignified little rhyme, which, however inappropriate to such a stately subject, seems to have some bearing on the critics and the case.

> Said the Reverend Jabez McCotton
> " The waltz of the devil's begotten ";
> Said young Jones to Miss Nye,
> " Don't you mind that old guy,
> To the pure almost everything 's rotten."

It is Lord Chesterfield's counsel on that problem which has concerned this generation — shall we say too much? — which has given its author most of his ill repute; and it forms another comment on human reputation, that had these eight passages been deleted and the letters containing them destroyed, his fame would have been far greater. That, as it happens, is the excuse for one of the great exponents of Victorian prudery, Thomas Bowdler, who in the age of Chesterfield's eclipse edited and purified the works of Shakespeare and of Gibbon, so that those works could no longer " raise a blush on the cheek of modest innocence nor plant a pang in the heart of the devout Christian."

Whether or not we have forgotten the old art of blushing or whether our moral standards have gone down, it is, perhaps, worthy of note that no edition of Bowdler's masterpiece has appeared since the beginning of the seventh decade of the nineteenth century, and that Lord Chesterfield's reputation meanwhile has gone up. Even as Bowdler disappeared, in the pages of the *Gentleman's Magazine*, with more than usuual aptness called the *New Series*, an essayist ventured to challenge the then popular opinion that Lord Chesterfield was essentially vain and weak. He declared Johnson's dictum on the *Letters* "wrong in both assertions." He noted the difference between the standards of his time and those of Chesterfield in regard to the seventh commandment, and to that he rightly attributed the current opinion of the noble author; concluding that, though not good reading for the young, a man will " find him a profitable study after his thirtieth year."

A dozen years later, another critic went still farther. " That he was a capable man, a polite man, and a cultured man, goes without saying; but now it appears that he was a more urbane and humane man than has been generally thought. Deep down in his nature there were serious and elevated thoughts," however " hidden and encrusted by worldly considerations."

The tide was turning with the century. Presently a contributor to the *Spectator* ventured to declare that " The life aimed at here is not that of a recluse or a philosopher, but that of a man of the world . . . in his most attractive aspect . . . at bottom a life of industry and mental activity. It is not a lofty ideal of human life, but it is an ideal of a kind, and a very useful kind. He who promotes *savoir vivre*, who tends to diminish the wear and tear of natural human intercourse, who compels to mental alertness is in very truth a real benefactor of his species."

So presently that eminent antiquarian-critic, Mr. Wheatley, was emboldened to declare that Chesterfield " was not unprincipled or heartless, and selfishness was by no means a marked feature of his character," and recently a contributor to the *Contemporary Review* dared to assert that " Among the many victims of what Lord Morley called defective and traditional criticism, Lord Chesterfield is perhaps the most distinguished." Endorsing Sainte-Beuve's estimate, he attributed unfavorable criticism to Chesterfield's French outlook, to the charges of immorality, and to the scathing censorship which Chesterfield had exercised over English manners.

That, in fact, was what Lord Chesterfield was to his own generation, a *censor temporum* if not an *arbiter elegantiarum*. His morals did not offend its standards; his manners charmed; his wit captivated all but its victims; and, doomed to eclipse in the Victorian period, the circle of his reputation has come round full at last. Beside more recent outpourings of a Freudian fiction, even his worst lapses seem almost innocuous; and with this changing spirit, as his reputation grew, his character has become, if not exactly white, at least a lightish gray. Whether the world has been tempted to forgive the man of fashion for the sake of the man of letters; whether the moral standards of the twentieth century approximate more nearly those of the eighteenth than those of the intervening period, the fact remains that Chesterfield's reputation is now higher than at any time since his death.

Yet here something remains to be observed. Like a great predecessor in a different field, William of Wykeham, who founded Winchester School and New College in Oxford, Lord Chesterfield was what we call to-day, though in a different sense, a great " behaviorist." Each had profound belief in education; each held to that great faith expressed in the New College motto " Manners makyth man " ; and to Lord Chesterfield that motto might have seemed — as it may be — the soundest principle of living, if not, indeed, of life. Put in its crudest form, it is that if all that one does is in good taste and spirit, he cannot go far wrong; for this, if nothing else, will keep him from excess, from the vulgarity inseparable from excess, and the excess inseparable from vulgarity. This, it is argued on the other side, is a low philosophy, unworthy of the man of God who gave it to New College, or of a great aristocrat. It omits conscience and honor and religious faith, to say nothing of future punishment, as motives of human conduct. It relies on externalities and trivialities rather than on the eternities and immensities; on the opinion of one's fellow-men, rather than on the inner light of righteousness, to maintain morality.

It is quite unlike that other product of the eighteenth century which, at the moment that Lord Chesterfield became ambassador to the Hague, set out on its long task of softening the lives of humanity. Between Lord Chesterfield's *Letters* and William Law's *Serious Call to a Devout and Holy Life* lies the whole basis of the great argument, which began long centuries before, and will persist long after we are gone. It is the fundamental antagonism between the real and the ideal, between life as it is and life as it should be. Yet, so various and complex is human nature, as the idealists have often not been indifferent to worldly interests, the realists have not always been careless of the higher attributes. No one can read Lord Chesterfield's letter to his godson about his duty to God and man without perceiving this. " God," as he wrote, " has been so good as to write in all our hearts the duty he expects from us, which is adoration and thanksgiving, and doing all the good we can to our fellow-creatures. Our conscience, if we will but consult and attend to it, never fails to remind us of those duties. . . . Your duty to men is very short and clear: it is only to do to him whatever you would be willing that he should do to you." Despite the accusations of worldliness and immorality, you will find in his writings as little of contempt for what were once known as Christian virtues, as little of cleverness at the expense of religion or morality as of hypocrisy — and no man was ever freer from hypocrisy than Chesterfield. He disliked the priestly profession; in respect to dogmas he was, in a peculiar sense, a Nonconformist; but he was at heart a religious man in the most modern sense.

It is easy to see why he was so heartily abused by certain types of men. He had the characteristic pose of aristocracy, that indifference to popular opinion, which is sometimes unconscious, sometimes genuine, sometimes mere protective coloration. Most men endeavor to evade envy and jealousy. Chesterfield almost seemed to challenge them by his frank acceptance of his blessings, without humility or hypocrisy; but one only needs to read his comments on pride of birth or fortune to perceive that he valued those blessings at their true worth.

> Never [he wrote to his godson] be proud of your rank or birth, but be as proud as you please of your character. . . . You are, it is true, of a noble family, but whether of a very ancient one or not I neither know nor care, nor need you, and I dare say there are twenty fools in the House of Lords who could outdescend you in pedigree. That sort of stately pride is the standing jest of all people who can make one; but dignity of character is universally respected.

He has been compared to his discredit with one of his contemporaries, Benjamin Franklin; and when we set the career of the poor Boston boy who made his way to place and wealth and power beside that of the child of fortune; when we contrast Poor Richard's maxims of thrift and industry with Chesterfield's advice; even when we compare the bland, benevolent countenance of the one with the shrewd, capable face of the other, who can doubt which was the better man and the better guide to life? The one seems to embody all the homely virtues of democracy; the other, the vices of an aristocracy; and the difference between their characters seems no greater than the contrast between the order of the Garter which glitters on the breast of Chesterfield and the almost if not quite studied coarse simplicity of Franklin's dress in their respective portraits.

It may be so. The spendthrift Lord Chesterfield gambled and lost; while that pattern of thrift, Franklin, speculated and made his fortune. Yet, making allowance for their spheres of life, there is no dubious passage in Chesterfield which does not find its parallel in Franklin; and it has been noted that the English lord was almost as bad as the American printer, since each had an illegitimate son, and Franklin's advice on morals differs from that of Chesterfield only in being more direct and brutal. Yet who pictures Benjamin Franklin as a corrupter of youth or a preacher of dissimulation?

But, one may urge, Franklin was self-made and Chesterfield a mere inheritor. The answer is simple. Rank and wealth bear no relation to enduring fame. When Horace Walpole wrote his lives of royal and noble authors, the thinness of his book is equalled only by that of its contents. When we compare the number of those whose birth or fortune have put them in positions of authority with those whose names are now remembered, can we believe that birth and wealth have much to do with immortality? No one, not even Franklin, ever tried harder to improve himself than Chesterfield. Few ever read as much in an attempt to strengthen his knowledge and understanding; no poor, ambitious author ever labored more to better his writing; and since Demosthenes mouthed pebbles on the Attic beach, few men have striven harder to become an orator. For what he was, and is remembered for, Lord Chesterfield was emphatically a self-made man.

Though he warned his son against more learning than became a gentlemen; though he kept him from the only profession which which he might have hoped for eminence and success, that of teaching; though he spoke of college professors with almost as much disdain as a successful business or professional man might speak of them to-day, he was, in fact, a scholar and a teacher all his life. He would have been a notable lecturer on politics and history; and, as Maty observed, it is a pity that he did not write a history of England. His letters form an educational system, not merely on manners, modes and elements of success but on rhetoric and composition, languages and philosophy. He was, in fact, a professor, not only of politics and etiquette, but of decorum in its oldest meaning, " whose essential nature," as Cicero declared, " is inseparable from moral goodness "; for he was at heart a moralist.

The educational system of Lord Chesterfield, indeed, differed from our own. It had nothing to do with fitting men and women for citizenship or for salesmanship; but it was no less vocational for that. It was intended to prepare his pupils for life in parliaments and courts, for what is known as " leadership " to-day. He was what would be known now as an " environmentalist " or a " behaviorist " — however little attention the latter school has paid to good manners, or with small result. He believed that he could make statesmen as well as gentlemen by proper training and environment; and his failure may hold a lesson for us all. It was the crowning irony of an ironic life that both son and godson grew into virtuous mediocrity; and it is greatly to his credit that his affection was not lessened by that circumstance.

But Chesterfield was more than a teacher; he was a social reformer, though of a sort which might enlist small sympathy in this age of much reform. He did not seek to raise men to higher levels by mass action and prohibitory laws; he was not much concerned with housing or sanitation or sentimental benevolence. He did not seek to play the part of Lady Bountiful. He never patronized the poor. He laid aside all comforting sentiments of superiority and chose the harder part, the far more dangerous and thankless task, of working with his class. He challenged the vices and pretensions of Society. He labored incessantly with tongue and pen to correct the evils of drinking and duelling; he even entered on a gallant, if hopeless, crusade against ladies' " face-paint." He derided unmercifully those "Men of Honour," who cloaked their vices under that honorable phrase.

In one sense the charges levelled against him are true. He advised his readers to take advantage of their fellow-creatures' frailties. " Endeavor to find out men's pre-dominant excellency, if they have one," he counselled, " and their prevailing weakness, which everybody has; and do justice to the one and something more than jus-tice to the other." " Please the eyes and ears; and they will introduce you to the heart; and nine times in ten the heart governs the understanding." " Women have, in general, but one object, which is their beauty; upon which scarce any flattery is too gross for them to swal-low." What could be more cynical — or untrue — than this? Is it any wonder he has been condemned for dis-simulation, or that he deserved it? Continually he stres-sed the *suaviter in modo*, the *leniores virtutes*, the *volto sciolto e pensieri stretti*, *le douceur*, *l'aimable* — all the old, tried recipes for social amenity and success, whose very language re-veals how old and how widespread they are. You may find them in Horace and La Rochefoucauld, in Shake-speare and in Cervantes, in a hundred proverbs in a hundred languages.

These he turned into clear and vigorous English for his son and godson. He urged on them the importance of correct grammar and spelling and composition. He told them how to enter a room, how to sit, how to carry on small talk. He advised them on drinking, dancing and the drama; on keeping clean and telling the truth; on hunting, letter-writing, marriage, health; on the amount of necessary sleep; on how to talk to princes; on how to behave to the Pope. One of his best letters has to do with the art of which he was a master, the art of conversation. Talk often, he advises, but not too long; tell stories very seldom; never buttonhole a listener; be patient with bores; adapt your conversation to your company, avoid

controversial topics in mixed company; avoid speaking of
yourself as much as possible, especially avoid boasting;
never seem dark and mysterious; neither receive nor re-
tail scandal; never resort to mimicry; do not swear nor
indulge in loud and unseemly laughter. Perhaps nowhere in like compass is such excellent advice; yet it
became the subject of one of the most violent attacks on
its author, for reasons which, looking about us, are, perhaps almost too obvious.

Yet despite some circumstances in his life, despite his
apparent tone of worldliness and his apparent indifference
to criticism, these are not the qualities which impress one
who reads his letters through. As Horace Walpole said
after that exercise, they seem to have been derived not so
much from " the quality of his head " but actually from
the heart. It may be this as much as their worldly wisdom which has kept them so alive. No one can read
these letters to " My dear little boy," " My dear godson," and, as they grew older, to " My dear friend," and
" Dear Phil," without feeling that somewhere behind
that highly polished surface there was a gentle heart; that
somewhere in that epitome of worldliness which was the
Lord Chesterfield whom everybody knew, there was a
sensitive affection known only to his friends. To say that
his vices were those of his time, his virtues were his own,
is to excuse by accusation. He would have scorned to
take refuge behind such a defence; for, whatever else he
was, he was neither a coward nor a hypocrite; and that,
at least, has worked to his advantage through the years.

And there is one thing more which has commended
him to succeeding generations, as to his own. It is the
quality which the French call " gay," a quality too rare
in the Anglo-Saxon world, whether of life or of letters.
It tinged his every thought; it lasted all his life. His con-
gratulations to his friend Dayrolles on an attack of gout,
as " a certain cure for other complaints . . . a proof of

present riches and a certain pledge of their future increase," testifies to that quality. His famous observation in his old age that " Tyrawley and I have been dead two years, but we do not choose to have it known," reveals that gallant spirit to the last.

With all of this there remains something to be explained about Lord Chesterfield. Though he succeeded in politics, though he held high office and might, perhaps, have risen to the highest, his life seems to lack something — it seemed to lack something even to him — and lesser men have sneered at what they called his " failure." The reason is obvious. Despite his too apparent worldliness, he had a certain high disdain of courts and parliaments. He saw through their pretensions too easily; he would not take them seriously enough, as one must take them to reach their highest posts. He had the most dangerous of all qualities in one aspiring to political eminence — a keen sense of humor. Finally, perhaps as a result of these elements of his character, he did not care enough for the prizes of public life. He was too like his grandfather, the Earl of Halifax, on whom, unconsciously or consciously, he may have modelled himself. Each was urbane and witty; each concealed his deep beliefs and affections under a cynical exterior; each held to dignified, if agreeable, deportment; each wrote and spoke with strength and grace; each shrank from committing himself to extremes in either church or state. Each believed, as Halifax observed of ecclesiastical dogmas, that God would forgive him if, unlike an ostrich, he could not digest iron; and each was charged, in consequence, with political inconstancy and religious indifference. From Halifax, it may be, Chesterfield inherited some of that detached, ironic, philosophic tolerance which marked the genius of the great Trimmer. It is easy to say that a man is born out of his time, that Chesterfield was a Stuart in a Georgian period — but Halifax lived in the preceding

century, and Chesterfield's other grandfather was a
sturdy royalist. It may be that this royalist inheritance
gave him a certain tenderness toward the Tories, intensi-
fied, perhaps, by a comparison of Stuart manners with
those of the early Hanoverians. Or it may be that, like all
thoughtful men, he endured with such grace as he could
muster the long absurdity of life.

It is, indeed, conceivable that, had he been given opportunity, he might have shunned the reputation he
achieved. He was not as wise as he was witty, nor as
wicked as he was worldly, nor as worldly as he was wise.
If his advice had not seemed good, it would not have been
so widely and enduringly popular. If it had been as
vicious as it was assumed to be, it would have been long
since forgotten, and he with it. It has, indeed, some
flaws; but, taken all in all, it has undoubtedly made the
world a better place to live in; for Chesterfield, with all
his faults, was, on the whole, on the side of righteousness.
He hated lies and liars with a bitter scorn; he neither
preached nor practiced dishonesty, even with himself, and
his strongest denunciations were reserved for it. He hated
cant and loathed hypocrisy; and it is not merely a change
in moral standards nor the decline of the Victorian
prudery which has brought him to the twentieth century
with an enhanced reputation. With each addition to the
bulk of his published letters that reputation grows. Nor
is it the enduring fallacy that " to know all is to pardon
all " which has enhanced his fame.

The real objection to him and his writings lies deeper
than all these. He held, or he professed to hold, all human nature at too cheap a rate. He stressed the weakness
rather than the strength. He saw too clearly into human
hearts, and described what he saw — yet missed some
part of its nobility — and serious souls resented the portrait. Unlike the comment on a later politician-author
who, it was said, " Knew men, and yet loved them,"

Lord Chesterfield knew them, and loved but few; and those he loved too well.

He was a great actor on the stage of life, as even the charges against him prove. He was, it has been said, incapable of appreciating the greatness of great men, as evidenced by his attributing Marlborough's success more to his perfect manners than to his intellect. The charge is measurably true. It was a natural defect in one who saw Life's drama only from the stage or wings. For Chesterfield never sat among the audience. He played the parts assigned him as best he could; he judged the other actors not as a spectator but as a participant. He spoke his lines with spirit and with wit, not always decorously. But underneath the tinsel and the paint, and between those lines, one may perceive somehow a very human man hiding a tender heart and an unquestioned honesty beneath the mask of worldliness and indifference which was the fashion of his age and class. The character he assumed was perhaps at first the natural effect of time and circumstance. It may have come to be a second nature in the course of years, as his life became " subdued to what it worked in, like the dyer's hand "; yet, as his letters prove, it never quite conquered his natural humanity. He played no inconsiderable part in the great human comedy, but few now remember what that part was. They only recall how he once played it; how he tried to teach two little boys to take his place upon the stage when he was gone; how his teachings have seemed, on the whole, helpful to many generations since; and, as the years go on, they incline to overlook, if not to forget, the less admirable advice and the less praiseworthy qualities with which his name was too long identified.

# VICTORIA THE GOOD

O N THE 24th of May, 1819, there was born in a room of Kensington Palace, London, a little creature described correctly, if not very elegantly, by a future biographer as a "female infant," and, according to report, still less decorously, after the fashion of an earlier age, by an eminent social contemporary of the event, as " a girl, by God! " The birth of one female infant more or less, as determined by that most, and perhaps only, veracious chronicler of the race, the census enumerator, however important it may be to the infant in question, to its parents, or to posterity, is not necessarily of any striking consequence at the moment to the world at large; nor does it appear that this particular infant was any great exception to this rule. However English " by birth," she was of German parentage and ancestry. A little more than a century earlier, her great-great-great-grandfather had come to England from Germany, where he had been born, where he and his successors had found wives and such consolations as their lives afforded in the way of manners and morals; and, despite their long residence in England where they enjoyed a great inheritance, they remained in some respects very German indeed.

This was peculiarly true of this latest addition to that family. Her parents, poor relations of this great connec-

QUEEN VICTORIA

*From a photograph*

tion, were living at this moment largely from its charity, indebted to it, in fact, for their food and shelter. Apart from her father's relations in Germany, her mother's connections in that country were almost innumerable. She was one of eight children, her first husband was a German, and besides her own two children by her first husband, she had fifteen nephews and three nieces, whose marriages extended the family connections proportionately. A woman of " homely intellect and domestic interests," with strong love of family and of fatherland, she retained and passed on to her daughter those qualities in an unusual degree. It was, indeed, only owing to the determination of her father to give his offspring whatever advantage an English birth might possibly provide, that she was born in England at all. According to the no doubt scandalous gossip of the time, lacking money for the journey from the little German principality where he found himself when her arrival became anticipated, he hired a carriage and drove it himself across Germany and France — bad roads, worse inns, and every discomfort of an uncomfortable period — all on the strength of what a Gibraltar gipsy had once prophesied of his own future and that of his daughter.

It is not surprising that he had snatched at even this slender hope of bettering his condition, for there was little in his life and still less in his prospects which gave much hope of happiness or even comfort, much less eminence. He was a retired officer of fifty-one, on a pension scarcely adequate to support his station, and wholly insufficient to meet the debts he had contracted earlier, a man of no great qualities or importance, the fourth of seven brothers, with most of whom, after the fashion of his family, he had quarrelled. He was a comparative stranger in England; and it appeared at this moment with small chance or none of bettering his fortunes by following his superstition and taking up his residence there. He had recently been married, to a German princess, indeed, but a princess almost if not quite as impecunious as himself. His marriage had been a business arrangement, for which, according to report, he had sacrificed a devoted mistress with whom he had lived for many years. By that marriage, after service in Canada, the West Indies and Gibraltar, he merely exchanged a round of travels through Germany and Belgium inspecting troops and a tedious existence in Brussels for a no less tedious existence at a small German court, of all places in the then known world reckoned the dullest and most depressing. There it is said that he put in what time remained from his court duties in the more useful and perhaps even more exciting pastime of mending clocks.

Such were the short and simple annals of the poor at the beginning of the nineteenth century. Nor, for the time at least, did the gipsy's prophecy seem to improve them. Contrary to his expectations, his elder brothers married almost at once, thus dimming whatever hopes the new-born infant's father had entertained by his belated access of virtue in his own marriage. He was mildly cheered by two things. The first was the belief — we will not say the hope — that his brothers would die before him and he would get the family inheritance. The second was the reflection that, being healthy and regular in his habits, he might make that possibility a certainty by his superior expectation of life. So, within a year, he went out walking on a rainy day, got his feet wet, caught cold, and died, without leaving money enough to enable his wife, who was away, to get back to London with her infant daughter, or to live there without help from her brother on the Continent.

Then the world changed, once he was out of it. The little girl's grandfather, who had been insane for many years, died six days after her father's departure from the scene of his earthly activities. Her uncles and her uncles' children, one by one, followed the same road to the grave, so by the time that she was ten years old, she was the heiress apparent to the family rank and property. When she was turned eighteen her uncle William died and she came into the great inheritance, and so, in that degree, bore out the gipsy's prophecy. Three years later she married her cousin Albert, a good-looking, serious, earnest young German who lived in the Absolute and devoted himself with extraordinary conscientiousness, enormous industry and considerable ability to assisting his wife in the management of her great inheritance. In turn she first fell in love with him, then became his devoted slave, showering upon him an affection, or rather an adoration, all but incomprehensible to the world outside, always speaking of him in her intimate letters as " my Angel."

Children came to bless his happy union, abundantly and rapidly — five in six years, four more in the nine years following. In them and in her husband her life was centered. The family moved from the town to the country. They took possession of the official family residences in London and Brighton; they built a house in the Isle of Wight and another in Scotland. In these they lived an idyllic domestic life of what seems to a more restless generation almost incredible homeliness, not to say dulness, walking, reading, and, in the evenings, music, cross-stitch, round games, spinning counters and rings. As time went on and the husband grew better acquainted with England and his work, he devoted more and more of his time and energy to it. He became, in fact, a slave to it. From early morning — earlier and earlier as the years went on — till late at night, he was engrossed in it. The student lamp he brought from Germany and which he himself improved, saw their mutual labors begin before the late sun of English winter rose; it saw them continued in the early English winter evening which begins in mid-afternoon, till ultimately, the work, aided by his wife's stubborn devotion to a doctor of apparently not too great competence made an end of him.

That was in 1861. His widow, who was then forty-two years old, could not bear her loss. She secluded herself almost entirely from the world and mourned her husband as husbands have seldom been mourned. Every day, according to the gossip-mongers of the time, she is said to have had his evening clothes laid out and water put in his basin. On the head of every bed in which she slept it is said by the same competent authorities that she had a picture of his head and shoulders as he lay dead with a wreath of immortelles on his brow, where she could see it as she turned on her pillow. Almost daily she visited the mausoleum which she had built for her husband. And this much, at least, of that gossip is true — his every word, his lightest opinion, became the law of her existence, the one infallible guide to her judgment. The way to her favor lay through praise of her husband, the way to her assent lay in convincing her he would have approved. Thus she lived for forty years, cherishing the memory of her perfect married life and of her more than perfect husband.

In all of this, save for her almost incredible devotion to her dead husband's memory and the merging of her individuality into his, there is little out of the common run of many human experiences. But there is one thing which makes it almost if not quite unique in history. It is the fact that this woman was Alexandrina Victoria, Queen of the United Kingdom of Great Britain and Ireland, Empress of India, a " wiser, gentler, happier Elizabeth " in Tennyson's earlier lines, yet for all time in common phrase, in Mr. Kipling's poetry, to herself and to the world at large, the " Widow of Windsor." That accident of birth conditioned the circumstances of her daily life; it affected her character; but it did not in large degree alter the fact that she was — with some qualifications — a wife and mother — though a royal mother — first and a queen afterward. It did something to influence history, but she was far more affected by it than even history. The nineteenth century is a great period in the annals of England and of the world; in it Queen Victoria was cast for one of the most conspicuous parts; and it is not without some interest, even some importance, to understand something of her character — and something more than that. For her life involves a great problem. The nineteenth century was the age of democracy. It saw the decline and fall of monarchy and aristocracy in many lands. What, then, was her position in the world; how did she manage to maintain it; what influence did she have, and with what result?

If, as has been said, nothing in the life of Charles I so became him as his leaving it, few things or none in Queen Victoria's life were more characteristic of her than her entry into the great post she occupied. Her uncle, William IV, died at Windsor about two o'clock on the morning of June 20, 1837. Before five o'clock the Archbishop of Canterbury and the Lord Chamberlain arrived at Kensington Palace to announce the news of her accession to this girl of eighteen who, roused from sleep, came in her dressing gown with her hair down her back to receive their homage. The best-known passage in her Journal records her sentiments. " Since it has pleased Providence to place me in this situation," she wrote, " I shall do my utmost to fulfil my duty towards my country. I am very young, and perhaps in many, though not in all things, inexperienced, but I am sure that very few have more real good-will and more real desire to do what is fit and right than I have."

In those few words lies the key to her reign, her character, her influence and her reputation. Her uncle William had been fond of her and had predicted with unusual

acumen her character and her future. She would be, he
said, a " good woman and a good queen," and, sailorman
as he was, or liked to be regarded, he declared " It will
touch every sailor's heart to have a girl queen to fight for.
They'll be tattooing her face on their arms, and I'll be
bound they'll all think she was christened after Nelson's
ship." As if to confirm his words, almost the first act of
her reign was to sign her public documents " Victoria."
In that act she revealed another quality of some importance in her life and character. She had been known in
the immediate family as " Drina," but she had never
liked that name; and when she was only four years old she
had signed a childish letter " Victoria." It had been suggested that she take the title of Elizabeth II, but she disliked the name and the queen who had borne it; and,
despite considerable public opposition to its " foreign
sound," she had her way — and made Victoria as great
a name as Elizabeth!

Her training and advisers for the great post to which
she had succeeded had provided her with a peculiarly
wide and thorough preparation for its duties and re-
sponsibilities. She was " a soldier's child " as she often
and proudly asserted; and to the end she took the greatest interest in the army. She was by nature pious, and
her clerical preceptor strengthened her devotion to the
church. She was exceptionally good at languages. Her
mother-tongue was German, but she learned to speak
English with an accent " thoroughly natural, although
refined," as one of her biographers observes with unconscious humor. To these she added French and Italian, so
that she was an accomplished linguist. In spite of this —
perhaps because of this — she had no taste for literature;
but, like many of her generation, she was a voluminous
letter writer and she kept a diary or a journal with great
and extensive care. Forbidden to read novels when she
was a girl, she never acquired a taste for those works

which were among the greatest contributions of her reign to literature. She had scarcely more artistic than literary taste; but she loved drawing and music and through a great part of her life she sketched and played the harp and sang. She was a skilful horsewoman; she loved exercise, especially outdoors; she danced well; and she was devoted to all kinds of games. Under the direction of her tutors she did her best to read history, and not without success.

Thus trained with more strictness than even most children of her age under a discipline all but inconceivable to-day, as she grew older and as her chances of succession increased till she was presently recognized as certain to be queen, her ambitious and intelligent mother began another and no less important enterprise. When Victoria was but twelve years old she was taken to Bath to open the Royal Victoria Park, thence to inaugurate the Victoria Drive at Malvern; and from that time forth she travelled over the greater part of Great Britain, visiting the country-seats of the nobility, giving prizes, laying corner-stones, opening fairs, examining cotton mills and universities, reviewing ships and regiments, and generally being trained for one of the great occupations of modern British royalty, as well as coming in touch with her future subjects of all ranks.

Meanwhile her formal education proceeded, first under the guidance of her governess Fräulein Lehzen, daughter of a Lutheran pastor and her lifelong friend. Her instruction in the art of being a sovereign was undertaken by her mother's brother, the shrewd, capable Leopold of Saxe-Coburg-Gotha, who, after his wife's death had for some years travelled in England and Scotland, till in 1830 — that *annus mirabilis* of the Saxe-Coburg-Gotha family — he accepted the crown of newly liberated Belgium. For many years he played the part of father to the child Victoria. Fully acquainted with British as well as

with Continental politics, through many years he guided
her political footsteps, and when it seemed she was about
to mount the throne their correspondence revealed their
mutual confidence and aims.

One of his earliest letters lays down his concept of a
modern monarchy.

Entrust Lord Melbourne, the Prime Minister [he wrote], with the
office of retaining the present administration. . . . They [the ministers
then in office] will serve you with great sincerity and attachment, for
they and the Liberals at large know that their offices depend on you.
Try to avoid great measures of state at first. Maintain the influence of
conservative principles and the Protestant church. Show yourself attached to it; for you are where you are because of it. Cultivate a feeling of right and wrong and be very true and honourable in your dealings. [And again] I should advise you to say as often as possible that
you were *born* in England. George III *gloried* in this. . . . You can
never say too much in praise of your country and its inhabitants. . . .
Your being national is the great thing. . . . You will be certain in this
way of the love of the nation you govern.

It was good advice. Long since it had been noted that
the English love a queen; and as her father had been a
Liberal, she had been bred in that school from her earliest
youth. To Leopold's counsel she replied in kind. " I am
not alarmed," she wrote at the prospect of her imminent
succession to the throne, " and yet I do not suppose myself quite equal to it all; I trust, however, that with *good-
will*, *honesty* and *courage*, I shall not at all events *fail*." In
that spirit she approached her task, and how strong was
the influence of her shrewd, kind uncle may be judged
from her first public utterance. " Educated in England,"
she declared, " under the tender and enlightened care of
a most affectionate mother, I have learned from infancy
to respect and love the constitution of my native country.
It will be my unceasing study to maintain the Reformed
religion as by law established, securing at the same time
to all the full enjoyment of religious liberty; and I shall
steadily protect the rights and promote to the utmost of

my power the happiness and welfare of all classes of my subjects." From these simple, homely, fundamental elements proceeded the Victorian policy; from them she never swerved; and they may be regarded as the clue to her reign, her character and her hold on her people.

To these influences may be added that of the first figure which presented itself to her on the morning of her accession, William Lamb, Viscount Melbourne, Prime Minister and leader of the Whig party. He was then a man of fifty-eight, who during a lifetime spent in politics, had revealed few talents as an administrator and still fewer as an orator, but had owed his rise to his personal qualities and his peculiar skill in politics. He had long been separated from his wife; he had no children; he bore a vivid, if not wholly deserved, reputation for gallantry; and he was at once one of the most astute and charming men in public life. He fell in love with the young queen at first sight; he loved her as he would have loved a favorite daughter; and with the utmost skill and tact he thenceforth devoted his time and talents to her political education. That devotion became a jest among his intimates, but it was as genuine as it was unselfish; and to the end of her life the queen never spoke of him without the epithet which was the height of her praise — " *dear* Lord Melbourne."

To these elements in her introduction into politics another was soon added. Scarcely was she on the throne when her solicitous uncle sent to her his most trusted adviser, Christian Friedrich, Baron von Stockmar, Swedish-born, bred in Coburg, sometime physician, then secretary to Leopold. He had retired from that office when his master became King of the Belgians to avoid the jealousy of his new subjects, but had kept in close touch with Leopold and public affairs from his retreat in Coburg. A profound student of men and measures, honest, disinterested, astute, he was one of those men who find their satisfaction not in exalted station but in helping their

masters govern.  Sometimes in England, where his foreign birth and his peculiar position made him unpopular,
sometimes on the Continent, for more than twenty years
he devoted his talents to Victoria's service.

How greatly he was trusted was soon apparent.  The
young queen must have a husband, and of the candidates
for that position her cousin, Prince Albert of Saxe-Co-
burg Gotha who had visited England three years previously, seemed most promising.  To him, therefore,
Stockmar was attached as guide, mentor and friend for a
year's tour in Italy.  His report confirmed the favorable
impression the young prince had made upon the princess
who had found him " extremely handsome " and thanked
her uncle for " the prospect of great happiness " he had
held out to her.  " He is so sensible, so kind, so good and
so amiable," she wrote, and " He has, besides the most
pleasing and delightful exterior and appearance you can
possibly see."  Thus, having received Victoria's approval
and passed Stockmar's scrutiny, he visited England again,
became definitely engaged, and married the Queen a
little less than three years after she ascended the throne.

The marriage was fortunate and happy and the royal
pair presented that spectacle unusual in royalty, a husband and wife absorbed in each other.  Prince Albert was
not merely a model husband.  He had been carefully
educated, especially in science and government; he was
intelligent and industrious; and he was an excellent man
of business.  Under his management, it is said, the estates
of the hereditary appanage of the Prince of Wales increased their annual returns from eleven thousand to
fifty thousand pounds, and the royal farm at Windsor became a model establishment.  Ten years after his marriage he promoted the first " World's Fair," the Great
Exhibition of 1851; and with the money derived from it
was founded the Victoria and Albert Museum of applied
art at South Kensington.  He was a great public servant

as well as a devoted husband and though he was given the title of Prince Consort only four years before he died, his influence over the Queen was reflected in the measures of her reign not only during his lifetime but after his death so strongly that Victoria's reign has sometimes been divided, after the fashion of geology, into periods in terms of the Prince Consort as pre-Albertine, Albertine and post-Albertine. But it would be nearer the truth to eliminate the last — for even when he had been removed from her side his memory remained a dominating influence in her life and policy. And though it is easy to say that influence was not good, that England suffered from too great Teutonic bias and "Albertinism," that if he had not wielded such great influence her fortunes would have been better served — there are no " ifs " in history.

Thus equipped with advisers and a husband, the young Queen set forth upon a reign of such length and importance that few or none in history compare with it. It is not easy for men in even middle life to realize that the Victorian era now belongs to the ages, that it is fast mouldering into a heap of memoirs and documents, that it is almost as much a part of history as the age of the Antonines. Yet if politics turns into history when it is no longer necessary to conceal facts; when once all those who knew its great figures are dead — and that will be no lengthy period — when the graves give up their memoirs and the archives their documents, Victoria will soon become as shadowy a figure as Elizabeth or Anne, as remote as Cleopatra or Semiramis. Before we have forgotten what her age was like, we may inquire what were the characteristics of the period into which she was thrown by accident of birth, how she met its requirements, what part she played in it, and how the institution of monarchy which she represented fared at her hands.

This last is, in fact, the real test of the other three, the

fundamental problem of her place in history. For, whatever else the century just past accomplished, it made
the situation of monarchs difficult or impossible. The
changes in the status of such rulers were, for the most part,
coincident with the reign of Queen Victoria; her fortunes
were bound up with them; at one moment they seemed to
threaten even her position, and at all times they conditioned it. That situation was recognized by all the
royal families. " The position of what is generally called
great people," wrote her uncle Leopold in 1833, " has of
late become extremely difficult. They are more attacked
and calumniated, and judged with less indulgence than
private individuals. What they have lost in this way
they have not by any means regained in any other. Ever
since the revolution of 1790 they are much less secure
than they used to be, and the transition from sovereign
power to *absolute want* has been as frequent as sudden."
To avoid this the good man advised his niece to study the
art of government; to give time to reflection — though,
as he observed, that is " difficult in a great town "; to
self-examination, " every evening to recapitulate the
events of the day "; to consider one's own motives and
those of others; to guard against selfishness and vanity; to
judge one's self and others with truth and impartiality;
and not to be intoxicated with success nor cast down by
misfortune. To that end he recommended books to her
— Sully's *Memoirs*, properly expurgated by Fräulein
Lehzen — Rollin's *Ancient History*, Russell's *History of
Modern Europe*, Gaillard's *Rivalry of France and Spain*, and
Clarendon's *History of the Great Rebellion*, which last she
found " drily written but full of instruction."

The situation which confronted an English sovereign
differed widely from that of Continental rulers even in the
seventeenth century, to which she had been referred for
guidance, and even England had altered greatly since
Clarendon wrote his great classic. Not only had Parlia-

ment become supreme but the commercial, agricultural
and industrial revolution of the eighteenth century had
altered the bases of society. Beside the old lords of the
soil, the new lords of commerce, manufacturing and
finance had ranged themselves. England had not merely
learned the secrets of machinery and power; she had acquired huge stores of capital. She had not merely become a hive of industry, she had bred an army of workers
and of men skilled in financial operations. So, despite
the debts incurred in revolutionary and Napoleonic wars,
she emerged from those conflicts the leading power of
the European world.

That eminence was bought at a great price. The many
had grown dependent on the skill of a few for livelihood,
till not only Great Britain's living but her life depended
on the capacity of her industrial and financial leaders to
meet the demands and the competition of the outside
world. For the masses, existence had come to depend on
the " job," the job on the ability of the employers, their
fortunes on the success or failure of crops half a world
away, the price of freights, the state of credit, the vagaries
of fashion, the threat of new inventions or competitors.

Nor was this all, for the .influence of the industrial
revolution was no greater than that of the upheaval in
France. New notions of liberty, and especially of equality, made way in the world. By the time Victoria came to
the throne, " democracy " had begun to infuse the spirit
of the lower classes, and as their numbers and resources
increased, they pressed forward to a share in government. To these elements was added the influence of a
new empire. In Canada, in Australia, in South Africa
the beginnings of self-governing colonies had been made.
The British power in India had overflowed its older
limits in area and authority, till a great part of that
peninsula owned British sovereignty. Thereafter through
the years that sovereignty was extended steadily, to far-

flung islands, to strategic points, through the dark continent of Africa, till by the time she died, the new Queen had become the visible, personal symbol of the greatest aggregation of lands and peoples the world had ever seen, now gathered " within the golden circle of the crown."

Nor did Great Britain grow merely in wealth and empire and popular government during Victoria's reign. No circumstance more clearly typifies the change which overtook her people in that period than the simple fact that those who first paid her homage drove six hours to get from Windsor to Kensington. Of all the changes which mark her age from all that went before, the one which most appeals to a generation like our own is the improvement in rapidity of communication. First railways and steamships, then telegraphs and cables, then automobiles and aeroplanes and wireless, mark that great development. Not even the transition from candles to oil, from oil to gas, from gas to electricity, is more striking; not even the enormous improvement in machines and power is more remarkable.

This great mechanical and scientific development is not only the most astonishing characteristic of the Victorian period, the one which marks it off from all previous times, but it reveals a fundamental fallacy, though a common one. In accordance with the modern rule that successive generations — or some of their members — strive to exalt themselves by depreciating their predecessors, " Victorian " has been used as a term of contempt. It has even been used in three degrees, positive, comparative and superlative, " Victorian," " mid-Victorian " and " early Victorian," as one should say, Neolithic, Paleolithic and Pliocene. Applied chiefly in the field of morals and aesthetics, it is not unlike the contempt of the eighteenth century for the sixteenth, the Restoration reaction against the Puritans.

Yet what was "Victorian"? An age which began with Wordsworth and Macaulay, which went on through Browning and Tennyson, Fitzgerald and Gilbert to Oscar Wilde and Rudyard Kipling and Dobson; which began with Bulwer-Lytton and ended with Wells, which included on its way Dickens and Thackeray and George Eliot, Hardy and Meredith, Barrie and Bernard Shaw, Conan Doyle and John Galsworthy — what an age was that, or how to be defined in any sweeping terms? An age which began with Turner and ended with Aubrey Beardsley, how is that to be described in terms of art? An age which saw its beginnings in *Friendship's Garlands*, yet produced *Punch* and the Gilbert and Sullivan operas — was that age humorless? An age which began with horsehair sofas and wax-flowers under glass and worked through Eastlake to William Morris — how is that defined in any single phrase, however devastating, as " Victorian "? It was not all mawkish sentiment and rigid morality, any more than it was an age of orthodox theology. For an age which could produce Charles Darwin and Herbert Spencer, which accepted and furthered " higher criticism " of the Scriptures, was little bound by tradition of whatever kind, least of all was it committed to unchanging dogmas in whatever field. What was " Victorian "? Was it Charles Dickens or George Gissing? Was it Landseer or Phil May; was it Carlyle or Gardiner; was it Frederic Harrison the Positivist, or Cardinal Newman? They were all Victorians.

Whichever way we look, whether to wealth or power, to science or invention, to economic or to intellectual affairs, to letters or to art, to politics or society, it is apparent that the Age of Victoria was not, as has been often and ignorantly conceived, a static period of dull stolidity. It was an era of amazing change, of rapid evolution in every department of human activity. It was infused with ideas, energetic, vigorous, amazingly alive.

Its favorite words were " progress " and " reform "; its favorite concepts those of change; its favorite doctrines, liberty and humanity. The political distance between the beginning and the end of the reign was greater than that between the middle of the seventeenth century and the middle of the nineteenth. The material and physical advance during her lifetime equalled or surpassed that between the nineteenth century B.C. and the year of her birth. To say " Victorian " in disparagement is to reveal one's ignorance of the almost incredible advance in almost every field of human activity. Beside the great achievements of her reign what have the Edwardians or the neo-Georgians to offer?

And what did Queen Victoria have to do with this? The first and natural reply is " nothing." She did none of the things which made her era great. She wrote no novels; she painted no pictures; she contributed nothing to poetry or philosophy, or to science or invention. She dug no mines and built no factories; she led no explorations, formed no companies to exploit new resources, founded no colonies. She did not even govern — she only ruled. She merely *was*. In consequence it has been fashionable to regard her, and rulers like her, in general, as mere ornaments if not excrescences on the body politic; to reckon monarchy as an outworn and useless, if not positively harmful, survival of an older stage of human existence, a functionless relic of evolution from lower to higher forms of social life. Not only that; it has been argued that, so far from being even a good figure-head, her personal characteristics made her almost absurd as the representative of the greatness of the people over whom the accident of birth had set her to rule.

To this view has been brought the evidence of the published writings of her early years; and it is true that no one can now read certain passages in those writings without astonishment that their author could have any capacity for government. It seems incredible to a professional writer, especially a clever one, and most of all to one depending on his cleverness for his audience, that the author of such a book as her *Journal of Life in the Highlands* could ever be a queen, much less a great ruler. To such a man such an existence as is described in it must not only seem insufferable, but certain to alienate the sympathies of a great people who looked to her to guide, or help to guide, its destinies.

It is the simple story of a simple life. Its highest spots are what to most of us would seem the dreariest of official or semi-official functions; its lightest moments a picnic or excursion to such points of interest as tourists or " day-trippers " are wont to visit while they eat. Its profoundest observations are those they might have made. Its deepest feelings are those commonest of platitudes drawn from the commonest of human experience — the anniversaries of her marriage, of the births of her children, of her husband's death. Its perpetual reiteration of the adjectives " poor " and " dear," its conscientious record of the days it rained, what have they to do with the world-compelling concerns of monarchy? It has in it no touch of great thoughts and high ambitions, no elegance of style, no touch of humor. It is unenlivened by clever sayings, amusing anecdotes, brilliant descriptions, penetrating observations, or striking thoughts.

It is, in brief, the kind of book which some millions of her subjects might have written, had they been so inclined. It is pre-eminently commonplace — and sympathetic. She sympathizes with " poor " John Brown, whose wet kilts made the back of his legs sore; with the " poor " Scotch woman whose little son was drowned; with the " poor " French Empress whose son was killed by the Zulus; with " poor " Mary, Queen of Scots. She writes sympathetically of " dear, good " Dr. McLeod, her preacher, of " dear " Princess Louise; of " dear, little

Albert " ; of the " dear, kind " Duchess of Athole; of
" dear " Madame de Weyer. It is all so simple and
homely and, to a modern taste, so dull. It is so unlike
what we have been accustomed to from more recent
authoresses, even royalties. It has in it little or nothing of
the pomp and circumstance of courts. Its pages chronicle no scandals or morganatic marriages, no pride of
power or social eminence, no changing of the guard, no
splendor or display, no shouting crowds, no back-stairs
gossip, no intrigues. And we forget that there are two
appeals, one of magnificence, one of simplicity, one of a
ruler far above ourselves, wrapped in the splendor of another world, and one of a human being like ourselves. It
recalls the story of the old lady who observed on seeing
Shaw's Cleopatra, " How unlike our own dear Queen."

It was to the humbler quality that this book appealed,
and its very dulness helps to explain her hold on her subjects. Like its author it touches the common heart. It is
full of homely experiences and homely observations such
as anyone might make. It is inconceivable that Queen
Elizabeth, whom Victoria disliked, should have written
such a book, as inconceivable as that Victoria should
have indulged in her predecessor's more vigorous language. An interview between those two great ladies
would have been a thing to enliven the centuries; yet
they are bracketed together in the public mind as great
rulers of a great people in a great period; nor has Victoria
suffered by the comparison. But why Victoria?

It is one of the insoluble mysteries of life. As described
by the sharp pens of clever writers, given only that description, the place of Queen Victoria in the world of
affairs and in the hearts of her people would seem incredible. Men and women being as intelligent as we
know — or think — they are, no such person as the author of the *Highland Journal* could ever gain or hold such
place in human hearts and history. It would be incredi-

ble but for two things. The first is that we have continually given our hearts, our minds and our affairs into the hands of politicians often of no more, often of much less ability, and still more often of far less honesty and character than Queen Victoria. The second is that her " dulness " her " stupidity," her " commonplaceness," did not exhaust the list of her characteristics.

She was a devoted wife and mother, with whatever virtues and defects that this implies; and, apart from the appeal she thus made to the women of her realm, whatever the declining force of wifely devotion nowadays, her maternal rôle might well move even such a generation as our own to its greatest depths. For what chord is touched so often and with such great success by all sorts of persons as the mother motif? What politician, orator, vaudeville artist, playwright, songwriter, criminal lawyer does not recognize its worth? What florist, telegraph company, candy manufacturer, does not strike that note on " Mother's Day " ? It is the surest and most universal of all appeals to the emotions of humanity, the deepest, the most affecting, the most certain of response; the one, unfailing, ever-fresh, perennial synonym of unselfishness in a selfish world.

And she was a woman. Every instinct of chivalry, every protective sentiment was aroused by that circumstance. She was, moreover, during a large part of her life a " lorn woman " ; and the " Widow of Windsor " inevitably moved men and women to a sympathy based on the finest and most enduring sentiments of the human heart; for she personified the common experience of death and deprivation. Above all perhaps, she sympathized with the misfortunes of others; and sympathy breeds sympathy.

It was the quality of all qualities which most appeals to the masses of a democracy. It may have seemed dull and commonplace to some; yet, incredible as it may appear,

most of us are dull and commonplace. Few live in the
high altitudes of statesmanship and epigram. Most of us
are absorbed in every-day affairs, in uneventful tasks, in
commonplace concerns, thoughts, sentiments, and relationships. We find vicarious romance in sports, scandals,
crimes, the moving-pictures and the daily press which
chronicle such things as — mercifully — life denies to
most of us. This element in some fashion monarchy supplies. Some rulers, like Elizabeth, met that demand with
high adventure and glittering court life; some, like
Charles II, with wit and wickedness. Victoria's appeal
was of another sort. It was to the every-day virtues, the
universal experience of men and women raised to what
mathematicians call the $n$th degree.

It has been said that a Prince of Wales often owes his
popularity to the fact that he is what every young man
would like to look and be and do — perhaps what all
young women would like to have them. In no small
degree that was the appeal of Queen Victoria. She
summed up in herself those precise qualities of humanity
which made a wide appeal. She was the average person
exalted to a throne. She was not merely the *ewig weibliche*,
she was ordinary life apotheosized. And most people
loved it. They saw in it themselves. It was the quality
which endeared Lincoln to the masses. Napoleon assumed it with his gray overcoat, his tricorn hat, and his
title of Little Corporal; Louis Philippe with his bowler
hat and his umbrella. Few politicians but practice it
sometimes; and many all the time. Victoria did not have
to practice it; it was her own nature.

It was not all her nature. She was, it was said, too vain
and too susceptible to flattery, like that of Disraeli's
adulation of his " Faery Queen." She had small sense of
humor of the livelier sort. She was too conscious of her
dignity. She was too utterly respectable. Her famous
observation, " We are not amused," revealed these quali-

ties in a phrase. She was too dictatorial; she ruled her own family too strictly; she lived up to her standards too rigidly and compelled submission to them too sternly. She disapproved of the conduct of her eldest son, of the too vivid company he kept, of the new elements he introduced into society.

It doubtless all is true, in part; and in part wholly true. But being a ruler is like being one of Swift's Brobdingnagians. Each quality is exaggerated incredibly. The little dominance of the home multiplied to the dimensions of a monarchy; the little idiosyncrasies of our family or our friends magnified to royal and imperial proportions; who could escape these and far worse complaints? Not merely does a fierce light beat upon a throne but we examine its occupants under the microscope. Each little blemish becomes a major fault; each little habit a matter of enormous consequence; each action and each word, however insignificant, becomes the subject of dispute. And which of us would come off better under such a scrutiny? With that the world of her subjects was not greatly concerned. It knew little and cared less about her relations with her court, her servants or her ministers. It took small account or none of her less admirable qualities — if it knew of them. It saw in her a good woman who happened to be Queen.

She had another and still greater source of strength. It has been said that one of the greatest of all qualities is that of being *there*. She was always there. Times altered and fashions with them, and standards and philosophies; but Victoria remained. She did not change with them. She had the quality of the stars or a great hill; one could guide his course by her. In a changing society she remained little changed. Her standards were fixed and elemental, and whether one approved or disapproved of them, he knew what he could count on; and that is something in a whirling world. That world, it was said, went by her; but the world goes by a hill — and the hill remains. She clung to the simple principles with which she began, to truth and honesty and good-will and what is called " virtue," in whatever form; and whatever men may say, these change but little through the changing years. In that lay a great source of her appeal. All the rest — the petty vanities, the obstinacy, the domineering qualities which offended some about her, all those lesser irritations which we all inflict on those nearest to us, these may well be forgotten in view of those greater qualities more observable from afar than by those close at hand. There all hills seem the same, and all have their defects. It is only as we recede from them that we perceive that one stands out above the others, that its minor imperfections lose themselves in the mass of the whole. We may forget the vain and crotchety old lady of the gossip-writers and recall that somewhere within that outward form there was a steady soul devoted to the fundamental virtues which from the beginning and evermore shall be those upon which we must finally depend for such stability as our unstable human nature may achieve.

A thick volume has been written on *The Tragedy of Edward VII*. That tragedy consisted in the fact that his mother denied him any share in public affairs so long as she was able; that the heir to the throne was deliberately, even jealously, excluded from activities which might conceivably have been regarded as his right. It is alleged in defence of his earlier courses that a first-rate political intelligence, deprived of its proper sphere of influence, was wasted on frivolities, and worse. This is not merely the tragedy of Edward VII; it is an indictment of his mother. There is some truth in it. Victoria clung to power, not only consciously as a sacred charge from her husband, but unconsciously as an expression of her own pride of rank. It has been urged that this was a symptom of weakness, not of strength; not of greatness but of litleness. Yet in such a place as hers who would not cling to power? It is the commonest failing of humanity. Had she not clung to it, there would have been no less hostile charges brought against her on the ground that she was a weak and vacillating character. For, to paraphrase what Lincoln said, you may please all of the people part of the time, and part of the people all the time, but not all of the people all of the time.

Her love of power was reinforced by another characteristic — her strong will — and to this she added courage and honesty. For she was honest; and that is a rarer quality in rulers, whether hereditary or elected, than most of us believe, since, as the ancient adage says, " he knows not how to dissimulate knows not how to rule." She was, moreover, not merely incredibly industrious but she was almost morbidly conscientious in her task. She kept throughout her life that high resolve to do her utmost for her country, and to do what she thought right. If there was one criticism levelled against her by her ministers, it was her insistence on seeing the documents in the case — in all cases and in every case. She was a hard-working public servant, and she loved her work. She had a passion for keeping in close touch with every phase of public life; and no one can read the history of her later years without astonishment at the amount of work she did in going through endless papers and passing some sort of judgment on everything. It had a tendency to irritate some ministers who regarded her, and felt that she should regard herself, as a mere constitutional ornament and themselves as divinely appointed by the voice of God — that is, of the people — to conduct affairs. But it witnesses the fact that she was more than a *reine fainéante*; she was, if not a queen-governant, every inch a queen-regnant.

She was no mere spectator of the game of politics; she took an active, if unobtrusive part in it. Whatever her literary gifts, or lack of them, whatever her personal idiosyncrasies, minister after minister testified to her judgment. No one who reads her later letters but must recognize that, whatever their qualities of style, whatever trivialities they contain, they have in them an unusual amount of sound common-sense. No one can read the lives of her prime ministers but must recognize that she was as often right as the ablest of her servants. She was not always right. She made mistakes; she did and said some injudicious things. She would have been more or less than human had she not; but the balance of sound judgment was strongly on her side. Taken all in all she knew how to play the part of a monarch in a society continually tending toward democracy. Unlike too many of her fellow-sovereigns, she kept not only her head and throne, but the love and respect of her subjects, in a difficult period for persons of her rank.

In that capacity she made but one serious mistake and that was when she permitted her feelings as a wife to overpower her sense of duty as a queen. Her long retirement from public life after her husband's death, joined to concurrent impetus among her subjects toward democracy, bred a party and a creed devoted to the principle that monarchy had no place in a democracy. She became, in fact, at one period of her life, almost violently unpopular. Men like Sir Charles Dilke began to ask why Great Britain should endure such an expensive and useless piece of antiquated furniture as a royal throne, especially when occupied by a crotchety and domineering woman; why not accept the rational solution and abolish it?

To that question one of the ablest and sanest of English publicists, Walter Bagehot, provided an answer which still stands. " No one," he wrote, " can approach to an understanding of the English institutions, or of others which, being the growth of many centuries, exercise a wide sway over mixed populations, unless he divide them into two classes. In such constitutions there are two parts . . . the dignified parts, if I may so call them; and next, the efficient parts, — those by which it in fact works and rules." " The use of the Queen in a dignified capacity," he goes on to say, " is incalculable; without her in England, the present English government would fail and pass away. Most people, when they read that the Queen walked on the slopes at Windsor, that the Prince of Wales went to the Derby, have imagined that too much thought and prominence were given to little things; but they have been in error, and it is nice to trace how the actions of a retired widow and an unemployed youth become of such importance."

The reasons for that, he observes, are simple enough. A monarchy is strong because it is intelligible, it is interesting in ways which people can easily understand, to have a *family* on the throne, for, among other things " the women — one-half the human race at least — care fifty times more for a marriage than a ministry." And, " to state the matter shortly, royalty is a government in which the attention of the nation is concentrated on one person doing interesting actions." To these he adds the other sources of the strength of monarchy as exemplified in Queen Victoria. It gives to government the strength of religion, the ancient faith, or superstition, of allegiance to an anointed sovereign. It is the head of society. It is — or, as he notes cautiously, it had come to be — " the head of our morality. The virtues of Queen Victoria and the virtues of George III have sunk deep into the popular heart; we have come to believe that it is natural to have a virtuous sovereign, and that the domestic virtues are as likely to be found on thrones, as they are eminent when there." Or, to put it into words which, could he have heard them sung, would have delighted Bagehot as they have delighted many others,

Hearts just as brave and fair,
May beat in Belgrave Square,
As in the lowly air
Of Seven Dials.

Finally — and this is what Continental minds would call British hypocrisy — he regards monarchy as essential because it "acts as a disguise; it enables our real rulers to change without knowing it. The masses of Englishmen are not fit for elective government; if they knew how near they were to it, they would be surprised, and almost tremble." As to the actual duties of the crown, as to the influence it may exercise — for English monarchy has influence but no power in the old meaning of the word — he finds that, too, invaluable. " The sovereign has . . . three rights: the right to be consulted, the right to encourage, and the right to warn; and a king of great sense and sagacity would want no others." " In the course of a long reign, a sagacious king would acquire an experience with which few ministers could contend." He has, besides, a certain advantage over even a minister in his social superiority; he has the actual right of dissolving Parliament; he is a permanent official; and he has a powerful, if not precisely legal or even constitutional source of authority by the tacit recognition that he is, after all, the head of the state in sentiment if not in fact.

There you have, in brief, the statement of the case for a good constitutional sovereign like Queen Victoria. It is — to apply to matters of government a simile taken from the great motive force of English life in her reign, the steam-engine — like a balance-wheel, which does no actual work by itself, but keeps the driving-wheel steady. It is like that aptly named device known as a " governor " which, apparently scarcely even connected with the engine proper, serves to regulate and preside over what might otherwise be the erratic action of the whole machine.

But Queen Victoria was — and did — far more than that. As Bagehot pointed out, in accordance with her earliest training and resolutions, she became a model of " virtue " to her subjects. It is easy to sneer at the homelier virtues which she personified, at the conventions and the " inhibitions " which guided all her life. It is easy to find witty phrases to cast discredit on her principles and practices, and to emphasize the stodginess of existence under such conditions as she laid down for herself and her subjects. It is easy, but it is not wise. For those conventions and those inhibitions, however restricting they have seemed, have lain at the root of sound society since the days of the Ten Commandments, and for long before; and the so-called " common people " have in general been wiser than some of their self-appointed intellectual leaders in clinging to those ancient platitudes.

Victoria had more than character. Despite her obvious limitations, she had ability. No one can read her letters to her ministers and to her fellow-sovereigns without consciousness of that. With all their little personal interests, family concerns and homely sentiments, no one can miss that quality. She exercised a great influence. She advised the choice of ministers, of leaders of the church, of diplomats, of generals. Her advice was not always good; it was not always taken; but it was not infrequently of assistance to statesmen.

Moreover, she had the courage of her character, her crown and her convictions. It took the " fountain of honour " to watch over the distribution of rewards and dignities; the titular commander-in-chief of the armed forces to abolish the purchase of commissions. It took a Defender of the Faith to guard church appointments and to protest disestablishment. It took a queen to suggest to Lord Rosebery that it was better for a prime minister to " take a serious tone in Parliament," and, being " so clever," not to be " carried away by a sense of humour."

It took an Empress to suggest to Lord Salisbury that " It is a very great danger to India to disregard the Mohammedans." It took a royal grandmother to advise and even correct the All Highest German Emperor, William II.

Finally, as the years went on — and on — there was added to these elements of strength her age. She lived to be eighty-two, and for sixty-four years she occupied the throne. If one of the requisites of eminence is to keep on living — and without that there is no worldly eminence — she was the greatest sovereign of them all. In English history there were but three reigns comparable in length to hers; and of them two were of rulers who lost their minds in later years. She never lost her mind. She had complete control of all her faculties, and not least her memory. She could tell Lord Rosebery what " *dear* Lord Melbourne " had thought about this or that problem — dear Lord Melbourne who had been dead some fifty years, who had died, in fact, about the time that Rosebery had been born. She could remember Wellington vividly; she could adduce political parallels from a past already historic. She had an experience of prime ministers which might command not merely reverence but awe — Melbourne, Peel, Russell, Aberdeen, Palmerston, Derby, Disraeli, Gladstone, Salisbury and Rosebery — and she came near outliving them all. She dealt with every president of the United States from Martin Van Buren to Theodore Roosevelt. She became more than an oracle; she became an institution. Like the Pope she might well have said in her later years: " Tradition! I am tradition! "

For what had she not seen and experienced? She had seen the monarchy of Louis Philippe succeeded by a republic, that by an empire and that by another republic. She had seen the rise of a united German empire and an Italian kingdom; the division of the ancient Hapsburg monarchy into a dual monarchy; half a dozen Spanish revolutions and as many governments; the rise of independent Balkan states on the ruins of a declining Turkish sultanate; the revolutionary movements of 1830, 1848, and the red " fool fury of the Seine " in 1871.

She had begun with Metternich, she lived through Bismarck and Cavour and Napoleon III to William II. She had seen the rise of new powers beyond the seas, of modernized Japan, of a reunited United States. She had seen the Indian Mutiny and had lived to be crowned Empress of India. She had seen a newly founded Australian colony named after her and lived to see the formation of an Australian Commonwealth. She had seen her own dominions grow from a handful of scattered settlements into a new empire; and she had grown with them. In more senses than that of the ancient jest, she had expanded with that empire. The slender, girlish figure which won all hearts at her accession had become every inch — and more — a Queen-Empress; and her concept of her office and her judgment had strengthened with the years.

She had seen more than that. She had seen her own kingdom turn from aristocracy to democracy and enter the path which led to socialism. She had seen its population doubled; its wealth tripled; its electorate quadrupled; and this last, at least, she did not like. By virtue of her office, her training and her character, she was essentially conservative. That, in a sense, is the business of monarchy. She felt that the world was steadily, if not rapidly, going down the hill; and she did what she could, though unobtrusively, to act as a brake on that progress. To those who felt that it was rising to new heights this was an irritation — to Mr. Gladstone and his followers in particular. She did not like that champion of democracy, and he did not like her. He addressed her, she complained with a rare touch of humor, as if she were a

public meeting. She addressed him, it was retorted, as if
he were a servant. On that antagonism was founded
much of the criticism of her later years. It was but natural and inevitable that the representative of the old order
should clash with the champion of the new. If she was
behind the times, he was in advance of them. It shows
what happens when the irresistible force meets the im-
movable object — the force goes on its way, the object
remains unmoved, but there remains, also, the heat of
their impact. Yet in a world like ours who is to say
whether the queen or minister was "right"?

As she began so she ended. " With good-will, honesty
and courage," she had written at the outset, " I shall not
at all events *fail*." She did not lose her old phrases as she
grew older. She speaks of " precious little May," of
" poor, dear Alice," of " dear Sir Henry Ponsonby."
But the words which occur most frequently are " duty,"
" responsibility " and " anxiety." She writes of " prestige," of an " England (not to speak of her Sovereign),"
which " will *never* became subservient." She was not
only the Widow of Windsor, she was the Sentinel of the
Empire. She was more than that. She was the Guardian
of the Throne. She set a new fashion in monarchy. She
laid the ghost of royal tyranny, incompetence and selfishness. Her wide relationships on the Continent; her
contact with almost every element in her own country;
her intimate correspondence with her ministers; her interest in every phase of politics which touched her realm;
her common-sense, and, above all perhaps, her sympathy, did more than buttress her own position. They
gained and held men's confidence in monarchy — however parliamentary — as a form of government.

Let us assume — for purposes of argument — that all
the stories of the gossip-writers, the scandal-mongers, the
enemies of monarchy and the court hangers-on are true.
Let us assume that Victoria was absurdly wifely and ma-

ternal, that she was at once the slave of her husband and the tyrant of her family. Let us assume that she was capricious and petty in her early life and crotchety and dictatorial in her old age. Let us assume that she did and said and wrote some very foolish things. Let us assume that she seemed better fitted to some about her to be the wife of a small middle-class tradesman than a Queen-Empress — for that is the impression which one gets from reading some memoirs.

Let us assume all that — what then? It is pleasant to think that great souls are encased in splendid bodies; that they have every grace of mind and heart as well as of figure. It is pleasant to think that all dukes are tall, slender, and aristocratic; that all duchesses are lovely and gracious; that all great commanders are stately and heroic figures; that all great scientists are immune to petty human weaknesses; that all great musicians are sweet souls; that all great writers are lofty characters; that all rulers are of impressive form and manners and moved only by the highest and most patriotic impulses; that, in short, great men and women are great in everything, as charming in appearance as they are admirable in character and eminent in talents.

It is pleasant, but it is not true. Is it not recorded that the fate of Asia once hung on the outcome of a conflict between a lame man and a man with only one eye? Has it not been noted that one of the great battles of modern times was fought between armies commanded on the one side by a feeble and asthmatic king scarcely able to keep his horse and on the other by a general so ill that he had to be carried in a litter? Yet no one has yet seen fit to challenge the capacity of either William III or Marshal Luxembourg. Only Marlborough conformed in his outward form to the ideal of a great nobleman, a great diplomat and a great general. He had capacity equal to his task, his station and his appearance — but he had other qualities which make him a far from attractive figure in history. Napoleon had generals both in his service and against him who surpassed him physically; there were a hundred diplomats who were more beautiful than Talleyrand. Beethoven was not a " sweet soul " ; nor Newton a wholly admirable character.

On such grounds, if no others, we may put in a plea of confession and avoidance for Victoria. It was not her business to write charming and intelligent letters; it was not her business to be an amusing and delightful hostess; it was not her business to be entertaining. It was her business to be Queen of England; and she did not even pretend to any other part. She did not try to write clever books, or utter clever observations; she did not pass public judgments on all conceivable aspects of life; she did not seek to be a recognized authority outside the scope of her office. She tried to do her work; to fulfil as best she could the duties of the high station to which, in Victorian phrase, God had called her. And all the rest may well be cast aside. We do not judge Shelley by his life but by his poetry; we do not judge George Eliot by her personal appearance or her personal morality; we do not even judge a great captain of industry by his opinions on politics, religion or philosophy; we do not judge a scientist by his vagaries on international affairs. The essence of us all is too often screened from the world by some trivial peculiarity of manners or appearance; greatness of mind or soul is too often obscured by superficial qualities. It is the business of biography not to stress the husk in which a soul is wrapped, but to find beneath that husk those elements which make for greatness; to rescue it and sweep away the rest.

In a sense rulers have no need to fear oblivion. The records stand, the names are there to read. Kings, queens and presidents, prelates, popes, dukes and dictators have their place reserved for them in history. Yet of them all how many can we name — and how, and why? This one because his hair was red and he was killed a-hunting, that one because he was a marvel among monarchs, a man of wit; this one because he was a conqueror, that one because he was beheaded. Some are dimly remembered as " the Bald " or " Fat "; some as " the Great"; some as " the Unfortunate "; some as " the Wise "; some as " the Simple "; some, whether in praise or blame, as " the Pious " — and one as a " Saint." A few are recalled as " the Good "; but only three in English history — Good Queen Bess, Good King George, and, though the fashion has gone by, Victoria. As she began, so she ended. Her uncle William's prophecy came true. She would be a " good woman and a good queen "; and unquestionably had she been born to the throne a thousand years before, she would now live in history as " Victoria the Good."

# THE HISTORIC CROMWELL

TO ANY thoughtful person who is interested in the past, — and most, if not all, thoughtful persons have an interest in the past — there must occur one question of importance, not only to history, but to all knowledge. How do we know what we profess to know? By what process has that knowledge been built up; on what foundations does it rest; in how far does it represent the truth; and in how far is it tradition or opinion, or mere hypothesis? To many, even to some professed historians, this question does not seem to have occurred; or, if it has, it has been dismissed as too vague, too difficult to determine, too "unpractical" to undertake without a study of such inordinate length and unsatisfactory conclusions as to repel the most patient of scholars and the most long-enduring of readers — if, indeed, there are any long-enduring readers left.

Yet such studies, however difficult and inconclusive, have not been found either useless or uninteresting to science, with which history nowadays professes to be allied, or even to literature, to which it was once supposed to be related. To know how knowledge has developed provides a measure at once of its achievement and of what remains to be accomplished. It reveals the methods of intellectual progress — that strange combination of investigation, imagination, industry and chance;

OLIVER CROMWELL
1658

*From a contemporary oil painting in the author's possession.   Probably the
last and best of the Protector's portraits*

nor is it without a fascination of its own, apart from that of the subject with which it is immediately concerned.

For such a study the development of the historic Cromwell offers certain advantages. The great Protector occupies a place in modern history second perhaps only to that of Napoleon; and he represented or opposed causes and parties that still play their part in affairs perhaps even more than did the Corsican. He lived in times when it was possible to make and preserve an ample record of human activities, and his period yields in interest and importance to no other in English history and to few in the history of any people. Moreover, however much we may add to the knowledge of his period, we are not likely to know much more of him personally than we do now. The story of the slow evolution of our knowledge of him and of his time is, in fact, the epic of our recovery of the past in miniature; and the career of the Huntingdon squire who rose to be the Lord Protector of England, Scotland, Ireland, and the dominions oversea — he whom we call Oliver Cromwell, though his family name was Williams — is scarcely stranger than the career of his memory once he had passed from life to history.

When Oliver Cromwell died, the world in which he played so great a part knew as much and as little of him as we know of the men of our own time. Week by week the newspapers, which had begun their great career almost if not quite in his lifetime, had chronicled the events of war and politics then reckoned their chief excuse for existence; and, more than at almost any other time, masses of ephemeral though serious literature had poured from the presses, informing, arguing, praising or denouncing him. Among the thirty thousand pamphlets which tradition says this period produced, a multitude owed their origin to him; and speeches, letters, ordinances, proclamations, petitions and treaties made him on this side, if on no other, the best-known ruler of his time.

There were, besides, many who had known him personally — but to what purpose for historians? Most of their knowledge was bound to perish with them; and what has history to offer in its place? The lively impressions of contemporaries, the intimate knowledge of events and characters — what is more obvious than that we cannot know such a man as Cromwell as well as those who knew him at first hand? Yet consider " contemporary history " — almost without exception it is dull and disproportioned, superficial, prejudiced; and lives written by contemporaries are divided between panegyric and depreciation. This being true, what can a revolutionary leader, in particular, hope from his own generation or its immediate successor?

He may expect just what Cromwell received. The characteristic product of the Protector's lifetime was Ricraft's *Survey of England's Champions and Truth's Faithful Patriots*, and it serves for all. It reads like what we call " campaign biography." Introduced by the weak verses of John Leycester, that " poor crumme of mortality," as he describes himself; adorned with "lively Pourtraitures" and lists of victories of those " prosperous Armies raised for the preservation of Religion, the Kings Majesties Person, the Priviledges of parliament and the Liberty of the Subject," far down the list — next to the last, in fact — of these brief sketches comes that of the " Religious, successful and truly Valliant Lieutenant General Cromwell," " who for his gallant actions, the Cavaliers have (Anabaptist-like) rebaptized (if I may properly so say) and given him a new name, called *Old Iron Sides*." Thus Ricraft sets the pattern for Cromwellian biography, reciting the list of his victories, from the skirmish at Stamford, through the " never to be forgotten fight at Marston Moor " and Naseby, where he " did bravely perform the day," till he returned from Oxford and the West to " take his place, as a member of the House of Commons, where I leave him to act by his counsell, according to the pattern he hath acted with his hands."

So, when he died, the first account of him, prefixed to a rude engraving of his lying in state, followed that pattern.

Oliver Cromwell L. ptor of Engd Scotd and Ierld borne at Huntington of the name of Williams of Glamorgan and by K. H. 8 changed into Cromwell was educated at Cambridge afterward of Lincons Inn at the beginning of the Warres Cp: of a Troop of Horse raised at his owne charge and by the Parlam made commander in cheefe reduced Ierld and South Wales, overthrew D. Hambletons Army the Kerkes Army at Dunbar reduced all Scotland defeted Ch: Stewards Army at Woster . . . Was declared L: ptor of Ed Scd and Ird 26: of Decemb: 1653. died 3 Sep: 1658 after 14 dayes sicknesse of an ageu with great assurance and serenitie of minde peaceably in his bed. Natus 15 Ap: 1599.

Then, as an afterthought, or because there was one line left, was added casually, " *Dunkerke in Flanders surrendred to him 20 of June. 1658.*"

Such was the recorded history of Cromwell at his death. All men knew him as a small landowner who had risen to the headship of the state; in politics, as in war, his every action attended with success. They recalled the steps of his ascent to power, the roll of his victories over royalists, Irish, Scotch, and finally foreign foes; how he had overcome opponents in his own party, lukewarm aristocratic leaders, Levellers, Presbyterians, Parliament itself; furthered the execution of the King, the formation of the Commonwealth and the Protectorate; and, as dictator of the Empire of England, had become the most formidable figure in the European world, the Puritan hero and the Protestant champion.

All this they knew, for it had been the fabric of affairs for nearly twenty years. What they did not know was how it had been done, and why, — the springs of action, the motives and machinations, the circumstances which he had faced and overcome. Not until the graves gave up their memoirs and the archives their documents, and their stories were compared; not until the great underlying currents of thought and action had been sounded and charted, would they know what part he played, and what sort of man he was.

Yet there was plenty of material. Of his own letters hundreds were preserved; of the letters of others many thousand more; the archives of foreign powers held the reports of agents and ambassadors regarding him and his country; those of Great Britain, masses of documents relating to his rule. His secretaries, Thurloe and Milton and Rushworth in particular, had kept their correspondence; his opponents, theirs. In many a country-house, in many an old bookseller's shop, lay masses of pamphlets, and even before his death men were collecting them. Especially a certain George Thomason of St. Paul's, as he went about his business among authors and printers, had gratified his collecting instincts and his interest in affairs by picking up these fugitive publications against the time when his professional judgment told him they would interest posterity, till he had gathered some twenty-three thousand of them to perpetuate his own memory with that of his times.

Even while this bookseller of St. Paul's went his unobtrusive way, the young Prince Charles's governor, Sir Edward Hyde, in his retreat among the Channel Isles, began to draw from his own recollection; from the state papers which he knew so well, for he had written so many of them; from his diary and correspondence, the story of the Great Rebellion and the Civil War. Meanwhile, too, the secretary of the Long Parliament, Thomas May, was publishing his history of that body to 1647; and various other men who had played parts in public life were busy writing their recollections or their *apologiae*. But to these men, for whatever reason, such documents were dangerous, especially to Cromwellians when in that *annus mirabilis* of 1660 King Charles II came to his own again; and each took steps to protect himself. Thurloe and Milton abstracted their letters from the Public Paper Office in Whitehall and hid them. Thomason stored his pamphlets in false table-tops; and even when Clarendon came back as Chancellor, he did not rush into print with reminiscences, for " indiscretion " was then a term of reproach and not, as now, a boast. So Cromwellian material went into hiding, for men feared what its possession might entail to them, a fear not lessened by the execution of the regicides.

Thus one who in those days aspired to write a life of the Protector had little more to guide him than common knowledge and the public prints, with what he might gather from the actors in affairs. Yet then, as now, no ignorance or half-knowledge proved a bar to authorship, and Cromwell was scarcely buried when biography began. In it three books are notable. The first — for despite its brave title, Dawbeny's comparison of Cromwell's career, his character, and even his appearance, with those of Moses, is no biography — was Samuel Carrington's *History.* Adorned with a portrait and " That never till now published incomparable Poem of the English Virgil, Mr. Edmund Waller," on Montagu's victory, it formed, in its author's words, a " natural panegyrick " of its subject, without adding appreciably to the knowledge of his life. But panegyric was unfortunate, for the little book was scarcely published when Richard Cromwell, to whom it had been dedicated, fell; and Carrington's volume accompanied him into obscurity.

It was followed within a twelvemonth by *The Perfect Politician,* usually ascribed — on what seem slender grounds — to its booksellers, Raybould and Fletcher, and usually known by the latter's name. In turn it was short-lived, and was soon supplanted by a far more famous book, James Heath's *Flagellum,* a contribution of no small

consequence to Cromwellian biography. This owed its
popularity to reasons far outside its merits as a truthful
history, and not least to its style. Where Carrington began prosaically enough, " My intent is to give you a
rough draught of this most excellent Personage," and
Fletcher still more abruptly, " It is very well known that
he was of an honourable Extraction," Heath strikes a
note of true grandiloquence.

Fate [he begins], when it had decreed and ordain'd the unhappy
birth of this *Famoso*, by her most secret and hidden malice brought him
into the world without any terrible remark of his portentous life,
neither Comets, nor earthquakes, nor such like Violences of Nature,
ushering or accompanying him to the declaring and pointing out,
that the Scourge of the *English* Empire and Nation was now born; as
she did by indiscernible methods train him up to the possession of the
Throne, and as secretly and cunningly, after all his bloody and ne-
farious actions, shift him out of it and with a blast of her spent Fury,
turned him into his wish'd for Grave.

Which is to say, apparently, that Cromwell was born and
died like any other man.

Moreover, Heath devoted much of his book to Cromwell's youth, perceiving in it the prophecy of the later
criminal. " Of a cross and peevish disposition," unre-
strained by his mother's fondness, " rough and intract-
able," " robust and outragious in his juvenile years, adult
and Masterless at Mans estate," the young Cromwell was
a robber of orchards and of pigeon-cotes, a " veritable
*Apple-Dragon*," thus preparing to ravish the " *forbidden
fruit of Soveraignty*." Insolent and incorrigible as he grew
to manhood, at college a cudgel and football player,
ignorant of Latin and leaving without a degree, he was
sent to Lincoln's Inn, where his debaucheries might be
obscured in the city's general wickedness. Returning
thence to plague the countryside, a terror to maids and
alewives, " a veritable Tarquin," a friend of tinkers and
pedlars, a player of filthy tricks, he was disowned by his

uncle Oliver. Then, left a legacy by another uncle, and marrying Sir James Bourchier's daughter, he became a farmer; grew religious and " eminent for Puritanism " ; paid his debts punctually; even " grew so cunning as to comply with those modes of Kindnesses and . . . Friendships " which brought him " very much in the esteem of the best of the Faction," or " the Household as they then termed the people of the Separation." He was a " stickler against Ship-Money " and the Scotch war, and so finally came into the Long Parliament by favor of a Cambridge alderman, one Tims, as " one Viper more to the exenterating of her bowels."

Thus fairly launched, Heath spends near half his volume on the rise of this monster, till " The Power was emptied from one Vessel to another," and Cromwell, having " passed and surmounted all the difficulties and troubles that the interest of the Crown had hitherto threatened," became Protector. Once in power, one sentence suffices for the Dutch war, whose success, like the victory of Dunbar, is attributed to Monk. Another does for Cromwell's dealings with the Northern Powers; scarcely more for intervention in behalf of Continental Protestants, the treaty with Mazarin and the war with Spain. " I must omit," Heath says naïvely, " the successes by Blake . . . and Sir Richard Stayner " ; and Dunkirk's surrender he feels constrained " to pass without further remark." Cromwellian legislation scarcely fills a page, and though Heath lingers long over Cromwell's complicity in plots against his own life, it is only when he reaches matters of real importance that he grows voluble. The Protector's " Guard of Halberdiers in gray coats welted with black velvet," his " Drol discourse," his mode of life, with the descriptions of his inauguration and his funeral, fill nearly as many pages as the story of his rule. Thus what the newspapers of his day omitted, Heath supplied, following, or founding, that great jour-

nalistic principle of giving the people what they want —
abuse and personal gossip; and, based on these unfailing
recipes for popularity, it is small wonder that his book
was a success.

Had Restoration knowledge been confined to these, it
would have been a barren epoch in Cromwellian historiography. But no such period of civil war fails to
record itself in memoirs and recollections as well as in
official correspondence, and it was hardly possible to
write much about it and leave Cromwell out. So when
Sir Philip Warwick published his recollections, and the
Duchess of Newcastle an apology for her husband; when
Monk's chaplain wrote his patron's life; when Aitzema
chronicled the Anglo-Dutch war, and Meadowes and
Manly the history of the Northern Powers, they contributed indirectly and unconsciously to Protectoral biography.

But the greatest contribution was neither indirect nor
unconscious, for in 1659 John Rushworth began to publish his *Historical Collections*. Few men were better qualified to recall the past. One of those characters invaluable
to historians who appear at every great crisis, Rushworth,
bred to the law, had busied himself in attending political
and judicial proceedings and making notes of them.
Appointed assistant clerk of the Long Parliament, he was
on duty when the King came to arrest the five members.
He reported Strafford's trial; then, as messenger between
the King and Parliament; as secretary first to Fairfax,
then to Cromwell, and finally to the Council of State; as
a member of Cromwell's parliament; in the service of
Richard, and finally of the Rump, he went everywhere,
knew everyone, and heard almost everything, and set
down most of it. Thereafter, through more than forty
years, the memoranda of this great reporter of the Puritan Revolution found their way to print, the first and still
one of the greatest contributions to its history.

Not to the satisfaction of the royalists, who, declaring

that he had omitted or suppressed much evidence favorable to their cause, commissioned the Reverend John Nalson to gather documents on the other side. To him the Duke of Ormonde sent Irish material; Lord Guilford, the Earl of Manchester's papers. Charles II gave him access to the state archives; and he collected a huge mass of notes, whose fate is characteristic of historical material. From them he published two volumes, with a shorthand report of the King's trial; then he died, with his story told only to 1642. His notes disappeared. Some found their way to the hands of that omnivorous collector, Dr. Tanner, and finally to Oxford University. Some, after a century of wandering, came into public hands; and, two hundred years after Nalson died, some twenty volumes of them were discovered in the Duke of Portland's library at Welbeck, too late to serve their author's purposes.

Such were the earliest efforts to recover the documents of the period; and just before Rushworth's third volume appeared, the first of the Cromwellian memoirs, Bulstrode Whitelocke's *Memorials*, saw the light of print. Eminent in affairs, an able lawyer, sometime ambassador to Sweden, honest, well-informed, he made a solid contribution to the history of his times. Accompanied and followed by more unconscious contribution to Cromwellian historiography, — this time chiefly from Ireland, where Cox's history provided some account of Cromwell's activities in that island and Petty recorded some of its results, — by the time of the Glorious Revolution of 1688 a beginning had been made in gathering material for the Protector's history.

That period took it a step forward. Four years thereafter the bookseller-author, Richard Burton, published the most popular of English lives of Cromwell, notable in that it followed Carrington, not Heath, thus fixing, as it were, the canon of Cromwellian biography; but only, as it chanced, for Englishmen. For on the Continent, meanwhile, Gregorio Leti's *History . . . of the Life of Oliver Cromwell . . . Tyrant without Vice, Prince without Virtue* captured the European fancy and held it for a century. The reasons for its long success are obvious. It provided an elaborate and picturesque account of a prodigious life; a selection of documents, chiefly from Milton, to give it verisimilitude; a genealogy and even a new birth-year (1603) for the Protector. Still more, it now endowed him with a youth of such appalling piety that at five he knew more hymns and prayers than others knew at ten, took such pleasure in sermons that he seemed destined inevitably for the church, and " What a happy disposition for the episcopate! " says the enraptured Leti. At ten he had " a tincture of mathematics and philosophy " ; at twelve he went to Cambridge to pursue the higher sciences. There he attracted Archbishop Ussher's attention; and Bishop Bayly of Bangor seems to have made a special pilgrimage to view this prodigy, " the admiration of the world," whom any professor would have been glad to have as a disciple, and who at seventeen, after six years of college, " possessed perfectly both mathematics and philosophy." One need scarcely pursue the later history of this amazing youth through Leti's thousand pages to perceive that the age of fable was not past in the late seventeenth century, nor pause to meditate imaginary conversations between Heath and Leti in Elysium.

The English lacked this masterpiece of historical imagination, but they had their compensation, for as the revolutionary century waned, its controversies entered into history. The narratives of the " Presbyterian Pope," Richard Baxter, and the Republican regicide, Edmund Ludlow, weighted the balance against their common enemy. The memoirs of Denzil Holles, the political Presbyterian, however hostile to Cromwell, impugned Ludlow's veracity; each provoked retort from royalists and Cromwellians alike, and thus began the age of controversialists.

It was illumined by one great event. In the first year of Queen Anne's reign there finally appeared the great classic of the Cromwellian period, long hidden from the world, Lord Clarendon's *History of the Great Rebellion and the Civil Wars*. The product of the " inexhaustible impulse to work " of a statesman who had spent half his lifetime in exile, with its magnificent periods and its quality of genius, it " fixed the circle of ideas for the English nation " for a century and a half, and from its time the measure of contributions to Cromwellian historiography was in no small degree their relation to the work of Clarendon. It not merely evaluated the characters and the movements of the period. It supplied a store of documents to supplement Rushworth and Nalson; and was in turn supplemented by Rymer's collection of treaties, which added some knowledge of Cromwellian diplomacy, and Walker's *Sufferings of the Clergy*, which became the Anglican martyrology. In such fashion the Age of Anne made its contribution to the memory of Cromwell.

Yet Cromwell himself was known but indirectly; it remained for Hanoverian England to recover him. Its earliest effort was that of a certain Rapin de Thoyras, a Huguenot refugee and follower of William of Orange, who, in an endeavor to explain to the Continent the people and the Revolution that had brought his master to the English throne, issued the first volume of his *History* in 1723. Translated into English, it was continued by the deists Toland and Tindal and the novelist Smollett. In its pages Rushworth and Nalson, Whitelocke, Ludlow, Baxter and Clarendon, and many more besides, had each his day in court, and for the first time the world had a substantial, connected, documented and relatively impartial narrative of the seventeenth century, the most widely read and popular history for more than a generation.

In a sense Rapin opened a new era. The age of Whig history had begun. Within a twelvemonth were published Burnet's *History of my own Time* and Oldmixon's attack on Clarendon, which he called a " critical " history of England. With these appeared the best biography of Cromwell yet written, whose author, one Isaac Kimber, a " General Baptist " minister, first ventured to print some of Cromwell's own letters, and so began another era of Cromwellian biography.

This development was presently reinforced by a new movement, not, indeed, historical, but of much influence in that field. In 1731 was founded the first English periodical of consequence, the *Gentleman's Magazine*, soon followed by the rival *London Magazine*. In their pages were embalmed an amazing number of references to Cromwell and his policy, derived from the contemporary journals, whose contributors found in the great Protector's foreign policy a convenient club with which to beat Sir Robert Walpole, then bent on keeping peace. Then as his ministry wore to a close, this was accompanied and followed by an unparalleled burst of publication relating to the revolutionary period and its great figure.

In quick succession, appeared Neal's *History of the Puritans* and its *Examination* by Grey; Peck's extraordinary collection of tracts, memoirs, letters, wills and epitaphs, which he called *Desiderata Curiosa*; Birch's *General Dictionary*; Carte's edition of the Ormonde papers; a general collection of State Trials; the first volumes of the journals of the Lords and Commons, whose first editor, oddly enough, was the novelist, Dr. Richardson; Thurloe's state papers; those of Milton; the Sydney papers; the " old " parliamentary history; and collections of tracts from the libraries of Lord Somers and Harley, Earl of Oxford. It is a most imposing list, quite overshadowing even the new life of Cromwell by John Banks, the first openly favorable biography of the Protector.

What was the cause of this outpouring of source material for the Cromwellian period? It was due in part to the fact that it was now safe to print it; but still more to the activities of two kinds of men who for a half a century had been collecting it. The first were the collectors proper, those great gentlemen who found refuge from politics in their libraries. High among them stood Sir Robert Harley, Earl of Oxford, who, known to history as a great Tory leader, deserves still greater reputation as a collector. Thousands of manuscripts salvaged from monastic spoil, a hundred thousand books, and more than three times as many pamphlets filled his shelves and those of his son. Next to him stood his rival, Sunderland; the Whig Chancellor, John, Lord Somers; and beside them still others of this noble company.

They were accompanied, assisted and followed by another set of men, peculiarly characteristic of the eighteenth century, the antiquarians, among whom the names of Hearne and Tanner, Birch and the brothers Rawlinson, were conspicuous. Seldom has any country had such a group at the same time. Unknown to fame beyond the narrow bounds of scholarship, without them we should know little of our past. They fell on happy times. Where the pedantic James I had perceived a danger to his throne in the meetings of their great predecessors, Camden and Cotton and Leland, and forbidden them, the Hanoverians, known to history as dull and ignorant men, perceived no such danger. George I chartered the Society of Antiquaries, which they founded. In time George III gave it quarters in Somerset House; and chiefly from its members proceeded this illumination of the past.

But where had collectors and antiquarians found their documents? The story of the Thurloe papers may suffice to show. Superior even to Rushworth in his opportunities as foreign secretary to the Protector, head of an unrivalled spy system, the most trusted of the Cromwellian advisers, Thurloe had made his peace with Charles II's government; but when he died, not even Clarendon, to whom he rendered useful services, knew where his papers were. To all appearances the secret perished with him. But a full quarter of a century thereafter, the then owner of Thurloe's chambers in Lincoln's Inn loaned them to a friend in vacation, and that inquisitive clergyman discovered a false ceiling in the attic and behind it Thurloe's documents. Thence they passed to Lord Somers, thence to his brother-in-law, Sir Joseph Jekyll, Master of the Rolls, thence to a bookseller, Gyles, from whom Rawlinson got some; and, in due course of time, the rest came into public hands.

Such was the career of many such collections. But as the great collectors passed from the scene of their activities, what was to become of their accumulations? One answer was at hand — the universities; and to Oxford the papers of Carte and Clarendon, Tanner and Hearne, in due time found their way. But the Harleys' were bought by a bookseller, Osbourne, and seemed likely to follow Rawlinson's to the auction-room and so be dispersed into original chaos. By the mid-eighteenth century the problem was acute; but a new remedy was found. Among these great collectors the fashionable London physician, Sir Hans Sloane, was eminent. When he died, he left his treasures to the nation in consideration of a payment to his estate of twenty thousand pounds. An act of Parliament authorized a lottery to raise that sum, with an additional amount to buy the Harleian collections and house them. To these were added those of Sir Robert Cotton, and in 1757 George II presented the new foundation with the royal library, which included Archbishop Cranmer's books and many more besides. Two years later Montague House, bought for this purpose, was thrown open to the public, and the British Museum was an accomplished fact. Its foundation was thus coincident with the Seven Years' War; and with the Peace of Paris, which brought it to a close, George III gave it the Thomason collection which, after vicissitudes scarcely less romantic than those of Thurloe's papers, found finally a safe resting-place.

In such fashion the age of institutions succeeded that of private collectors and antiquarians. Nor is it, perhaps, unworthy of note that it was marked by the first volumes of Hume's *History of England*, which found their inspiration in the Stuart period and replaced the Whig Rapin's account with one more suited to Tory proclivities. Still more important for Cromwell's life, Harris, following the precedent of the periodicals, included in his biography of the Protector his letters and orders now emerging from the obscurity of a century. The publication of Cromwellian material now became, indeed a characteristic feature of both periodicals and histories, and found its chief exponent in Mark Noble's monumental *Memoirs of the Protectoral House of Cromwell*, whose very title reveals the altered state of his biography.

Yet even this landmark revealed, as well, its great deficiencies. Much had been published about Cromwell; but the great mass of evidence remained, preserved in safe places, but in what a state! Uncatalogued, or listed in wretched calendars, it remained for a new type of man to carry on the work of the collectors and the antiquarians. This was the cataloguer; and among such the name of the Reverend Samuel Ayscough must hold high place in the minds of that small and obscure fraternity concerned with the invaluable, little recognized and less rewarded task of making knowledge available. The indexer of those reservoirs of eighteenth-century life and letters, the *Annual Register*, the *Gentleman's Magazine* and the *Monthly Review*, the author of the earliest concordance to Shakespeare and of the first catalogue of books in the

British Museum, he set himself to list and describe the manuscripts in that growing collection, and make them available to students. Following him, a Scotch doctor, Robert Watt, compiled a monumental bibliography of pamphlet literature, the *Bibliotheca Britannica*, and thus opened another field to historical scholarship. And it is an ironical reflection upon our self-complacence that on the labors of such humble men as these depends so much of our knowledge of the great ones of the world.

With the French Revolution and Napoleonic wars, among infinite parallels between Cromwell and Bonaparte, came a new burst of interest in the seventeenth century. Drawing upon the work of the collectors and the cataloguers, the compiler of new parliamentary history which goes under Cobbett's name made the chief contribution to Cromwellian biography. From the newspapers in the Thomason collection he extracted the notices of the Protector in a volume entitled *Cromwelliana*; and to this mass of information that all but forgotten prodigy of learning and public spirit, Baron Masères, presently added a collection of tracts to supplement those of Harley and Somers.

Still more important to the cause of history was another force. In the first years of George III's reign, three gentlemen, taking advantage of the great interest in historical collections, secured a commission to catalogue and arrange the public documents. By 1800 it was evident that, after the manner of many such ingenious gentlemen, they had done little but draw salaries for a new sinecure. In consequence they were replaced by a Keeper and Register of Public Documents, who embarked upon the task of setting in order these huge accumulations, which had long attracted and infuriated antiquarians. As the Napoleonic period wore to a close, this work was reinforced by another agency. The sale of the Duke of Roxburghe's collections revealed that these memorials might be dispersed and lost, and a new group bestirred itself, in different fashion from the eighteenth century, to preserve them; forming for that purpose the Roxburghe Club, to publish the rarer and more important documents.

From these two circumstances proceeded the earliest advances of the nineteenth century. Beside the publication of such diaries as those of Pepys and Evelyn, two lives of Cromwell by his descendants, notable for their documents, and the work of the French historian, Guizot, whose series of the memoirs of the revolutionary period is still the most complete, these great collections began to influence history. From the pamphlet literature Godwin drew much of the material for his *History of the Commonwealth*; and in 1825 His Majesty King George the Fourth gave, or sold, his father's collection of eighty thousand volumes to the British Museum. He was, besides, " graciously pleased " to appoint a royal commission to consider the publication of historical material from that source. In 1829 the commission was renewed, and on February 7 of that year, a momentous date for English historical scholarship, the commission voted that the letters of Cardinal Wolsey to Henry VIII and other like material be printed. With this event the authority and resources of government were at last invoked in the cause of recovering the past.

Meanwhile, private enterprise went on. John Forster's life of Cromwell gathered up materials that had been accumulating for a century; Robert Vaughan drew a history of the Protectorate from the Thurloe papers; Cary wrote his *Memorials* of the Civil Wars, which added many Cromwell letters, from the Tanner manuscripts; and Lister utilized the Clarendon papers for his admirable life of the chancellor-historian. Finally these, with lesser contributions to the Cromwellian story, were crowned in 1845 by the appearance of Thomas Carlyle's

*Letters and Speeches of Oliver Cromwell*, the chief landmark
thus far in this long historical pilgrimage.

In it was summed up all, or nearly all, of the development of Cromwellian historiography. It was, and it remains, the greatest literary monument to the Protector's
memory. Carlyle's principal contribution was the as-
sembling of the material in convenient order and his
vigorous plea for his hero; and no one familiar with the
period but must perceive that his actual additions to
knowledge yield in importance to the emotional stimulus
of his " appreciation " of his subject; for virtually all the
documents he published were already in print.

The enormous popularity of his work drew from its long
hiding a new store of Cromwell correspondence, trans-
mitted to the press, or to him, to be included in his later
editions. And, characteristic of the late nineteenth century, there was founded almost at once a periodical to
meet the miscellaneous curiosity about the past which has
filled the pages of *Notes and Queries* from that day to our
own. Its answers to questions about Cromwell and his
times form a perfect encyclopaedia of information,
chiefly, as is usually the case, about minor points. Still
more to the purpose of historians was the progress of publication among the learned societies, which, following the
lead of the Roxburghe Club, and its worthy successor,
the Camden Society, still further illuminated the Cromwellian period.

Thus firmly established, precisely two centuries after
the Protector's death began a new age of Cromwellian
historiography, an age that may properly be described as
that of the scholars. In 1859 David Masson's monumental *Life of Milton* led the way, soon followed by Leopold
von Ranke's *History of England chiefly in the Seventeenth
Century*, which opened new sources of information to historians. If this prototype of Carlyle's famous " Dryas-
dust " did not, as has been humorously said, " invent "

archives, he at least pointed the way to the great treasures of the Continent whence his materials were chiefly
drawn. And even while his work was coming from the
press, Andrew Bisset, in his *History of the Commonwealth*,
introduced its readers to the last, or almost the last, of the
sources for Cromwellian history, the Domestic State
Papers, soon to be made public through the activities of
the Public Records Commission.

It is an interesting question as to when we may expect
" authoritative " history of a given period. In this age of
publicity it may be that one generation will suffice for
reasonable accuracy. But it was not until three-quarters
of a century after his death that enough material was
available for an adequate life of Napoleon; and, as we see,
it was two centuries before there was sufficient evidence
for an adequate Cromwellian biography. Even so, the
era of the Puritan Revolution was, historically, a good
deal of a wilderness. To clear its undergrowth, to chart
its paths, to make it viable and understandable, was the
work of Samuel Rawson Gardiner, whose first volume of
the *History of England from the Accession of James I* appeared
in 1863. Thereafter for nearly forty years he devoted his
great talents to this single task; and his epitaph might well
be the encomium pronounced upon his work; he found
the early Stuart period fable and he left it history.

With prodigious industry and great gift of tongues he
uncovered new masses of material in public and private
collections in the British Isles, in the archives of Brussels,
Paris, Rome, Venice, and Simancas. Scarcely less, he
inspired and informed no small part of that tremendous
addition to the knowledge of the period which he made
his own, partly by the stimulus of his writings, partly by
his personal encouragement to other individuals and
agencies. Of these the greatest was set in motion six
years after his first volume appeared, when, to supplement the labors of the Public Records Commission, there

was established a Historical Manuscripts Commission to publish material in private collections; and it is notable that its first publication begins with an illustration of its purposes drawn from the letters of Charles I captured at Naseby.

Meanwhile its sister commission reached the same period, and working side by side, they uncovered an amount of evidence so rich in the Cromwellian period that, to take one instance, Carlyle's latest editor was enabled to add, chiefly from these sources, more than a hundred Cromwellian documents unknown even to his latest edition and hundreds more escaped even her industry. Finally, in 1886 was founded the *English Historical Review*, to meet the needs of this expanding profession of historical investigation. To all of these, to *Notes and Queries* no less than to the *Review*, of which he became editor, Professor Gardiner contributed of his vast knowledge; and as the nineteenth century went on, did one not know of the work done in other fields, it might seem that its historical energy was devoted chiefly to the elucidation of the seventeenth.

The monographists and the archivists joined in these labors; and education lent its aid, for the training of historical scholars and teachers evoked the doctoral dissertation, which now took its place among the agencies in the recovery of the past. All nations joined this generous rivalry, Scotland and Ireland, Germany and Austria and Italy and France. From points as distant as Nebraska and Japan came men to study Cromwell's policy. Specialists lent their aid to the elucidation of finance and trade, war and diplomacy. The archives were ransacked, the most minute points investigated; historical societies, like those of Massachusetts and Rhode Island in particular, published studies and documents relating to him. Even New Zealand sent its contribution of Cromwellian material which had somehow found its way to that far-distant shore. Above all, Professor Gardiner's great colleague and successor, Professor Firth, not merely in his exhaustive study of the Cromwellian army, his continuation of Gardiner's history to its conclusion, and his study of the House of Lords during the Civil Wars, but in his discoveries of new sources of information, like the invaluable *Clarke Papers*, stands as the dominant figure in the latest phase of Cromwellian scholarship.

Thus the knowledge of the historic Cromwell, like his reputation, reached its height just three centuries after he was born, and the turn of the nineteenth century was signalized, like his death, by three lives of the Protector — but with what a difference! To that task the talents of Professor Gardiner, Professor Firth, and John Morley were summoned, and each in his way produced a notable biography. In them were reflected the labors of two centuries of scholarship; and the differences between them and the work of Heath and Carrington were no longer matters of opinion. As a result there came into being a new conception of Cromwell and his period, based on more accurate knowledge of the motives and manoeuvres of the leaders of both sides than even Clarendon possessed; of the great forces which they directed or by which they were influenced; the circumstances which confronted them, and the results of their activities.

To determine the facts of any given period and set them down in order seems a simple formula to explain its history. But it has not been quite as simple as it seems, for it has meant more than mere determination of the truth — though that was hard enough: it has meant destruction of error, which is still more difficult. The problem of Cromwell was not to be solved by emotion or by argument; it was neither literary nor dialectic in its method. It was not the determination of " rights " and " wrongs," by justification of one side and condemnation of the other, but the determination of the facts by judicial processes. If this new solution was, as its opponents claimed, merely a subtler method of defending Cromwell than by open championship; if its " cold, dispassionate attitude " was but a more ingenious mask of advocacy, it was not consciously that, nor has that view been generally accepted. Whatever the interpretation of his motives and his character, the facts of the historic Cromwell are now available.

What, then, is the modern story of the historic Cromwell as distinguished from that of Leti and of Heath? In one way it differs little from Heath's chronicle. The main facts of Cromwell's life were seldom in dispute. The problems that remained were, in effect, but two — the grounds of the quarrel between the King and Parliament, with the motives and manoeuvres of the leaders of each side; and Cromwell's part in these activities. Was he from his first entry in affairs a shrewd, far-sighted, cunning, hypocritical, ambitious seeker after power; or was he a characteristic product of his time and party, led by the circumstances of his time and his ability to the conduct of affairs? Throughout there is but one issue, that of his character, good faith, motive, or whatever the springs of action may be called. In view of his beliefs and principles, could he have acted otherwise than he did — or were those beliefs and principles genuine?

To that the verdict of history seems thus far in his favor. Admitting the motto of Carrington's biography to be true — that " he who knows not how to dissimulate knows not how to rule "; admitting that all men have their imperfections, the balance has inclined to Cromwell's side. Nor is this merely because the world has changed, that triumphing democracy has perceived in this undemocratic figure a champion of its cause. It is largely because of the activities of those who have preserved and interpreted for us all this historical material, —collectors, antiquarians, cataloguers, editors, monographists, and historians, — and thus enabled us to reconstruct the period and the man.

So, as this last age shifts

> Into the lean and slippered bibliographer
> With spectacles on nose and pouch at side,

we find a different Cromwell from that of the preceding generations. If to each of his biographers the character of the historic Cromwell bears a somewhat different aspect, as his features seemed slightly different to each of the artists who painted his portrait while he was still alive, there remains, none the less, as a result of all these scholarly activities, a figure which we all recognize as Oliver Cromwell, with small chance of error in what he would have called " the fundamentals," whether of actions or of character. Who can doubt that, apart from the more favorable estimate, were Cromwell himself to read these later lives, he would prefer them to those of Heath or Carrington or Leti? Who can doubt that, imperfect as all human knowledge is, in history or in any other field, they represent, so far as may be, what we call the truth; or that truth in history is, in the last resolution, the product of what we call scholarship?

# DAVID HUME:
## PHILOSOPHER–HISTORIAN

IT HAS now been almost precisely two hundred years since a young Scotch student, then resident in the Jesuit college of La Flèche, which had once housed " the father of modern philosophy," broke in on his companion's discussion of a recent miracle with an argument against all such phenomena which not only, as he said, "very much gravelled" his companion but became a standard refutation of miracles in general — except to believers. That circumstance may have been in some degree, perhaps, a tribute to the educational skill of the Jesuits, then reckoned the best schoolmasters in Europe, and the faculty of La Flèche was doubtless fortunate in being able to attract such talented students. Yet some of its members may well have wondered sometimes whether their instruction was not, possibly, too good, the intellectual stimulus they afforded possibly too great. For one of these pupils was René Descartes, the other David Hume; and each of them, so far from contributing to the spread of the true faith, as it was understood by the good fathers of La Flèche, worked mightily to the undermining of that faith.

Between the moment when the youthful Hume took issue with his companion on the subject of miracles and

DAVID HUME

*From a contemporary portrait*

the moment that he died, just as the news of the American Declaration of Independence reached Great Britain, his life took tone from two great influences. In philosophy he was reckoned in his day an advanced thinker of radical tendencies; in politics — though Johnson said of him that he was " only a Tory by chance " — he was an equally pronounced conservative. He was, like so many of us, a paradox. Though he was long an office-holder under the British government, he resented Puritanism and English demagogues so much that he even hoped for the triumph of the Americans over the " barbarous " countrymen and followers of John Wilkes. He was a scholar who never attained a professor's gown but who had to be content with a post as librarian. He was a philosopher who filled many public offices, who was in-ordinately proud of his family, fond of food and drink and cards, concerned about his health, still more concerned for popular applause, and most of all concerned for the financial rewards of his reputation — and who made a fortune out of philosophy and history and the offices they brought!

To those entirely unacquainted with philosophers, such mundane interests may seem astonishing; but this is only half the tale of Hume and human inconsistency. Philosophers are popularly, if incorrectly, supposed to be men of mature years, immune from human frailties, long pondering the mysteries of life, experienced in its infinite complexities, indifferent to popular opinion and applause, still more indifferent to financial gain — and no doubt some are. Yet nothing could be further from the truth than popular conceptions of the age at which genius manifests itself. Poets, musicians, painters, orators, even, we are told, some mathematicians, develop before thirty; historians and economists seldom before forty; great scientists between forty and fifty, and great statesmen and administrators often seem to reach the height of their powers, ripened by reflection and experience, at sixty or even seventy. Hume was no exception to this general rule. He published his *Treatise on Human Nature* when he was twenty-six, and when it fell " dead-born from the press," he was profoundly disappointed — yet being, as he said, " naturally of a cheerful and sanguine temper," he went on. His first *Essays* he published when he was thirty-one; and he was as deeply gratified at forty with the success of his *Political Discourses* as he was depressed by the reception of its immediate successor, his *Enquiry concerning the Principles of Morals*, which, though " incomparably the best " of his writings, he said modestly, " came unnoticed and unobserved into the world."

Whether or not as the result of his failure to gain such recognition and such rewards as he desired from philosophy, at the age of forty-one he turned to other courses. The Faculty of Advocates of Edinburgh elected him librarian, and in such favorable surroundings, with ample leisure and plenty of books, with a fortune of a thousand pounds which, to his friends' amusement, he declared made him independent, he turned historian, on the principle, perhaps, of Bolingbroke's pronouncement that history is philosophy teaching by example. For that pursuit, besides his studies in philosophy, he was equipped with some knowledge of the world, acquired first as a student in Edinburgh; then as a clerk or apprentice to a Bristol merchant — an atmosphere which he found " stifling " ; then as a student for three years in France; still other years in Scotland, as a tutor to the son of the Marquess of Annandale; then as secretary and aide-de-camp to General St. Clair in Venice and Turin. It was a varied and fruitful preparation for his new enterprise, and to it he added other qualifications for his task. He was at the age when, it is said, good history is written; he was financially at ease; he had long training as a writer; and he had leisure. Such were the prime requisites for historical composition, and so Hume undertook the writing of a *History of England*.

If Bolingbroke was right, there is nothing surprising in a philosopher turning historian; it is, in fact, a natural transition. But in Hume's methods, and in his anticipations, there lies another paradox. Most historians begin at the beginning of their task and pursue it chronologically. Hume, in a sense, began at the end and wrote, as it were, more or less backward. " Frightened," as he said, " with the Notion of continuing a Narrative through a period of 1700 years," he commenced with the accession of the House of Stuart to the English throne, that period, he declared, when " the Misrepresentations of Faction began chiefly to take place " — that is to say with the dawn of modern politics, or democracy, or whatever one chooses to call it. The writing of the history of the first two Stuart reigns took him some three years; and the unfavorable reception of his book was so astonishing and so depressing that he thought of going to France, changing his name and spending the rest of his life in some obscure provincial town.

His disappointment at the lack of popularity of his *History* seems as surprising as his idea that he could expect a favorable verdict — or it would be if all authors were not more or less like that. The reason for his failure to gain immediate recognition seems simplicity itself. He wrote a Tory history in a period of Whig ascendancy. Incredible as it may appear, despite his long experience of the world, and, as a philosopher, presumably skilled in the workings of the human mind, he dreamed that though, as he declared, he " was the only Historian that had at once neglected present Power, Interest and Authority and the Cry of popular Prejudices," he might expect " proportional Applause." That is, indeed, precisely what he got. He was, as it seems to us, unreasonably amazed and disappointed when, as he tells us, he was " assailed by one Cry of Reproach, Disapprobation and Detestation; English, Scotch, Irish, Whig and Tory; Churchman and Sectary, Free Thinker and Religionist, Patriot and Courtier, united against a man who had presumed to shed a generous Tear for the Fate of Charles I and the Earl of Strafford."

Yet though, as he went on to say, he scarcely " heard of one Man in the three Kingdoms, considerable for Rank or Letters, that could endure the Book " — except the Primates of England and of Ireland — he proceeded with his *History*. He could not go to France, for the outbreak of the Seven Years' War made it impracticable; and after that the fear that, if he went, the charming Comtesse de Boufflers might marry him despite himself, made it inadvisable. Two years later, he published his second volume, which covered the period from Charles I's death to the Restoration. In " the year of victories," 1759, while England rejoiced over the conquest of the French in Canada and India, he published the history of the Tudor period, which, according to him, was as badly received as his first volume. By that time he was, as he observed, " callous against the Impressions of public Folly " ; and, as the war wore to a close, he issued the two final volumes covering the earlier part of English history. Meanwhile he published his *Natural History of Religion* with some lesser works; and meanwhile too, despite his incessant complaints of his unpopularity, his royalties made him not merely independent, but, as he conceived it, wealthy.

As one reads his letters and compares his grumblings with the facts, Hume seems at least disingenuous, and his accounts of his ill reception both untrue and exaggerated. What more could he expect? His first volume sold, it is said, but forty-five copies in its first twelvemonth, and it is difficult to believe that forty-five copies could have raised such a tremendous outpouring of objurgation as he credits himself with in that period. On the other hand, he received four hundred pounds for the first edition of that volume; seven hundred for the second, which, as he said, helped to reinforce the first; then eight hundred guineas for the copyright of the two; then fourteen hundred pounds for the last two volumes. In all, his "copy money" exceeded, as he said, that of any previous English writer.

Moreover, his reputation brought him further rewards. As the Peace of Paris was being signed, Lord Hertford made him secretary to the British Embassy in Paris, where he was loaded with civilities and compliments and acted for a time as *chargé d'affaires* at a handsome salary. Thence, much gratified with his honors, and, as he takes pains to say, " with much more money and a much larger Income by means of Lord Hertford's friendship," he returned to Edinburgh. For two years he was an under-secretary in the Grafton-Pitt ministry; and, returning to Edinburgh again, he built himself a new house and lived in luxury the rest of his days. Besides his royalties he had been paid generously for his public employments; Bute conferred a considerable pension on him and he had, besides, half pay for his quasi-military services, to which he clung as long as possible. This, for one who had been " passing rich on forty pounds a year " and had early ambitions for a not overly well paid professorship of " ethics and pneumatic philosophy " in Edinburgh, seems no ground for complaint, least of all for a complaint of " public Folly."

He was a recognized leader in European thought; he corresponded with Voltaire, with d'Alembert, Horace Walpole, and even Benjamin Franklin. He befriended, then quarrelled, with the ungrateful and unbalanced Rousseau, whom he had brought to England. He was an intimate friend of Adam Smith, and Lord Kames; and, apart from his great reputation in philosophy, he was, with

Robertson and Gibbon, one of the great triumvirate of British historians. Thus, with an income of a thousand pounds a year, rich, respected and vastly pleased with a career which had brought him reputation which he valued much, and a fortune which he valued certainly not less, he passed his declining years as an eminent member of that brilliant circle which made Edinburgh in his days not only " the Athens of the North " but one of the great intellectual centers of the world.

He was fully conscious of his eminence and he enjoyed it all. Even now one may find amusement in his letters to his historical colleagues. Hume's writings and those of Robertson were translated into French by the same lady; and Hume, writing to Robertson in regard to this, cannot forbear to tell his Scotch confrère of his good fortune. He had been received and complimented by the Dauphin's family; he had been applauded by every class of French society, especially the highest. " I eat nothing but ambrosia, drink nothing but nectar, breathe nothing but incense, and tred on nothing but flowers," he adds with pawky Scotch humor lurking in the words. And when the first volume of Gibbon's *History of the Decline and Fall of the Roman Empire* appeared, Hume wrote him in a certain patronizing strain. " Whether I consider the Dignity of your Style, the Depth of your Matter, or the extensiveness of your Learning, I must regard the work as equally the object of Esteem; and I own, that if I had not previously had the Happiness of your personal Acquaintance, such a Performance, from an Englishman in our Age, would have given me some surprize." Such was the esteem in which Hume was held in France; such the regard for Englishmen in Scotch minds; such the qualities which made for eminence in eighteenth-century historical writing — first style, then " matter," then learning; and such the qualities which made for Hume's reputation as a historian. And, finally, such was the vanity of Hume that he could write to men like Robertson and Gibbon in such terms.

He was, then, besides being a model for the young, an admirable example of the race at that time busily engaged in the conquest of the nation to which it had been united some four years before Hume was born. He was a shrewd, able, thrifty, ambitious and successful Scotchman. Yet even here there was a paradox. While his ingenious fellow-countrymen had been busy making their fortunes in law and politics and business, Hume found fame and fortune both, not in commercial and professional activities, but in what seems the least promising of fields, in contemplation of the eternities and immensities, in the pursuit of history and philosophy. He deserved it all; for David Hume, if not " the intellectual king of the eighteenth century," was one of its greatest intellects. If he was not " the last great British philosopher," he was certainly one of the most eminent. He was, and he remains, one of the chief philosophical forces of modern times; and, as Carlyle once pointed out, he was, unlike Johnson, a European rather than an English figure. And even if one cannot quite admit, with the sage of Chelsea, that Hume is the " pontiff " of the modern world, his works are still read and studied, his ideas debated, his influence still powerful.

He is, in fact, perhaps, as potent an influence in the field of philosophy as ever. But his fate as a historian has been far different. Who now reads Hume — at least for history? Or, for that matter, who beside professional philosophers reads his philosophy? Yet a hundred years ago men read him for both things; read and attacked him both. In his lifetime he wrote that he " possessed the love of all men, except all the Tories, all the Whigs and all the Christians." The Whigs denounced him for his political teachings, the Tories and the Christians for his theological principles. So, taken all in all, he should have been well satisfied — as, barring his vanity, he was. One cannot but suspect that this complaint, like all his other grumblings was, merely " the pride that apes humility " ; for David Hume was a great man, and fully conscious of that fact.

Of his influence, even his historical influence, there can be no doubt. He wrote his *History* at the flood tide of Whig success. Almost romantically attached to the House of Stuart — for such a fat man — he challenged the principles of the party which had overthrown that house and contributed powerfully to that Tory tradition in which, even as he wrote, the Hanoverian prince, George III, was being reared to overthrow the Whigs. With Bolingbroke and Blackstone he broke the Whig hold on the minds of people and sovereign alike, and did his part in establishing the Tory supremacy which lasted sixty years. No book since Clarendon did so much to rehabilitate the cause of the old Cavaliers; no book until Macaulay did so much to change a people's attitude toward its past. For Hume replaced Rapin's defence of the Revolution of 1688 with a defence of the Stuarts whom that revolution overthrew; and as the Huguenot follower of William III had interpreted their history to the English people in terms of Whig principles, this Scotch follower of the Stuarts reinterpreted that history in terms of Tory traditions. In how far it was the cause, in how far the effect, the great age of his *History* coincided with that of Tory dominance, and the Age of George III was no less the Age of Hume.

For three-quarters of a century his great work held the field against all comers as the " standard " account of English history. Not until that " resolute, learned and industrious Whig," the now forgotten Brodie, ventured to challenge Hume in the eighteen-twenties did the Whigs pluck up courage to attack his *History*; and the very essay in the *Edinburgh Review* which led the charge is the best proof of Hume's great influence and enduring charm. " The great support of . . . Tory opinion," it agreed, " has of late years been found chiefly in Hume's history." " Both the prejudices which infect the few genuine Tories of the present day," as well as popular sentiments, " may be justly ascribed to the impression which the artful colouring and delusive reasonings of that book have made on public opinion — an impression which the excellence of the writing, the acuteness of the observations, and the apparent fairness of the deductions, have all tended powerfully to confirm." " We are aware," it went on to say, " that to many practical politicians it may appear fantastic and even ridiculous to ascribe such effects to a book, and especially to a book in four quarto volumes published near seventy years ago. But when it is considered how universally, and at how early an age, it has been read, especially during the latter half of that period, how pleasant it is to read, and how easy to understand and remember it," the conclusion is, as the writer observes, neither fantastic nor ridiculous.

With all his learning, his industry and his resolute Whig principles, Brodie's effort to dethrone Hume failed; but the Whig attack went on. Their greatest champions entered the lists against him; among them John Stuart Mill and Macaulay, each then beginning his career. Mill's charge was curious. " Hume," he admitted, " possessed powers of a very high order; but regard for truth formed no part of his character. He reasoned with surprising acuteness; but the object of his reasoning was not to attain truth, but to show that it is unattainable. His mind, too, was completely enslaved by a taste for literature; not those kinds of literature which teach mankind to know the cause of their happiness and misery, that they may seek the one and avoid the other; but that literature which without regard for truth or utility, seeks only to excite emotion." " The latter part " of Hume's history, he goes on to say — though owing to Hume's curious method of composition, it is hard to know whether Mill refers to the end or the beginning — " has no title to be considered as a history . . . it is really a romance, and bears nearly the same degree of resemblance to anything which really happened as Old Mortality, or Ivanhoe."

To that the young Macaulay added his strictures. " Hume, from whose fascinating narrative the great mass of the reading public are still contented to take their opinions," he asserted dogmatically if with a certain sophistry, " hated religion so much that he hated liberty for having been allied with religion, and has pleaded the cause of tyranny with the dexterity of an advocate, while affecting the impartiality of a judge." It is an odd commentary on life and reputation that this last charge, at least, Macaulay lived to see levelled against himself. As for the rest, it has been properly observed, " Hume sympathized with the Stuarts because he was a Scotchman, and disliked popular government because he was a skeptic."

But Macaulay was not satisfied. Three years later he returned to the charge; and once more in phrases which anticipate his own critics. " Hume," he said, " is an accomplished advocate. Without positively asserting more than he can prove, he gives prominence to all the circumstances which support his case; he glides lightly over those which are unfavorable to it; his own witnesses are applauded and encouraged; the statements which seem to discredit them are controverted; the contradictions into which they fall are explained away; a clear and connected abstract of the evidence is given. Everything that is offered on the other side is scrutinised with the utmost severity; every suspicious circumstance is a ground for comment and invective. What cannot be denied is extenuated, or passed by without notice; . . . but this insidious candor only increases the effect of sophistry." It is a curious charge from such a source; one might think one was reading a review of Macaulay by Croker in the eighteen-fifties, not one of Hume by Macaulay in the eighteen-twenties.

But the diatribes of Mill and Macaulay broke as harmlessly on that magic style as the charges of inaccuracy levelled by Brodie; for as Hume's work had long been almost a requisite of polite education, it still remained the "standard" history of England. It was reprinted, re-edited, revised, abbreviated, even expurgated; and among the curiosities of literature there remains the title of one of these latter works—*Hume's History of England. Revised for Family Use, with such Omissions and Alterations as may render it Salutary to the Young, and unexceptional to Christians.*

Moreover, Hume's influence was not confined to the effect of his *History* on the popular mind; nor is this the end of the extraordinary paradox that was David Hume. He was, he once declared, equally opposed to the Whig doctrine of the contract theory of government and to the Tory doctrine of passive obedience; and Carlyle observed that he was " the father of all succeeding Whigs," as Samuel Johnson was of all succeeding Tories. There is some ground for that apparently paradoxical statement. Hume's influence on Bentham, and even on the republican Godwin, was profound; and in the field of economics he had the distinction of influencing Adam Smith and Malthus. For among his other qualifications as a great man, and even as a historian, was his insatiable curiosity in almost every field of human interest, and he adorned whatever subject he discussed. He even wrote an essay on public credit, and he was vastly concerned over what seems a peculiarly modern problem, that of savings, investments and public revenues. His was, in fact, a universal intellect, and its impact on problems of politics and public economy was scarcely less important than on those of religion, morals and human nature.

That, among other things, is what made his *History* so long-lived and popular. There is scarcely a chapter in the book which does not consider both the situation of the world at large and the social and economic problems of the times of which he writes. The price of food and drink, the problems of wages and taxation, the habits and customs and occupations of the people, fill many pages of a work which for the first time in English historiography found space for what is too often regarded as the product of our day. In a true sense Hume was the father of the " new " history.

But most of all he owed his popularity to his style — clear, luminous, if slightly Latinized prose, with a touch here and there of Scottish influence, and more of Gallic lucidity, easy, graceful, interesting and eminently readable. Whatever he may have lacked in scholarship he made up in mind. For he applied, as has been aptly said, intelligence to history; he wrote with judgment, insight, even humor. He made good reading out of history; good reading still; and, with all his faults of facts, there are few faults of style. Even what seem to us incredibly long sentences are clear and logical. Given modern punctuation, they would often seem lively, and he survives that hardest of all tests — being read aloud — far better than most of his successors. It was not learned history. No man could write the chronicle of the reigns of James I and Charles I in three years, in accordance with the scholarly standards of our time — despite the fact that Mr. Wells wrote a world history in that period. It took Professor Gardiner a lifetime to cover the ground of Hume's first volume, and he did not live to finish his account of the Puritan Revolution.

In consequence, the three great forces which make against historians' immortality set to work to break down

Hume's long rule. The first was the changing temper of the times; the second, scholarship; the third, the altered taste in literary style. The first great Whig attack of the eighteen-twenties broke down, but the reaction against the Tory dominance which it voiced went on to the Reform Bill of 1832 and its succeeding practices and philosophy. That was accompanied by the onslaught of scholars against Hume. The solid learning and massive style of Hallam's *Constitutional History*, which traversed much of Hume's ground, presented a very different picture of Tudor and Stuart times and made great breaches in Hume's argument. The more violent and direct attack of that eminent mediaevalist, Herman Cohen, better known as Sir Francis Palgrave, had less effect than Hallam's more measured discussion. "Flaws in the metal — specks in the rind," which showed the rottenness within; the charge that it was " the one end and intent " of Hume's *History* to attack religion; that only Hume's " sagacity taught him in most cases to avoid absolute falsehoods " — these are not the stuff by which historical reputations are made or marred. More damaging by far was Carlyle's apotheosis of Cromwell which turned public attention into other lines and served to reinforce the rising spirit of democracy. With the appearance of Burton's *Life of Hume* in the eighteen-forties, the controversy flared afresh. With all its faults, the judicious Burton wrote, Hume's *History* had been kept alive by two great qualities, its attention to " the living progress of the people in all that increases their civilization and their happiness," and its " purely literary merits " which maintained it " as a classical and popular work."

This roused the ancient animosities, now reinforced by the obvious decay of Tory principles. " Hume," said the *Edinburgh Review*, " had got from history no confidence in man nor in society." It rejoiced that his " subtle and attractive influence " was waning and that the Toryism which was in part attributable to it was vanishing. " Its varnish is wearing out; and the mischief apparently is nearly over." Even the *Quarterly*, that old Tory champion, added its voice to the clamor; and the *North British Quarterly* betrayed Hume in his own country, chiefly on the ground of his skeptical philosophy, which " melancholy as it may be to think, all the consolation it afforded its author was the conclusion that all was darkness and uncertainty." It was not without reason that across the sea in the *North American Review* it was observed, caustically, that " The estimation in which Hume's great work is held is rather remarkable. It is the fashion to abuse it; every year or two we have a fresh exposition of its errors, its deficiencies and its misstatements." So, the author declares, " The book is immortal . . . and the best advice that can be given even now to the diligent student of English history is to read Hume first " ; and, he concludes, the highest compliment ever paid to Hume was that his old critic, Macaulay, began his history approximately where Hume left off.

Had Macaulay ever read that statement, which is improbable, he would scarcely have appreciated the implication that he feared comparison with Hume. His work was determined by his Whig principles and by the fact that he had Mackintosh's notes. And yet this much is true — Macaulay's triumph marked the beginning of the end of the long reign of Hume. In part as the effect of the development of Liberalism in politics and thought; in part as the effect of that great change in style — and punctuation — which came in with Macaulay; in part as the effect of the advance in scholarship, the great prestige of Hume's *History* began a long decline. Yet it was not until the late eighteen-fifties and the ensuing decades that it was finally broken. Then the Stuart period became the subject of such intensive study as few if any periods ever had before, as the talents of Professor Gardiner began to unravel the tangled skein of seventeenth-century politics. Gardiner's history spelled the epitaph of Hume. As he had been damned as un-Christian in an earlier age, he was now damned as unscholarly and uninteresting in this later time.

Of these charges only one will hold — he was unscholarly. " No one," observes the latest history of English literature, " now reads Hume's *History*." And yet — and yet — it still goes on to say, " Our more conscientious and more enlightened historians might learn much from it as regards the form in which the results of their labors might be presented; its defects in matter, therefore, are of little consequence, while its dignity, its masterly composition and its excellence of expression, render it a literary achievement of the highest order." Hume gave too little time to preparation; he did not always walk across the room to check his facts — he was too comfortable with his feet propped up as he wrote in his lap. He did not trouble to use all the authorities he had. Yet his dramatic skill, his care for social and economic phenomena, above all his style; these make him well worth reading even to-day.

Above all his mind; for even that high priest of the newest school, Strachey, has declared that " one may still find entertainment and even instruction in Hume, especially in his study of the Tudors and the Stuarts." For Hume, he says " was an extremely intelligent man, and anything he had to say on English history could not fail to be worth attending to." His knowledge was insufficient; his metaphysical cast of mind was not suited to history, for " the virtues of a metaphysician are the vices of a historian " ; his " formality, which Hume doubtless supposed was required by the dignity of the subject; his Latinized vocabulary; and a habit of *oratio obliqua*; these were his faults of style; yet he is well worth reading for all that."

Such is the epitaph of the great eighteenth-century historian and philosopher as written by the exponent of the twentieth century. It is an estimate of Hume and of his century; it may not inaptly be regarded as an estimate of Strachey and our times. In its every phrase one may perceive that its author had read and pondered Hume. It has no word of skepticism or the lack of a religious element; it has no word of Tory or of Whig; and this marks a distinction from Hume's critics of a former age. Hume was no orthodox Christian in an earlier sense. That he was deeply concerned with religion, his long attention to religious subjects proves. He tried his best to know and understand what that religion was. His skepticism offends this generation not at all, for it is even more skeptical than he. Nor is it now concerned with Tories or with Whigs; for its political philosophy has long since passed the limits set by them, whether to left or right.

" Two strong angels," says De Quincey in his essay on Joan of Arc, " stand by the side of History, . . . the angel of research on the left hand, that must read millions of dusty parchments and of pages blotted with lies; the angel of meditation on the right hand, that must cleanse these lying records with fire . . . and must quicken them into regenerated life." Such is an older version of history as a science and as an art, as research and as literature. In Hume's case the angel on the right was far more potent than the angel on the left. That ministering spirit was too little active in the composition of his *History*, as the spirit of research is too feverishly active now in comparison with the torpidity of the angel of literature.

And yet one thing remains. In a time when what we now call " facts " threaten to overwhelm men's limited capacity to handle them and find out what they mean; when masses of information seem impossible of such literary treatment as he gave them; when statistics tend to replace the operations of the human mind; when fluent journalism supersedes the literary dignity of such history as he wrote; what then becomes of Hume? The answer has been given — no one reads his *History*. It remains one of those great monuments of the past, which hurrying throngs glance at and pass by. However much scholars might improve their style by studying it, they scorn it for its inaccuracies; however little the multitude may care for those inaccuracies in their current books, they shun it for its style. And both are poorer for neglect of it. Yet to have ruled the field of history for nearly a full century; to have moulded men's conceptions of their past and so influenced their present policies for such a period is an achievement of which few men can boast; and, though his day is past, Hume must be reckoned among the great historians.

What, then, of his philosophy — but how shall a mere layman speak of that? For philosophy is not merely a mode of thought or a scheme of life, which, consciously or unconsciously, each one of us enjoys. It is not merely a code of morals or a view of our relations to the universe and of the universe to us. It is also a terminology which, like French or German, physics or chemistry, one must learn to use. We all have our philosophies; but only those who are conscious of that fact and vocal about it are " philosophers " within the special meaning of that word. In that sense Hume was preeminently a " philosopher." He was acutely conscious of his thoughts and speculations, and vocal about them. He was deeply concerned — as most of us are not — with his relation to the universe; with this life and the next — if there was one; with religion; with the operations of the human mind and emotions. In what spirit, then, did he approach the mystery of human life and thought; what did he think about it all; and what have other people thought of him as a philosopher?

His great claim to distinction in philosophy, as in his work in history, is that he had a mind which he applied to the problems of life; and he lived in an interesting period for the exercise of his faculties. The scientific age had dawned; and, among its infinite manifestations in the form of those tools and toys which it connotes to most of us, it had tremendous influence on men's intellects. The religious phase of human experience had lasted from the beginning almost to Hume's day. In whatever form, dogmatic, supernatural theology had dominated thought as well as emotion. For a millennium and a half the form of religious faith known as Christianity had held the allegiance of the European mind and heart. But in the century and a half before Hume's birth, the venerable edifice of Christian belief had felt the powerful impact of two forces; the one was the challenge of the Reformers to the authority of the Roman church, the other was the challenge of a new kind of men, so-called " scientists," to Roman and Reformer both.

The first was not so dangerous to the ancient faith. The new theologians spoke the language of the old. They met on the same ground. They argued in like terms and from essentially the same premises. They recognized the earth as the center of the visible universe; the heavens as the abode of the blessed after their departure from their earthly activities; and somewhere below the earth's surface a place of punishment for the wicked, known as hell. All these, like man himself, were the creation of an omnipotent, omnipresent, omniscient Deity whose chief concern was man, toward whom His purposes, however they made for righteousness, were inscrutable and incomprehensible — except to those who found in everything some argument for their cause.

But " scientists " were different. They attacked the problem of the universe and man from a wholly different side. They did not use the methods of scholastics, commentators, controversialists or exhorters; they did not speak the language of theology, new or old. They were not interested in angels, saints or martyrs, in conversion, justification, election, regeneration, sanctification or salvation. Without denying His existence, they were not interested in the God of the theologians and His purposes toward man. They were rather concerned with His handiwork. They wanted to find out what the universe was like; what laws, if any, governed it; of what it was composed; and how, in general, it worked. They were concerned with man, not as a child of God but rather as a living organism with material qualities and functions. They were interested rather in bodies than in souls, in the material rather than in the spiritual aspects of the universe and man. They had no concern with the great argument as to the chief end of man and his relation to the Deity; they lived and thought and worked upon a different plane and in a different dimension. They were at once broader and narrower than the disciples of the humanities and of theology. They were concerned, so they claimed, rather with reason than with revelation, or even than with faith.

In consequence, they fell foul of theologians of whatever kind; and equally in consequence they revolutionized all thought. From Copernicus to Newton, their astronomy revealed the heavens not as the abode of disembodied spirits but as the Milky Way, planets and stars and infinity beyond, with some of the laws which governed it — wherein the earth and man receded into a minor place. Whether or not this universe was deocentric, it was certainly not geocentric, and still less homocentric. As a result men took up three positions in regard to this new scientific gospel. They rejected it altogether as inconsistent with revealed religion; they accepted it, whatever effect it might have on revelation; or they sought to find a way to reconcile the new discoveries with the old beliefs.

Into the middle of this vigorous argument, which in some form has lasted to our time, Hume was plunged by accident of birth. A highly intellectual eighteenth-century Scotchman, of a race which had long excelled in splitting the theological hair between the south and south-west side and framing sects whose hope of salvation hung on the slender filament of that divided hair, it was impossible for him to escape his fate. Like so many of his race and age, he was inevitably destined to philosophy and no less inevitably to a philosophy in some sort based upon the scientific spirit then spreading through the world.

Yet here, like his great predecessors, Spinoza, Descartes and Locke, he was confronted with a great problem which concerned the old theology little if at all, but was fundamental to the new discipline. It was the human mind, on which, when all was said and done, depended the validity of all scientific work. What was this thing called " mind " ; of what was it composed; how did it work; what of emotions or passions; what was thought itself? As Kant was to observe later, the business of philosophy is to answer three questions: " What can I know? What ought I to do? For what ought I to hope? " To answer the first, on which the others depend, one must know how one knows. In consequence, eschewing the metaphysics of Spinoza and Descartes, and following the more concrete example of Locke's *Essay on the Human Understanding*, the title of Hume's first and most important book reveals his whole design. It was called *A Treatise on Human Nature, being an Attempt to Introduce the Experimental Method of Reasoning into Moral Subjects*. It fell, as he observed, " still-born " from the press; and, despite the fact that upon it rests the greater part of his reputation as a philosopher, it is some consolation to the non-philosophical to be assured by a historian of philosophy at the end of the nineteenth century that " even at this day there are professed philosophers in England itself who have never read it."

It is apparent from the title of his book that he would nowadays be classified as a psychologist. In that long, complicated and difficult speculation as to space, time, reality, causation, the relation between the external world and ourselves, the question as to whether there is any reality at all, or whether it is a creature of our own imagination — these are problems which have concerned man almost from the beginning. It is a long-debated question as to whether there could be a sound if there was no one to hear it. The relation between mind and matter is one of the great puzzles of existence. " What is matter? Never mind! What is mind? No matter! " is an ancient jest. To the great problems of the theologians as to free-will and foreordination succeeded the psychologist's problem as to what the will was; to the questioning as to the mind of God succeeded that of what was the mind of man. And into that ancient and honorable philosophical argument Hume plunged.

Into that argument only philosophers may follow him. But there was another issue in which all men were much concerned. Hume was reckoned a " skeptic." That is to say, his speculations led him, like many before him and many more since his time, from questioning the validity of theological dogmas into the whole problem of religion. For he, like many others of his kind, was not content with applying reason to matter or even to mind; he was moved, or driven, to apply it to belief; and there he came in conflict with the theologians and with the masses of believers in general. For faith, whether in science or theology, is not a matter of reason. It is instinct or emotion or whatever one may call that realm which lies more or less outside our " rational " processes — if they are rational!

Had he been satisfied to let his early writings take their chance and trust to later generations to recognize their merit, he would never have attained the reputation that he had. But he was not content. His reaction to his disappointment over the failure of his work to give him the recognition he believed that it — and he himself — should have, was characteristic of the man. He rewrote the book. His first volume *On Understanding* he transformed into *An Inquiry concerning Human Understanding*, whose simple style and anecdotal character, with the " omission of acute analysis," gave it a wider public than the earlier work. His volume *On Passions*, with that *On Morals*, which he believed incomparably the best book he ever wrote, were treated in like fashion. But even this would not have given him the notice he deserved, had it not been that, reverting to his early success with the good father of La Flèche, he inserted as the tenth section of this latter work his argument against miracles.

It seemed to many then and since an extraordinary thing to do. It infuriated every section of theological opinion from Roman Catholic to Scotch Presbyterian. His editor and his biographer agree that this essay was both " violent and irrelevant," They further agree that Hume, so far from being a fanatical and heroic anticlerical champion of free thought was an amiable and easy-going man of the world. The only reason they can suggest why an agreeable hedonist should burst forth into a fierce attack upon the " bigotry, ignorance, cunning and roguery " of " that considerable part of mankind " which professed belief in miracles is that it was Hume's passion for notoriety.

If that were true, his formula was simplicity itself. It was the oldest and the newest recipe for gaining the world's attention. It was to shock men by attacking a cherished faith. It succeeded. He brought his philosophical speculations not only into the study and the drawing-room but to the market-place and sold them with much profit to himself. He became a scandal to the orthodox; he was attacked, denounced and vilified; his name became anathema — and his sales revealed the virtues of publicity.

Whatever the reflection on Hume's character, the explanation is simple, if not convincing. It may be true; yet there may well be others. It may be that Hume liked his argument and put it in, despite irrelevance, to give it greater permanence. It may be that, as in his *History*, he loved to take the other side, as part of his ironical view of life. It may be that he perceived the question of miracles to be the real issue between the theologians and the scientists. It may be that he merely posed it as a paradox, that even here he was not serious, but played with all such speculations as a part of his great intellectual superiority to his fellow-men.

If so, it was a characteristic of the man. Though he took the side of the experimental scientists, he argued plausibly that since science depended in the last resort on the human mind for its facts and conclusions, all scientific processes should begin by study of that mind, its characteristics and its qualities, its strength and even its weakness. Though he did not go the length of Bishop Berkeley, who pointed out the close analogy between the faith required for religious and for scientific purposes, Hume was among the first to challenge the scientific as well as the theological dogmas. For he infuriated many by remarking that, save for what we may derive from " figures or numbers," our knowledge of the " facts of science " is only a form of faith, or, at best, a " moral certainty " that things having followed the " law of nature " in a certain course must, of necessity, continue to do so.

Others he infuriated by asserting that, though we regard ourselves as rational, reason is never a cause of action. It merely teaches us whether a thing is true or not, and " such knowledge never moves any one to anything."

Thought he regarded as merely memory plus imagination; and he added in words that must bring sorrow or anger to many 'hearts, that " to have impressions was only to feel, that to think one must have ideas." The only motive force of human action he considered to be emotion; and, when all was said and done, pleasure and pain and their derivatives—joy, sorrow, hope and fear—were the mainsprings of life. When Hume discussed ethical principles his critics were strengthened in their opinion of his cynical philosophy, for he defined the virtues as those qualities in ourselves which are useful to others, or to society, and which, in consequence, are extolled by men as a sort of self-protection.

Were this not bad enough to those who view themselves as moved by very different and much superior motives, he went on to anger others in another field. He vigorously attacked the contract theory of government then so fashionable through the influence of Locke and Rousseau, and so popular as being useful to various elements on their way to power. Finally as to religion he committed himself, apparently, beyond dispute. " The whole frame of nature," he wrote, " bespeaks an intelligent author, and no rational inquirer can, after serious reflection, suspend his belief for a moment with regard to the primary principles of genuine theism and religion."

How, in the face of this, could he have been regarded as an enemy of religion? Such a declaration to-day would be regarded as a certificate of admission into almost any church. The answer is two-fold — first, that theological thinking, even among the clergy, is so rare nowadays that most persons even of that profession would not recognize this as unorthodox; and second, that science has permeated and revolutionized theology. To theologians of an older time his confession of faith smacked not only of skepticism but of atheistical principles. By many of them it would have been regarded — as it was — not as confession but denial of the Christian faith. For it was based not on the Word of God but on His works; on Nature as the product of an intelligent Creator, whose existence was argued from His deeds. It was a common trait of Hume's period. As Linnaeus said, " I think God's thoughts after Him " ; and the American Declaration of Independence spoke of " Nature and of Nature's God."

In Voltaire's epigram, " God created man in His own image and man returned the compliment." To eighteenth-century Christians that was not enough. Man must believe not in a Creator moved by the same rational processes as himself, not in an eighteenth-century scientist who, given immeasurable power, intelligence and opportunity, would have constructed just another such universe, framed just such laws to govern it, and peopled it with beings like, but far inferior to, himself. He must believe in a Being not merely superhuman but supernatural; not merely unknown but unknowable; not comprehensible but inscrutable to man; and not necessarily with the same rational processes, the same code of morals or the same concept of human life as His creatures.

Between these two concepts was a great gulf fixed, a gulf not to be bridged by taking thought — not even, perhaps, to-day. Yet, from one point of view, it was only a reflex of the theologians. One needs but to read those splendid passages in *Paradise Lost* where God expounds to the heavenly host the plan of creation, the mysteries of predestination, free-will and election in the best manner of a Puritan divine, to see that from one point of view the doctrine of science was only a new version of the old theology, transformed from Word to Works, and requiring faith, of whatever different character.

It was with reason that Hume seized on miracles as the crucial point in the scientific-theological dispute. To the old theology there was, so to speak, nothing miraculous about miracles. To it all was miraculous. To it there was no " order of nature," only the will of God which moved in a mysterious way its wonders to perform. To it the raising of the dead was no more a miracle than the rising of the sun, save that it occurred less often. From a Deity concerned with every minute detail of human life such things might be expected when occasion served. But to a scientist such a " miracle " or " prodigy " was unthinkable. It was against the law of nature — and that was impossible. They were not ready to say *Credo quia impossibile* — I believe because it is impossible. They perforce accepted the fundamental miracle, that of Creation and its laws, and argued a Creator from that miracle. All lesser prodigies, such as those recorded in saints' lives, they rejected as incredible — just as the Reformers rejected Roman miracles while clinging to their own. It was unthinkable that there might be more things in heaven and earth than were dreamed of in their philosophy. If there was testimony to that effect, it only proved human credulity, not that the thing occurred.

A miracle, wrote Hume, must be " a violation of the laws of nature," " by a particular volition of the Deity, or by the interposition of some invisible agent." There must " be a uniform experience against every miraculous event, otherwise the event would not merit that appellation. And as an uniform experience amounts to a proof, there is here a direct and full proof, from the nature of the fact, against the existence of any miracle; nor can such a proof be destroyed or the miracle rendered credible but by an opposite proof which is superior." That argument lasted into the nineteenth century and troubled even such a scientist as Professor Huxley, who regarded it as wholly indefensible. As he properly observed, a law of nature was only based on our observation and experience, and they might well be incomplete.

It is not necessary to go through the dozen points of Hume's long argument against miracles. It is enough to say that it has greatly contributed to his permanent reputation. Within a generation it has produced a whole series of volumes. Not merely Professor Huxley but, within six years, among others, the professor of philosophy at the oldest of the Scottish universities has discussed this hardy perennial of scientific theological controversialists. So, however defective or ironical his argument, Hume has had his way. He gained and held attention to his work, by means, some have declared, he must have known were of the essence of sophistry.

Yet even here his fallacies give way to still another element of his fame. What even his argument on miracles failed to do, his *Dialogues on Religion* bid fair to accomplish. Translated into various languages, especially toward the close of the nineteenth century, his " naturalism " has found many followers. A British prime minister turned philosopher heads the long, imposing list of men who have concerned themselves with the problems which hark back to Hume. His so-called " causal reasoning " has been acclaimed as a triumph of insight worthy to be set beside that of Socrates. All the new schools of thought and terminology — pragmatism, humanism, realism, experimentalism — bear echoes of his work. And what can man expect of human immortality more than this?

For after all he was a very human man. After his death his great friend Adam Smith wrote of his last days.

He had been reading Lucian's *Dialogues of the Dead*, and he told fancifully of the pleas he himself might make to the ferryman of the Styx. "I could not well imagine what excuse I could make to Charon in order to obtain a little delay. I have done everything of consequence which I ever meant to do; and I could at no time expect to leave my relations and friends in a better situation than that in which I am now likely to leave them. I therefore have all reason to die contented."

It would seem that, barring a wife and family, he had no more to ask of life, nor any more to get from it. None the less he procrastinated and delayed and made excuses. Finally,

upon further consideration [ he added], I thought I might say to him, "Good Charon, I have been correcting my works for a new edition. Allow me a little time that I may see how the public receives the alterations." But Charon would answer: " When you have seen the effect of these, you will be for making other alterations. There will be no end of such excuses; so, honest friend, please step into the boat." But I might still urge: " Have a little patience, good Charon; I have been endeavoring to open the eyes of the public. If I live a few years longer, I may have the satisfaction of seeing the downfall of some of the prevailing systems of superstition." But Charon would then lose all temper and decency: " You loitering rogue, that will not happen these many hundred years. Do you fancy I will grant you a lease for so long a term? Get into the boat this instant, you lazy, loitering rogue."

So he died as he had lived, keen-witted, shrewd, ironical, in love with life to the very end, conscious of himself, his contribution to the world and his enjoyment of it — and no less conscious of his relation to the universe. It was, one might remark, as many doubtless did, the death of a pagan, not the glorious hope of a true Christian in life after death. It would have confirmed the worst that his worst enemies said of him. It proved his skeptical, humorous approach to problems to which humor and skepticism were inappropriate and in the worst of taste. The present generation finds less to cavil at in such a death-bed scene. For faith like that has disappeared from many million hearts. To its departure Hume contributed; and whether the world is richer or poorer for its loss, each must judge for himself. Yet as theology has been influenced by science, so has science itself developed a mystical element, and, as Hume might have pointed out, that in a sense has done something to justify his position in regard to both.

EARLY AMERICANA

# I. JAMES BLOXHAM: FARMER

WHETHER the effort to drag a forgotten man from oblivion is worth while, whether the contribution to the already overwhelming mass of human knowledge is desirable, much less desired, is always questionable. Indeed we have long since been warned against

> The fond attempt to give a deathless lot
> To names ignoble, born to be forgot.

Yet there is not merely a certain human interest about the subject of this essay, but on at least one side he deserves to be remembered. He was, in a sense, a characteristic figure in the development of that pursuit which, however overshadowed nowadays by industry, is not only the basis of our existence but was at the time of which we write the most important of all American industries — that is to say the cultivation of the soil. He was the representative of a not inconsiderable proportion of the elements which earlier helped to people this continent; and, finally, and most important of all, he played a part in the life of one who did the most to make this nation what it is, George Washington, and so, however unconsciously, achieved a little niche in history.

Let us consider, then, the story of James Bloxham, Farmer. It begins with one of a series of letters written by

Washington to Arthur Young, traveller, writer on agricultural subjects and sometime secretary to the British
Board of Agriculture, published by that eminent theorist
and not very successful farmer after Washington's death.
In it occurs the following passage:

> By means of the application I made to my friend Mr. Fairfax of
> Bath and through the medium of Mr. Rock, a bailiff is sent to me,
> who, if he is acquainted with the best courses of cropping will answer
> my purposes as a director or superintendent of my farms. He has the
> appearance of a plain honest farmer — is industrious, and from the
> character given of him by a Mr. Peacy (with whom he has lived many
> years) is understanding in the management of stock and of most
> matters for which he is employed. How far his ability may be equal to
> a pretty extensive concern is questionable. And what is still worse he
> has come over with improper ideas, for instead of preparing his mind
> to meet a ruinous course of cropping, exhausted lands and numberless
> inconveniences into which we had been thrown by an eight years war;
> he seems to have expected that he was coming to well organized farms
> and that he was to have met ploughs, harrows and all the other im-
> plements of husbandry in as high taste as the best farming counties of
> England could have exhibited them. How far his fortitude will enable
> him to encounter these disappointments or his patience and persever-
> ance will carry him towards the work of reform remains to be decided.

Beyond that brief reference there seemed to be no trace
of this somewhat unpromising new bailiff in Washington's letters, or in his other writings of any sort, as published in the ensuing hundred years. Nor would anyone,
in all probability, have known even of this, had not
chance, which is a part of all such investigations, revealed some documents relating to him and to Washington's experience with him in the form of certain letters of
the bailiff and his master to the Mr. Peacey in question,
in the hands of whose descendants they were until recently preserved. But who was this Mr. Peacey, and who
were these other gentlemen who combined to transmit
the English Agricultural Revolution to America, among
other ways in the person of James Bloxham?

With regard to the first question, at least, there is a

reasonably satisfactory answer. Among that class of gentleman-farmers which reached its zenith in the latter part of the eighteenth century the name of Mr. William Peacey of North Leach, Gloucestershire, stood very high. This was no small distinction in the days when " farmers could let half their land lie idle and live like gentlemen on the proceeds of the other half "; when the greatest states-men in the country reckoned their interest in agriculture and their knowledge of its practical side as not the least of their accomplishments; when King George III himself took such keen interest in such matters that he not only delighted in cattle-fairs and agricultural exhibitions but even contributed to the periodical *Annals of Agriculture* under the name of Ralph Robinson. Not only was Mr. Peacey awarded the great gold medal of the Royal Agricultural Society and invited to become one of the editors of the *Agricultural Cyclopedia*, but he numbered among his friends and correspondents many of the most famous public men of his day.

It is of him, too, the story is told, and embalmed in the yellow pages of the *Gentleman's Magazine* for 1791, how, in order to save an innocent man from the gallows, he rode ninety miles to London in one night with proofs of the man's innocence, which he had secured at great trouble and brought almost, as it were, to the foot of the scaffold, on the morning set for the execution. There is another story, too, equally redolent of the atmosphere of the time, how once King George came to see him in his absence. The busy and irritable housekeeper grumbled vastly at being disturbed in her work by the tall footman for whom she opened the door. " You make," said she, " as much noise as if it was the King." " It *is* the King," replied the footman. " Then," said the undaunted house-keeper, " the King can just go on to Cheltenham to see Mr. Peacey, for he 's not at home." And the King went. Such a man was Mr. Peacey, probably the only man, or very nearly the only man, in the world on friendly terms with George III of England and his greater namesake in America.

It was, then, by a natural sequence of circumstances and events that Washington's new farm bailiff came to him as a result of the connection between Mr. Peacey and Mr. Peacey's friend, Wakelin Welch, Washington's London man of business, and Washington. Humble as the new bailiff was, in a sense he personified the great movement then altering the face of England. The changes in British agriculture which go under the name of the Agricultural Revolution were then in full tide of achievement. Fifty years earlier Jethro Tull had published his epoch-making work on what he called with nice alliteration *Horse-Hoeing Husbandry*; and Lord Townshend, " Turnip " Townshend as he was called from his devotion to that vegetable whose cultivation was one of his ruling passions, not merely revolutionized agriculture, but made farming pay so well that it became fashionable as well as profitable. The discovery that more cultivation meant better returns from the land, that rotation of crops meant less exhaustion, or even renewing of the soil, the introduction of root-crops and of " artificial " grasses, were achievements which may well be set beside those more spectacular inventions which were beginning to stud the land with the new monstrosities called " factories." Moreover, the breeding of cattle which substituted " blooded " stock for the previous " promiscuous union of nobody's son with everybody's daughter " was no less notable, as Robert Bakewell with his " New Leicester " sheep took his place on the roll of Britain's benefactors beside George III who in the very years of which we write it is said helped to introduce merino sheep into England.

As a natural result of this great interest in scientific agriculture came the development of societies and of competitions as the great landlords who fathered it sought means to increase and extend the new knowledge by making it a sporting event as well as a learned pursuit. Scientists lent their aid, and the President of the Royal Society himself, Sir Joseph Banks, was not above proposing a new remedy for scab in sheep. To this again English inventive genius was enlisted by the demand for better agricultural implements, ploughs, drills, harrows, cultivators, even mowing-machines and threshers.

In societies, at least, Scotland led the way with its oddly named Society of Improvers in the Knowledge of Agriculture in Scotland, founded as early as 1723. In England the Society for the Encouragement of Arts, Manufactures and Commerce, founded in 1754, offered prizes for agricultural as well as industrial achievements. A whole new literature of agriculture made its appearance. Local organizations were formed, for meetings, papers, and above all, perhaps, for exhibitions which stimulated competition and made farming a great outdoor sport. Finally, in 1793, this development was recognized by the government in the establishment of the Board of Agriculture with Arthur Young as its secretary.

Among these local organizations almost if not quite the first was the Bath and West of England Society formed in 1777 at the crisis of the American War. To it belonged most of the leading farmers and landlords of the region from which Bloxham was drafted to carry the new gospel to America once that war was done. In this respect there was a striking difference between agriculture and manufacturing. The secrets of the new machines were guarded with such strictness that it was a felony to carry them out of the country. The story goes that Silas Deane was as anxious to bring back from his diplomatic labors James Watt's new-fangled steam-engine, with whatever other machinery he might be able to lay his hands on, as he was to secure a French alliance, but with less result, for all his

Yankee shrewdness. Samuel Slater, stopped from smuggling out the plans of spinning machinery, was only able to introduce them into the United States, it is said, by committing them to memory and so carrying them literally in his head, to Pawtucket. But seeds, plants, agricultural machinery and livestock were subject to no such embargo and began to find their way across the Atlantic almost as soon as the war was over.

There was need of them. The war, as Washington observed, had left American agriculture, especially on such estates as his, in a bad way. The soil, in the older regions especially, was no longer that deep virgin mould which the pioneers had cleared. Much of it doubtless had never been; and, even where it had, the crude methods of cropping, and the planting of tobacco in particular, had long since begun to exhaust its fertility. To remedy this condition, Washington himself had experimented in crop-rotation after the English model, in drainage, and in fertilizing not only with manure but with marl. He finally turned to seek the help of an expert manager; and thus in much the same fashion in which the English had attacked their problems, the Americans began to follow their example.

In societies not the least, for scarcely was the war over when they began to spring up everywhere. In Charleston and in Philadelphia such organizations were formed in 1784–1785, and within six or seven years New York, Massachusetts and presently Connecticut had followed suit. Experimental farms had been proposed by the Charleston group, and agricultural education in schools and universities by Philadelphia; and all the societies had begun that publication of proceedings which is one of the chief occupations of such bodies. The leading men of America, like those of England, belonged to these societies — Washington and Franklin to the Philadelphia organization, the Adamses, Hancock and Fisher Ames to the Massachusetts body, one of whose members, the Reverend Samuel Deane of Portland, had even published a book with the somewhat forbidding title of *The New England Farmer or Georgical Dictionary, containing a Compendious Account of the Ways and Means in which the Important Art of Husbandry, in all its various branches, is, or may be, practiced to the greatest advantage of this country.* Moreover, English agricultural publications found many readers in America, and among the volumes in Washington's library are enumerated nearly fifty titles of works dealing with farming and kindred topics.

It was, indeed, not only the war nor even the exhaustion of the land by long cropping of tobacco which affected the value of Virginia holdings. The decline in the demand for that commodity, as for most American products, in England after the war, with consequent general demoralization of trade, made it necessary to turn to other crops, chiefly wheat. The local overseers were utterly unable to meet the new situation, and even when wheat was grown it was necessary to find a market for it. In that respect, at least, the Father of his Country and his fellows were woefully behind the times. They did not clamor for state aid, they sought no legislation, nor appropriations from the government. It would, of course, have been futile in a day when government itself was so weak, and when men like Patrick Henry were too busy opposing the Federal Constitution to give such support to Virginia planters as he had earlier given to the Parsons' cause. In consequence, Washington sought to develop trade with the West Indies; to make, it is said, ship-biscuit out of his wheat; and in various other ways to escape from the very uncomfortable dilemma in which he found his fortunes.

Such, then, were the circumstances of the Agricultural Revolution in England and of the Agricultural Depression in America, when, at the height of the former and the depth of the latter, the greatest, if not, indeed, the largest farmer in the United States sought for guidance from one of the fountain-heads of agricultural knowledge in Great Britain. In that enterprise he secured assistance from the members of the Bath and West of England Society in the person of this James Bloxham, who, it would appear, had got into some difficulty, probably financial, and was not unwilling to leave his native country, for a time at least. That worthy would, no doubt, have been enormously surprised to know that he was the representative of such a movement, and much abashed to find himself in such great company. What his sensations would have been had he known that he would have become the subject of an essay a hundred years and more after he was dead, we can only dimly imagine.

Least of all could he have realized what, politically speaking, he was getting into. Not the least interesting part of his story lies not in his own adventures but in the circumstance that he arrived in this country at one of the greatest crises of its history, that his new employer had been not merely the commander-in-chief of the victorious American army — which Bloxham doubtless knew — but that he was at this very moment the man above all other men to whom the new nation looked for guidance in this most critical epoch of its beginnings. Bloxham's connection with Washington, indeed, so closely parallels the period of the formation and adoption of the Constitution that, among other surprising things about this little story, none is more astonishing than that Washington had time or inclination to note the details of his relations with his new farm manager. They were some time in arriving at an agreement, for it was not until Monday, May 19th, 1786, that Washington noted in his diary that he had " Agreed this day with James Bloxham who arrived here the 21st day of April from England, to live with and superintend my farming business upon the terms mentioned in a specific agreement in writing."

That agreement, so characteristic of Washington's methods, runs thus:

ARTICLES OF AGREEMENT entered into this 31st day of May in the year 1786 between George Washington Esqr of the County of Fairfax and Commonwealth of Virginia of the one part, and James Bloxham lately from the Shire of Gloucester in the Kingdom of England, Farmer of the other part Witnesseth, That the said James Bloxham for and in consideration of the Wages, Allowances, and privileges herein-after mentioned, doth agree with and oblige himself to serve, the said George Washington for the space of one year; to commence the first day of the present month, in the capacity of a Farmer and Manager of such parts of Husbandry as shall be committed to his charge; and will, to the utmost of his skill and abilities, order and direct the same (with the approbation of the said George Washington) to the best advantage. — That he will at all times, and upon all occasions, suggest such plans for the improvement of the said Washington's Farms, and the stock of Horses, Cattle, Sheep, Hogs, &ca which are on them as to him shall appear most conducive to his interest, — Will keep regular Accts of the said stock — and will strictly observe and follow all such orders and directions as he shall from time to time receive from his said em-ployer; for this and for other purposes. That when thereunto required, he will buy, at the expence of the said Washington, Cattle, or Sheep for feeding, or for Store; and will dispose of the same or any others, to the best advantage; attending particularly to the care and manage-ment of the Stock of every kind, both in Winter & Summer — as well those for the use and benefit of the farms, and for family consumption, as those which may be fatted for the Market — That he will use his utmost endeavours to encrease, and properly distribute, the Manure on the farms; and also will improve to the best of his judgment, the implements of husbandry necessary thereto — and will instruct, as occasion may require, and opportunities offer, the labourers therein how to Plow, Sow, Mow, Reap, Thatch, Ditch, Hedge &ca in the best manner. — And generally, that he will consider the said Washington's interest as his own, and use his true endeavour to promote it accord-ingly. In consideration whereof, the said Washington doth agree to pay the said James Bloxham Fifty Guineas for his year's Services, to be compleated on the first day of May, 1787; and will allow him, the said Bloxham, ten Guineas besides, towards defraying the expences of bringing his wife and family to this Country. — That when they shall have arrived, he will provide him, & them, a decent and comfortable House to reside in, by themselves; will lend them two Cows for Milk — a Sow to raise Pigs for their own eating (but not to sell) and give them as much Bran as is sufficient to brew Beer for his Family's use. — And moreover, will allow them for the part of the year which will remain after the arrival of his family and leaving his present board, at the rate of Six hundred pounds of Pork and Beef, and Eight hundred pounds of Middling Flour, per annum: — and likewise a piece of ground sufficient for a Garden, and firewood. — The said George Washington also agrees to provide the said James Bloxham with a horse to ride on for the purpose of superintending the business herein required — or, if the said Bloxham shall find his own horse, to allow pasturage, & reasonable feed for him. — Lastly it is agreed between the said George Washington and James Bloxham, that if the said James Bloxham shall not return to England at the expiration of the year for which he engages, and his conduct shall be such as to merit the approbation of the said George Washington, that then and in those cases, his wages for the next year shall be Sixty Guineas; and the other allowances and priviledges the same as the present year. In testimony of all and each of these Articles, and for the full and perfect compliance therewith, the parties to these presents hath interchangeably set their hands and seals, and to the other, doth bind himself in the sum of One hundred pounds Currt money of Virginia, the day and year first written.

Signed, Sealed &ca
in the presence of
Geo. Washington. [1]

Go Washington     seal
James Bloxham     seal

What did they think of each other, these two men so very different in every way, thus brought together by this curious chance? That, too, we are permitted to know, for we have, in the first place, the remarkable communication of Bloxham, not to himself as one might infer from its beginning, but to his patron and benefactor, Mr. Peacey. It may be necessary to explain that " sanfine " or sanfoin of which he makes so much, is a kind of pasture grass, and from the Young letters it seems probable that the unsatisfactory seed came from that gentleman and had, perhaps, spoiled in transit. A " shupick " is a fork, and, like " biddick " in Devonshire, seems peculiar to Gloucester,

[1] George Augustus Washington, nephew of George Washington.

Worcester and Wilts. As to the gentle insistence that the ploughs be " Light and Deasant," his anxiety will not be surprising to anyone who has observed the difference of weight between English and American soil, probably nowhere greater than between North Wilts and Glouces- ter and the neighborhood of Mount Vernon. In his let- ters to Young, Washington complains of the trouble he has had to make his hands use the heavy English ploughs and comments on his land as " light loam." With these explanations we may attack the Bloxham letter.

FOR MR. PEACEY ATT NORTHLEACH FARM
GLOUCESTERSHIRE

Virginia July 23 1786

James Bloxham Sr. this to inform you that I arrived Safe att the generls Washingtons the 20 3 [23] of aprel which was Ester monday. I have ordered for 10 Bushels of Sanfine Seed and other Seeds from you which the generel Washington will aplie to you for and I should be glad if you would take the Best Care you Can to send it over good ass you Can for he have been Deseved in some sanfine seed from England which I Recemend him to you and let me have good that the generl sends for of all sorts if posable and send it along with my wife ass soon as possble and I should bee glad if you could get a Clever Little Deasant D plow which must go without a weeal for the Land is not Level and to be Shoor to make him Light and Deasant and be Shoor to make him turn the worke well for they have som most shoking Plows that Ever was Seen in the world the land is Light and very easy to plow they go with two horses only and Doble the same ass your Norfolk plows. But no weel but very light as they have no noshon of making a plow to turn the work they are very stupet in thare one Con- sait but send on that is Light and Deasant and that it will turn the work well I Rot in my other Letter to my wife to Com over but I thinke it not worth while for I think thatt I Shall not Stay no Longer than my yeare is up which is the first of next may for things Are verey Desagreable to Do Bisness it is impossable for any man to Do Bisness in any form the Genral have a Bout 25 hundrd akers of Clear Land under is on ocyping. Ther is nothing agreble about on the plase which I can not Do no Bisness form nor no Credet but I have you send the plow And the Seeds which the Genearel will send for to you and send half a Dosen of Good Clean made Shupicks for they have nothing but wooden forks I have got one or two made but in a very bad manner that I should be glad if you would not for this Contey is verey pore and there is no chance for any Body to Do any god and I should be glad if you and my Brother Thomas would See if these velins would Com to any terms or I would go to any part of Englun to be out of thare way But this Countruy will not Do for me but to Be Shore what the General have offered in wages is quite Well he Gives for this year we have a Gred for 50 English ginnes per yeare and Bord and washing and Lodging and if I Would send for my wife and famly he would alow me ten Ginnes towards thare Coming to this Contry an if I would Stay and to alow me 8 hundard weight of flower and 6 hunderd Wait of pork and Bef and to alow me two milche Cows for the youse of my famly and to alow me a Sow to Breed Som pigs for my own yous but Not to Sell and to alow me a Comfortable house to Live in but it apears to me not Any Inheretance [inducement?] thear is another thing Which is very Disagreable these Black People I am Rather in Danger of being poisind among them which I think I Shall Leave the Contrey ass son Ass      I Can But the general and I have agreed and articld for one yeare But my wife may youse ore one will A Bout Comming over.  But I hope Sr you I hope will Be a frend to my Poor Deer Children and Wife And I Hope you will Remember my Brother Thomas to a Sist them what he can my heart have yarned for my family a gret maney time and I think Im allmost Like a transport convict  But I hope that the Sun will Sine upon me wonce more the general have some very [good?] laynd But badly manedge and he never well have them no better for he have a Sett About him which I nor you would be troubled with But the General is goot them and he must keep them but they are a verey Desagreable People and I will leave the Contey But I Should be glad of answer Immedatly to know how afares Stand and then I sall be a better Judge of the matter the General have som very good Shep which he sold for 40 Shilings a pes of thar money a English guina is 28 Shiling of m o ney and I hope mrs and all the famly is Well and I have whent thro a greatt Dele Since I laft England.

And Lett me have a nanswer Imeadetly Rember me to all frens and no mor from yor frend and well wisher

James Bloxham

But if one gathers from Bloxham's communication that he was not wholly satisfied with his new surroundings and occupation, it is scarcely less apparent from Washington's letter which accompanied it that the new farm manager had tried even his monumental patience.  It also was addressed to Mr. Peacey and makes a shrewd guess as to what its companion contained.

SIR, Excuse the liberty I take in putting the inclosed Letters under cover to you. — It is to oblige Mr. Bloxham who now lives with me, but who scarcely has sufficient knowledge of his own mind to determine whether to continue more than the present year (for which he is engaged) or not. — In a word he seems rather to have expected to have found well organized farms, than that the end and design of my employing him was to make them so. — He makes no allowance for the ravages of a nine yeare's war from which we are but just beginning to emerge, nor does he consider that if our system of Husbandry had been perfect as it may be found on your Farms, or in the best farming Counties in England, there would have been no occasion for his Services.

What the old man has written to you respecting the coming over of his wife — sending over plows seeds and so forth I know not; because at different times he seems to be of different opinions. I can only add, therefore, if his family are to come, and by the way of London, that it would be well for some person on their behalf to open a correspondence with Mssrs. Forrest & Stoddart, Merchants, of that place who have Ships that pass by my door in their way to Alexandria, and would render the passage in one of them much more convenient & less expensive than to any other place; 'tho in a vessel bound for Norfolk in this State (Virginia), or Annapolis, Baltimore or Patuxent in the neighbouring one of Maryland, it would not be very inconvenient. In case of her coming, whatever Implements, seeds, &c. may be requested by Mr. Bloxham on my Acct had better be paid for by his wife, and settled for here.

I am sorry to be thus troublesome, but as Mr. Bloxham considers you as his Benefactor, and Friend — has addressed one of his Letters to you — and his Wife, if she finally resolves to come, will stand in need of advise and assistance, it is necessary that the best mode should be suggested. — A ship from Bristol to either of the places above named, may, probably, be more convenient than the rout but of this you can judge better than I, I am Sir, Yr most Obdt & Humle Servt,

G. WASHINGTON.

Such were the unpromising beginnings of a connection which, on the face of it, seemed destined to be of few days and full of trouble, if one did not allow for the characters of the two men involved, the shrewd patience of Washington and the obvious inclination of Bloxham to follow the instincts of his race and put his worst foot forward. For it is apparent that the new bailiff was already at work. Two months after he had written to Mr. Peacey, on Wednesday, September 20th, Washington noted in his diary:

My Farmer sowed this day the lay land which had been broken up at this place by his own directions, part of which, at the east end adjoining the Corn had been plowed        days. The other part at the West and also adjoining the Corn had been plowed        days. The first contns. about        Acres; the 2d about        . This Wheat was put in in the following manner, viz. sowed on the first plowing, which tho the ground was well enough broke, the sod was not properly turned. In the roughest and heaviest part the Seedsman was followed by a heavy harrow the same way as the ground was plowed; in the lighter part by two light harrows, side by side (fastened together), and the whole cross harrowed with the light double harrow to smooth and fill the hollows. Alongside this I set two plows as above to break up        Acres more of the lay, and directed it to be sowed as fast as the lands were finished, and to receive the same harrowings to try (the land being nearly of the same quality) wch. method will succeed best.

Despite their original differences, by October Washington was taking Bloxham's advice. On October 21st he recorded once more in his diary that:

At first the People had finished sowing Wheat about Noon yesterday; and today were picking up the fallen Corn and gathering the residue of the Pease. The Plows were preparing the Wheat Stubble for rye, and sowing it. At Dogue run the Plows had got into the drilled corn, the Stalks of which were cut down and entirely taken off the ground. The ground with the plowing seemed to be in perfect tilth, and in good order. I was about to harrow it after sowing, but my Farmer advised the contrary and I desisted.

Again on November 7th he noted that " My old Farmer thinking the nights had got too long tho' the weather as yet had been mild, to keep the cattle in open pens on the naked ground I ordered the whole not to be penned till proper shelters had been made for them." And on the day following he discovered that his new bailiff knew

little of the subject of surveying in which Washington
had been, if he was not still, something of an expert, for
he wrote:

> The Farmer having carrd. the level and staked it for conducting the
> water on the South side of Muddy hole swamp below the fork of
> Manley's old house and Cornelius McDermot Roe having done the
> same on the No. side from the plank bridge on Muddy hole (where the
> farmer also began) I tried with a water level across in several places
> within Manley's field and found that the farmer was higher on his side
> than the other by between 16 and 18 Inches. But this will make no es-
> sential difference in a ditch for water 18 Inches deep.

Washington did not, indeed, devote all his attention to
his farm, much less to Bloxham, in these days. On Sun-
day, November 2nd, he recorded:

> Mr. George Mason came here to dinner and returned in the Eve-
> ning — After dinner word was brot from Alexandria that the Minister
> of France was arrived there and intended down here to dinner — Ac-
> cordingly, a little before Sun setting, he (the Count de Moustiers) his
> Sister the Marchioness de Breton Brienne — the Marquis her Son and
> Mr du Ponts came in.

On Monday, November 3rd:

> Remained at home all day. — Colo Fitzgerald & Doctr Craik came
> down to dinner — & with a copy of an address (which the Citizens of
> Alexandria meant to present to the Minister) waited on him to know
> when he would receive it.

Yet even these visits of friendship and ceremony were
not unconnected with the humble Bloxham, for the General's account book shows that in November, probably at
the time of this visit, he took occasion to pay Colonel
Fitzgerald the sum of eleven shillings " freight of yr. chest
&c " duly charged in the Bloxham account.

As they worked together, it is apparent that each began
to modify his opinion of the other, and Bloxham in
particular began to be reconciled to his new surroundings,
for on November 13 Washington noted in his diary:

Told James Bloxham, my Farmer, who was about to write to England for his wife and family, and who proposed the measure that he might write to one Caleb Hall, a neighbour of his in Gloucestershire (who had expressed a desire to come to this country, and who he said was a complete Wheel right, Waggon builder, and Plow and Hurdle maker), that I wd give him 25 Guineas a year for his Services & if he paid his own passage to this country) the first year, and I found he answered my purposes, and we liked each other, that I might give him 30 guineas the next year, and held out encouragement, if he chose to work for himself, that I would provide him with some place to live at. Whilst with me that he should be found with Provisions, Washing and lodging.

What, meanwhile, had happened to the letters sent in August? In a day when it took from three to six months for a voyage across the Atlantic, it is not surprising to find that it was apparently only in January, 1787, that they reached London, and came into the hands of Mr. Wakelin Welch, Washington's correspondent there until 1791, and were, as it appears from his letter to his friend Mr. Peacey, duly forwarded:

Mr. PEACY,

By this post have sent you a packet which came by a vessel, just arrived, addressed to us from Gen. Washington in his letter to us — " he mentions that he had a Farmer sent to him from Gloucestershire by a friend at Bath, he has written for his wife to come to him with her children & to bring with them some Seeds Implements of Husbandry &c to this country. Bristol is their nearest port, but Oppo from thence to this River rarely happening I recommend it to their Patron Mr Peacey to open a correspondence with you that she may be advised of the Sailing of a Vessell from London to this River as a more speedy & certain mode of conveyance. Your compliance therein would be very pleasing to me & Serviceable to an old English Farmer

I am Sr
Yr Most obedient humle Serv.

G. W.

In Conformity to the above I am to inform you that a fine Vessell named the *Mary* Capt. John Andrews, & who sails by Gen. Washington's Seat will go from hence in all February if it suits your Friend to go by that time & from London, she should let me know as I might engage for passage which sometimes cannot always be depended upon. am Sr Yr H Servt

W. WELCH.

LONDON the 17 Jan. 1787.

The charge of a Passage from hence is high & paid for before the departure of the Ship how far will this be convenient for the Family.

Matters, it appeared, moved more rapidly once the business reached England. It took only six days for Mr. Welch to send and receive his correspondence with Mr. Peacey, as is evident from his next letter:

WILLIAM PEACEY, Esq.

SR. I am to thank You in the first place for your kind present of a Hare which I rec'd very safe & in Consequence of your desiring my engaging a passage for Mrs. Bloxham & her two children I this day have done it — the Captain one Andrews is a very good Man, his ship is Brittish & one of the first character, the Vessel goes very near Gen. Washingtons Landing so that Mrs. Bloxham has not far to Travel.

The Usual Charge for passengers who lay in the Cabbin & are found with fresh Provisions & Wine during the Voyage is twenty Guineas each, but for Mrs. Bloxham & her two children to go in that agreeable State, the Captain has agreed for thirty Guineas for the Family & which I do not think unreasonable, as to the things necessary for Mrs. Bloxham to take depends on Mrs. Bloxham her Self. Goods & Cloaths in Virginia as they mostly come from hence are very dear, therefore it would be necessary for her to Lay in a good Stock of them, on board Ship anything does, the Captain was saying some Beding might be wanting for the Cabin, but the expence of which can not be great as to everything else is included in the thirty Guineas, the Seeds will be particularly taken care of & let the package be marked Seeds so that they may be known when on Board, pray wil there be any quantity so as to fill Casks, if they do we must take a warehouse for them if not they may be sent to out Counting house no. 19 Fenchurch Buildings near Fenchurch Street, the place of my Residence is in the country about 4 miles from London.

The Ship sails in all Febr. so that if Mrs. Bloxham has any Acquaintance in Town she might come by the last week am very Respectfully yr obliged & humb Serv

W. Welch.

23 Jany. 1787.

If Mrs Bloxham should alter her Mind let me know as the Captain keeps the Cabbin for her Accomodation & therefore cannot dispose of it to any else.

In spite of this the fretful Bloxham was destined to remain in single blessedness for a considerable time, while, apparently, Mrs. Bloxham made up her mind and her other preparations for this great venture in a new world. We find in Washington's accounts only one record against Bloxham for 1787, a bill of eighteen shillings and sixpence debited to him on December 31 for " work done for you by my Shoem'r and Taylor as per act." Moreover, some time in 1787 it appears that Mrs. Bloxham did not alter her mind but was shipped along with the " sanfine " seed and other farming necessaries (of which we may hope that the ploughs proved " Light and Deasant ") as we may perceive by the following letter. From it also appears that Bloxham had not been poisoned, that he had apparently reconsidered his determination to leave the country to its fate as soon as his agreement with Washington expired, and that his services had proved more satisfactory than the previous letters would have led us to believe. Under date of 7 January, 1788, Washington writes to Mr. Peacey.

MOUNT VERNON, 7 Jany 1788

SIR: — I have received your letter of the second of Feby 1787. I am much obliged for your attention in sending me the seeds, which arrived agreeable to the bill. Mrs. Bloxham received of Wakelin Welch Esq. of London £10–1–10 which sum she informed him was what she paid you for the seeds on my account. I am not sorry that Caleb Hall did not come out for I proposed his coming more to please Bloxham, who was very desirous of having him here than from a want of his services myself. I thank you, Sir, for your obliging offer to furnish me with Blacksmiths and a Millwright: — I have two of the former occupation, who, though not very neat workmen, answer all my purposes in making farming utensils etc in a plain way — the latter I shall have no Occasion for as I have not work enough to employ him in his own line: — and indeed I doubt whether they would find their advantage in coming over at present for although I should be extremely glad to see the honest and industrious mechanic come into this country from any and every part of the Globe, yet I would not wish to encourage them unless they would be benefitted by it. Whenever we have a regular and firm government established the prospect for these people will be much more pleasing than it is at present. Bloxham and his family are in good health and appear to be contented with the country. I am Sir

Yr most obed: Servt

G. Washington

William Peacey Esq.

The seeds, as the General's diary notes, were put in the ground as soon as the weather permitted, for we find on

*Monday, 7th April 1788*

In the Vineyard Inclosure below the Stables I sowed in a bed in the No. Et. Cornr. the Seed of the Runkel Recbar, or Root of Scarcity, and adjoining this in two other beds, ranging therewith, the Seeds of Sulla were sown; the Middle bed was sent by Mr. Peacey to my Farmer. Below these again will be sown the seeds of the Fancy Grass, given to me by the Revd. Mr. Massey.

Moreover, Washington and Bloxham had begun to look after the family of the bailiff, for we find on May 9, 1788, the farmer was debited with 1000 herrings at five shillings, 100 shad at two shillings, and a barrel and a half of salt at four shillings, fivepence, the whole amounting to £1/9/6. Beginning with June 7, 1878, the Bloxham household began to receive " middlings " from Washington's mill, with which it was duly charged on March 1, 1789, with 1755 pounds at twelve shillings, or £10/10/8. With that, apparently, there began a new relationship between the master of Mount Vernon and his bailiff, for we find that these earlier sums are carried forward to what Washington calls a " new account," made out, it may be noted, not, like the old, to " James Bloxham (Farmer) " but to " Mr. James Bloxham," which argues possibly some obscure alteration in social status. The first item, the first of its kind on the books, indeed, is a charge of £19/12 in wages paid him on March 14, 1789, and again on that same day a cash item of fourteen guineas apparently included in the former sum.

Thereafter in 1789 is no account, perhaps because Washington was journeying through New England, but in February (13) 1790 is a payment to " your wife Mary Bloxham on account of wages due you £15 "; in June " 1255 lb. Midlings furnished you since the 1st March 1789 @ 15 / £ /9 /8 /3 "; " 1734 lb. for Beef and Pork furnished you from the time you commenced housekeeping @ 25 / pr. hundred £21 / 13 / 7½ "; " 35½ lb. Bacon @ 6d 17 / 9; 21 lb. Mutton @ 4d. 7 / " ; " 150 shad furnished you in 1789 £1 / 2 / 6; and 2 Bus for Salt 6 / 8 /." All of which is interesting not merely for the comparison with present prices but as an example of Washington's elaborate system of bookkeeping which might well give pause to some of the most advanced of modern farmers, to say nothing of the shock it might give to some others.

Moreover, two things are apparent from these otherwise dull accounts. The first is that Bloxham seems to have been rising in the world. On June 12, 1790, he was paid the very respectable sum of £200 on account of wages, which he had evidently not drawn until then; and in the April following there is an item of £80 paid to Mr. Alexander Smith in his behalf. In June, 1791, the account was closed with an item of " Cash pd. to you in full of all demands as pr. Receipt of this date, £19 / 11 / 8½ " making a total of £367 / 19 / 8 from the beginning to the end of the connection.[2]

The second consideration is the relation between Bloxham's activity and that of his master in these eventful days. At the very time that the new farm manager ar-

2. The difference between this sum and five years at 50 or 60 guineas a year is probably explained by the difference between English and Virginia currency, perhaps with incidental arrangements and expenses not specifically noted in the agreement or accounts.

rived at Mount Vernon, the farmers of western Massachusetts were beginning that movement for cheap money which presently led, among other things, to Shays' rebellion. When Bloxham sent his first letter home, that movement was finding expression in county conventions; and when Washington first noted Bloxham's labors in his diary, that little rebellion was getting under way. The whole country was similarly disturbed with the now desperate financial situation. Virginia was moving for what was to be a constitutional convention, with Washington as one of the leading spirits. By the time that Mrs. Bloxham came over, Washington was presiding over that convention in Philadelphia, while Congress was busy with the Northwest Ordinance.

When Washington wrote to Mr. Peacey in January, 1788, the struggle for the adoption of the Constitution was being waged, and Washington was throwing his influence into the scale for its acceptance. His letter on the subject of importing blacksmiths and a millwright, indeed, comes in between one to Jefferson on the subject of American interference in foreign affairs, and one to Governor Randolph urging the support of the Constitution. As the news of Massachusetts' adoption came to Virginia, it found Washington watching the sprouting of his new seeds of the " root of scarcity," the fancy grass and the sulla in the vineyard enclosure. While Bloxham's " new account " was being made up, his master was beginning his first term as President of the United States, and by the time that account was closed the reports of Hamilton on public credit, a national bank and protection of domestic manufactures were beginning not only to bring comfort to farmers and business men alike throughout the country, but were restoring that confidence so sadly lacking before, and, as Washington noted in his letter to Mr. Peacey, so essential to sound national life.

It is, perhaps, a mere coincidence, scarcely worthy of

note, yet it seems somehow typical of the times, that it was at this precise moment that Bloxham finally cast in his lot with this country.  In spite of those who from that day to our own have professed to see in the Constitution little or nothing more than an effort of the capitalist, " exploiting " classes to oppress the " plain people " of the country, Bloxham seems somehow a symbol of the new day which had dawned in the United States of America.  As is apparent from the next chapter in his story, he, like many of his kind, now felt that there was some substantial foundation for their affairs, enabling them, as well as the government, to go on.

With this last entry in June, 1791, all knowledge of Bloxham seemed to end on the severance of his connection with Washington.  There even seemed a possibility that he had gone back to his beloved Gloucestershire.  But in studying the accounts it appeared that there might be some significance in these last large payments and the name of Alexander Smith, that, instead of going back, he might have taken his accumulated savings and bought some land of that gentleman in the neighborhood of Mount Vernon.  An application to the Register of Fairfax County more than confirmed that conjecture; and from the information supplied from the records of the Circuit Court of that county it is possible not only to determine this fact, but in some degree the end of Bloxham's story.

For from that record it appears that on July 20, 1795, Mr. Alexander Smith completed a deed to Mary Bloxham and her children, William, Elizabeth, James and Thomas, confirming to them a tract of some forty acres, " Beginning at a red oak corner to the land of Peter Wise on an old ditch, and running thence with the said Wise's land to the new Turnpike road, thence Eastwardly binding with the said road to William Ward's corner on the said road, thence with Ward's land, thence with the said

Ditch a Southwardly line to the beginning." That land was bought in 1790 by Smith from one Thomas West, and, it would appear, was contracted for by Bloxham shortly thereafter, for £310 Virginia money. But Bloxham died when he had paid Smith about half of the purchase price, without making provision for paying the remainder or receiving a conveyance. Thereafter it appears that his wife Mary, instead of being cared for by a Society for the Encouragement of Mendicancy among Immigrants, carried on, paid the balance and so received the deed for her lifetime, with her children, the deed is careful to state, as tenants in common and not as joint tenants, for the further payment of one dollar. Moreover, the clerk of the court discovered that Mary Bloxham qualified as administratrix of her husband on Jan. 22, 1793, which fixes approximately the date of his death, and gives the amount of his estate at that time as £52 / 2 / 0.

This is then, apparently, the end of the career of James Bloxham so far as human records go. Yet to it, as to all things human, there is an epilogue. For in the records of the Fairfax County Court there is another entry, dated January 8, 1853, which carries the story one step further. It is the will of Bloxham's eldest son, William, a somewhat pathetic document with which this paper may well close. It reads as follows:

> Know all men buy thees presents, That I William Bloxham of the County of Fairfax & State of Virginia, Do will and bequeath to my son Joseph Bloxham and Mary my Daughter all my Real and personal property, after my just debts are paid which is my Desire that after I am laid in my last resting place there my repose in peace and In making this my Last Will I do it for the regard to my two children has allways shew me and in providing food and rament for me in my old age and Joseph being a cripple.

So ends the story of James Bloxham, Farmer. It has an interest in itself as what is called a " human document." It has a greater interest in its connection with the life of Washington. Yet its greatest interest lies in the fact that, thanks to that accidental circumstance, it has lived till now. It is a comment on the ways of fame. There were hundreds of men of more consequence in the eighteenth century than James Bloxham, important in their day and wholly forgotten since. Yet by a curious turn of Fortune's wheel, by chance preservation of his letters and his inclusion in the note book and correspondence of George Washington, in short by the accident of his connection with a great man, this obscure Gloucestershire farmer has outlived them all.

"CONSTITUTION HALL"

THE OLD PRISON

LANE UNIVERSITY

THE "ROWENA" HOTEL

LECOMPTON

## II. LECOMPTON

TO CERTAIN types of mind, to most minds, in fact, once their attention has been called to it, there is a fascination in what may seem, at first sight, a most unpromising source of interest — the index to an atlas. It is not merely that the origin and meaning of place-names rouse our curiosity. It is not merely their hint of distant lands and possible adventure inviting us to leave our little daily round. It is not merely that some names stir like the sound of a trumpet, that others echo the music of wave-lapped tropic shores, and still others plumb the depths of commonplace; that some bear in their syllables a threat, and others a promise or a hope. All these touch the imagination as we run through the list, from the Holms of Ire to Namouna, from Terror Point to Dull; but there is something more. It is that these names reflect mankind in all its aspects and its circumstance; its hopes and fears, its superstitions, its achievements, its greatness and its littleness, its romance, even its humor, its imagination and the lack of it.

It is, in short, that they suggest so much. Thermopylae and Waterloo; Stratford and Weimar; the saints' calendar wherever Spain and Portugal and France have gone; the English names borne to all corners of the earth by her far-wandering yet home-loving sons; these are material for history and romance. Capes Fear and Hope, Despair Bay, Heart's Content, one Hell and many Paradises, reflect extremes of man's infinity of moods. There are names which reach the heights of imagery, and those where all imagination seems to fail, names out of the arithmetic, from Seven to Ninety-Six, and places known only by their distance from somewhere else.

In that long list the greater part are, naturally, drawn from Nature, animate and inanimate, real and imagined; from birds, beasts and flowers, reptiles, fish and trees, and the infinite phenomena of weather and geography. Next come descriptive names like Glasgow, the dark glen, and Dublin, the black pool; or human creations like Stockholm, or stockade island, and Copenhagen, or shopping haven, with a small infinity of variants on man's chief occupations, fighting and trading, as he has made his way around the earth. Then come the names of men, especially in new lands, or lands once new, from Alexandria to Cassopolis, from Barcelona to Washington; not least in the United States, where, from the first chief executive to the last, few presidents or none lack such distinction as town names confer; with many lesser men, and some, perhaps, greater. It is a kind of hero-worship, of others — or one's self. It is a part of man's long striving for immortality.

Yet towns are like the men who founded them. Who can predict which one will have a place in history? Some seem to be born famous; some acquire fame; some have it thrust upon them. The accident of geography which makes this one a great fortress and that one a market-place, even that depends on shifting currents of trade and power, developments in war, or, it may be, on climate changing through the centuries. But most of all their greatness rests upon the strength and energy of their inhabitants. For where are Tyre and Sidon now; and what was New York before the white man came? Who now relies upon the strength of the Black Rock of Angers; who worships now at Angkor; who dwells in Petra; and where was Sybaris? Why should Boston and not New York have been the early home of liberty and letters in the United States; Virginia, not Maryland, the home of statesmanship?

There is no answer to the great riddle. Despite the dreams of sociologists, there is no recipe for greatness in men nor in the towns they found; there is no formula for immortality. At any moment some individual or some place may rise to fame; and none can predict that strange phenomenon, much less determine it. For a brief instant man or place may touch the universal at some point, and all unconsciously, perhaps not always willingly, achieve a place in history. Towns may receive that impulse from outside. Why should not any one of half a dozen Belgian villages or Pennsylvania towns have seen the downfall of Napoleon or the high tide of the Confederacy? Why was not Shakespeare born in Warwick or in Coventry? And who can think that those who lived in Waterloo or Gettysburg welcomed the event which made their villages immortal; who can conceive that Stratford planned a Shakespeare in its midst? As in all things human, whatever may be said, time and chance are vital elements of life's unending mysteries; and, among them, this.

To most of these reflections the little Kansas town of Lecompton provides an illustration. It is but a name to students of American history; to others scarcely that. It is, apparently, the only place so called in all the world; and had it not been for a series of events largely beyond its own immediate control, it would have lived out an uneventful life under the more distinguished name of Douglas by which it was first known. Unless one thinks with the determinists that every circumstance is the result of forces at work from the beginning and tending inexorably to a given point, it would appear that Lecompton's place in history was in the nature of an accident. It was achieved in a few hours and by a few score words. It was not won by its inhabitants; it was, one may conceive, hardly desired by a great part of them. It rests largely upon a single document, the so-called Lecompton Constitution, which not merely gave it a place in American history but brought it in touch with even greater things, among them that struggle for liberty which filled the nineteenth century.

Moreover, save for that, it is now virtually unknown. It is no goal of pilgrimage like Gettysburg and Waterloo. It has developed into no great center of trade and population like Chicago and New York. It is no longer, as it was once, a seat of government. Its sole claim to fame is that its name is bound up with a lost cause. Yet none the less it has an interest. For while historians may be trusted to preserve the memory of men and places that succeeded in the world, it is of scarcely less moment to know something of those that failed. To understand all human happenings it is not enough to know who won and how. It is no less significant to know who lost and why. To all these things the story of the brief moment when this little western town touched world-wide conflict at one point and then sank back to its old nothingness again, is at once a romance and a comment on human plans and ambitions, as well, perhaps, as a footnote to history.

In the vast sweep of man's activities that story is, indeed, only a speck upon the stream of time. Viewed in the long perspective of the ages, it was only yesterday that Lecompton played its little part upon the stage of politics. But nowadays the world moves fast. The story of the struggle for the West between slave states and free already belongs to the middle ages of the United States, those strenuous years between the Constitution and the Civil War. Already it has its legends and its myths; its heroes, saints and martyrs; its epics and romance, and even its crusade. In that the village of Lecompton played a major part. Yet it is scarcely more than two generations since this Kansas town was for a time the focus of a struggle which looked forth to civil war. Not a few of those who walked its streets were destined to great parts upon the larger stage; and the issue defined within its narrow limits was to spread across the continent and cost half a million lives.

Justy eighty years ago the United States was rent with the great argument over Negro slavery which for the moment centered in the West. Beyond the states then part of the Union until one came to California, lay the Great Plains, stretching from the Missouri River to the foothills of the Rocky Mountains. They were still inhabited by Indians and buffalo, but white settlement was imminent. The folk-wandering which had filled the land to the Missouri and found its way to the far western coast was by no means spent. It had, indeed, been recently reinforced by that other folk-wandering which was then pouring thousands of Irish and German immigrants into the eastern states. Already pioneers were straining at the leash; already plans were being laid to rush into that region once the bars were down; already politicians schemed to win it for freedom or slavery. The North regarded it as good as won; the South looked at it enviously; for on its possession depended in some sort continuance or decline of southern power in national affairs.

At this moment, in January, 1854, the Democratic leader, Stephen A. Douglas, Senator from Illinois, moved, his enemies declared, by his ambition to be president, but more probably by genuine desire to see his country grow in wealth and power, introduced a bill to organize this trans-Missouri region, then known as Nebraska, and throw it open to settlement. In his proposal there was nothing remarkable. It was the usual method by which the western states, his own among them, had been formed

into " territories," settled, and in due course of their increase of population, admitted to statehood. It was desired by his fellow-countrymen, especially in the West,
anxious to secure the way to California and to extend the
national boundaries and power. It seemed, in fact, to the
fast growing Union and its ambitious citizens, an admirable solution for their expansionist activities.

But Douglas' bill contained a dangerous element. For
a full generation the United States had been divided between North and South on the question of Negro slavery.
Within that period two efforts had been made to solve
that great problem. The Missouri Compromise of 1820
had determined that slavery should not exist in the territory of the Louisiana Purchase north of the parallel of
36° 30', which marked the southern boundary of Missouri. In return for that concession by the South, Missouri was admitted as a slave state in the year following.
Thirty years later the question arose again; and the
Compromise of 1850 marked the second stage of the great
dispute. By that agreement, California was admitted as a
free state; but as the committee in charge of the measure
reported, " all questions pertaining to slavery in the territories and the new states to be formed therefrom are to be
left to the decision of the people residing therein. . . ."
Such was the principle popularly known as " squatter
sovereignty " ; and in it there was a certain inconsistency which the long controversy on Douglas' bill
brought out. For his proposal raised two great issues;
the one was that the old Missouri Compromise was un-
constitutional in that it limited the right of property; the
other was that Congress had no authority to intervene in
territorial affairs, any more than it had authority to in-
fringe on the rights of states.

Adopting this principle of squatter sovereignty, first
proposed by Cass, Douglas proposed to organize the
territory on that basis. From that position he was forced,

chiefly by Southern opposition, to a proposal to repeal the Compromise; divide the territory into two parts, the one west of Missouri to be known as Kansas, the rest as Nebraska; and allow the people to decide the question of slavery for themselves. And though it was nowhere so stated formally, it was tacitly assumed that the southern area might well become a slave-holding state in time.

Such was the " Little Giant's " effort to organize the trans-Mississippi territories, leaving the question of slavery, as in the Compromise of 1850, to judicial action by the Supreme Court, through the motion of the people themselves. At once the northern Free State party was aroused. From the Senate its leaders appealed to the country at large in passionate denunciation of Douglas and his plan. In the Senate itself began a furious struggle and only after desperate resistance was his proposal forced through the House of Representatives by administration aid. During that four months of violent debate, the controversy spread throughout the nation to the exclusion of all other issues of politics. The North, already irritated by the Fugitive Slave Law, passed four years earlier, was furious. Press and pulpit poured violent denunciations upon Douglas and his " Nebraska iniquity." Party lines were cut sheer across; and within three months of the passage of Douglas' bill, a new political organization, the Republican party, took the field. The anti-slavery movement swept the West like a prairie-fire. In the ensuing election Douglas' party lost nine states and sixty-two seats in Congress; and it was evident that a new political era was about to dawn.

At that moment the settlement of Kansas began. It was not wholly political, for the debates in Congress and outside had called attention to a land pre-eminently fitted for human settlement; a land where it was said one could plow for five hundred miles and never strike a rock; a land whose deep, rich, virgin soil could raise such crops as farmers dream of but so seldom see; a land which would need houses, stores and towns, goods, citizens — and slaves. The prospect of cheap land, the chance to grow rich from business, land-transfers and town-site speculation, combined to draw the more adventurous to this new empire. It was not wholly new. For five years men had braved the passage to California; and now the plains which saw the covered wagons make their way to the western Eldorado became the goal of others in a new search for wealth and adventure, as the " Kansas fever " began to rival even the rush for gold. Unlike that gold-rush this new venture involved deep and far-reaching political interests. The eyes of North and South were directed to a region which might turn the scale in national affairs, then nicely balanced between the rival powers. Thus Kansas became the battleground between slave states and free, the proving-ground for squatter sover-eignty, the prize, perhaps, of national dominance; and North and South, each in its own fashion, bestirred itself to gain that prize.

The Douglas bill was signed on May 30th, 1854, and by that time the exodus had begun. Into the new terri-tory poured men and women from nearly every part of the Union. It was easier for them in that the trail was already blazed. They came for the most part up the Missouri River to where, nearly fifty years before, Zebu-lon Pike had set forth from its junction with the Kansas or Smoky River to find a way to the Rocky Mountains and the western coast. There had sprung up a trading-post which presently became a gateway to the West. Through it had poured, and was still pouring, a stream of settlers and gold-seekers, and with them it grew in ambitions, wealth and numbers. A year before the Douglas bill was passed, it had been chartered as a municipality, and, developing from Westport Landing to Kansas City, it aspired to be, what it has since become, the principal metropolis of the great Southwest. Farther north, a dozen years before, one Joseph Ribideaux had founded a post which he called St. Joseph; and through these two entries came the chief streams of emigrants.

With its slave-holding commonwealth of Missouri on the eastern border of this land debatable, the South had an advantage which it hastened to improve. First from Missouri, then from the farther South, her sons poured in to win an empire and perpetuate their power. The government land-agents, officers and surveyors, preceded, accompanied and followed them; and in that hectic summer of 1854 and thereafter, Kansas, which had been the home of eight Indian reservations, three army posts and here and there an isolated trading-post or house, became the scene of a land-rush unequalled hitherto in American history.

Under that favorite form of frontier enterprise, townsite promotion, almost overnight new settlements sprung up along the eastern border. Within a fortnight after the bill was signed, the Leavenworth Company was organized to lay out a town about the Fort, and by October it was selling lots. It was not far ahead of its competitors. Under the lead of some Missouri men, among whom its Senator, Atchison, was prominent, the Atchison Town Company was formed on July 27th, and at once established a settlement on the Missouri north of Leavenworth. Between them another, known as Kickapoo, sprang up; and within three years there were some fourteen of these mushroom cities established between Atchison and Kansas City. Backed by Missouri forces just across the line, there was thus formed a strong proslavery nucleus in the northeastern corner of the new territory.

Meanwhile the North had not been idle — New England in particular. Its entry into the struggle took characteristic form, that of a corporation. When the Douglas bill passed the Senate, one Eli Thayer of Massachusetts, supported by various rich and philanthropic individuals, among them the textile " magnates," Amos and Abbott Lawrence, secured a charter for a New England Emigrant Aid Society. Its purpose was to found settlements, build houses, mills, set up a hotel and a newspaper, and, in brief, reproduce in a modern dress the organizations which had founded New England two centuries earlier. The movement turned almost at once into a new crusade for liberty. The churches took it up, and, among others, the great pulpit orator, Henry Ward Beecher, made the cause his own. Funds were raised and settlers enlisted with such rapidity that four days after the founding of the Atchison Company the Emigrant Aid Society's pioneers set up their tents at a point on the Kaw River, forty miles west of Kansas City where, according to tradition, their leader, Dr. Robinson, five years earlier, had camped on his way to California. There they founded a town named from their chief benefactors, Lawrence, and established a Free State headquarters.

To it and to adjacent settlements men of that party hastened to emigrate. Within six months the town of Topeka was founded farther west on the Kansas River; and thus was established the beginning of a Free State stronghold over against that of the pro-slavery men. Almost at once a Free State hotel was built in Lawrence, and by October the *Herald of Freedom* was spreading the Free State gospel. It was more than a business venture; more even that a crusade; it became a second Pilgrim Father episode. As Whittier wrote:

> We cross the prairies as of old
> The Pilgrims crossed the sea,
> To make the West, as they the East,
> The household of the free.
>
> We go to raise a wall of men
> On Freedom's southern line,

And plant beside the cotton tree
The rugged northern pine.

Upbearing like the ark of old
The Bible in our van,
We go to test the truth of God
Against the fraud of man.

It was an open challenge to the South and was received
as such. From the first it was denounced with virulence;
and its " Hessians," its " mercenary hirelings," and its
" hypocritical promoters " became a favorite theme of
Southern editors and orators. It became an issue in
national affairs; and on its support or opposition the lines
of sectional and party cleavage were still more sharply
drawn.

Such was the situation of affairs in eastern Kansas in
the summer of 1854. But Kansas was not settled wholly
by " fanatics " or " fire-eaters " as the rivals called each
other in those violent days; there were other elements.
Among them, in the midst of these activities, a little party
of Northerners, chiefly, it appears, from Pennsylvania,
entered the territory by way of Kansas City, made its
way up the Kaw River beyond Lawrence, and half way
between that town and Topeka established a new settlement. To it, as to the county in which they and the
Lawrence Free State men had settled, was given the
name of their party idol, Douglas. And there, save for
forces outside themselves, and in which, for the moment
at least, they seemed not vitally concerned, the matter
might have rested and their town never have emerged
from the decent obscurity to which it seemed destined.

But while its founders were staking out their claims,
Fate took an active hand in their affairs and presently
gave their town a place in history unmatched by that of
any of these new foundations save, perhaps, Lawrence.
For during the autumn of that fateful year of 1854, the
new territorial governor, Reeder, arrived with his official

family to take up the task of government. Almost his first act was to call an election for a territorial delegate to Congress; and with that blazed up the bitter struggle between Free State and slave state men which filled the next five years with tragic interest. It began with an " invasion " of sixteen hundred Missourians under Senator Atchison who carried the election — and Reeder let it stand. It went on with a like movement in the following spring, again led by Atchison, whose five thousand followers cast over six thousand ballots and elected a proslavery legislature. That body not merely threw out the few Free Staters who had managed to be chosen; it passed an act confirming slavery in the territory, reinforced by a measure excluding anyone opposed to slaveholding from a jury to try cases which involved that species of property.

The South was satisfied; the North and the anti-slavery party were furious. Under the lead of Dr. Robinson, the Free State men repudiated the legislature's action; sent for rifles; named that " vessel of wrath," James H. Lane, sometime lieutenant-governor of Indiana, as commander of their troops; called a convention of their partisans; and in October met at Topeka to frame a constitution prohibiting slavery. Thus was the issue drawn; and events moved rapidly to armed conflict and an appeal to the national government and the people at large. The pro-slavery men met at Leavenworth to form a " law and order " party, and with this began not merely border war but a national conflict.

The capture of some Free State men; their rescue; the summoning of aid from Missouri by the sheriff; the siege of Lawrence by fifteen hundred " Border Ruffians "; their repulse by Lane's men armed with " Beecher's Bibles " — as Sharpe's rifles were nicknamed from the preacher who had raised money to buy them and shipped them out as copies of Holy Writ — these are the fabric

of Kansas history. The legislative victory of the Free
State men, their election of Robinson as " governor,"
their appeal for admission to the Union and President
Pierce's denunciation of the Emigrant Aid Society and
Free State men, brought the question into national politics; and thereafter it took the center of the stage not only
in Kansas but the country in general.

But what of the village of Douglas amid these stirring
scenes? For more than a year after its founders arrived,
Kansas had been torn with political dissension, which, in
comparison with its neighbors east and west, seemed to
pass Douglas by, though doubtless its people were profoundly moved by it. But men cannot devote their time
entirely to politics. The new settlers had to stake out their
claims, find food and shelter, and somehow make a living
if they could. They had, as one of them observed later,
little enough to live on save bacon and flour brought in
by boat or wagon, with some parched corn which they
managed to raise. They had, according to all accounts,
plenty of whiskey — and within three years, apparently,
not merely whiskey but champagne and oysters! For,
strange as it may seem, money was plentiful. Nor is this,
after all, surprising; for they possessed a fundamental
source of wealth. They were the first comers in a new
country, rich, unoccupied and sure to be the goal of
thousands of home-seekers. They had land on which
they planned to build cities — and sell lots. They had
the backing of what was known as " Eastern capital,"
ready and anxious to speculate in that great source of
wealth.

Moreover, they would have to have a seat of government; and on its location turned not merely a great
political issue but a great land speculation. In consequence, the second controversy which arose was that of
the determination of its site. The Douglas bill had desig-
nated Leavenworth as a " temporary " capital, and that

dignity it enjoyed for some fifty days. But its promoters were apparently not strong enough politically to make it permanent, or they were, perhaps, too much concerned with other things, and the capital was moved to Shawnee Mission, southwest of Kansas City. Thence it migrated to Pawnee Mission, near Fort Riley, where, as it happened, Governor Reeder had taken up land claims. Thence it returned to Shawnee Mission; and, after some fifteen months of wandering, in August, 1855, it was " permanently " located at " Lecompton," as the town of Douglas was re-named.

The reasons for these rapid shifts were characteristic of the time; nor were those reasons wholly, or even largely, political. They were chiefly due to the activities of the town-site companies. It was obvious that the location of the capital would largely benefit those fortunate enough to secure that great advantage to their real estate, and pressure of every kind was put on the new territorial officials to lend their influence to this place or that. Seldom, if ever, in Kansas history has there been more intrigue than in those months when it was trying to make up its mind where it should have its seat of government.

That mind was finally made up. The officials themselves organized a town-site company. Its president was the territorial chief-justice, Lecompte, and among its members was the governor's secretary, Woodson, who presently became acting governor. While new settlers poured in, while political animosity rose to fever heat and matters shaped themselves to civil war, these enterprising gentlemen had fixed on Douglas as the site of the new capital. In more senses than one, perhaps, they plotted a town-site of nearly a square mile; and against the opposition of all rival schemes they pushed the matter through the legislature, named the place after their president, and prepared to reap the profits of their plan.

Thus was Lecompton born; and here in the autumn of 1855 was established the seat of government. Almost at once the place became much more than that. Partly for that reason, partly because of its proximity to the center of Free State activity, Lawrence, it became the pro-slavery headquarters. From Lecompton men went to take part in the so-called " Wakarusa War." To it were brought six Free State leaders with their chief, Dr. Robinson, in March, 1856, as prisoners. It was here that chief-justice Lecompte charged the jury which indicted those leaders for the murder of a pro-slavery sheriff, and denounced the Lawrence newspaper and hotel as accessories. As a sequel to this, in May, 1856, Senator Atchison led another invasion from Missouri which captured Lawrence, and, in accordance with Lecompte's denunciation, burned the hotel and wrecked the printing-press. It was against Lecompton that Lane, finding the Missouri River route closed to him, brought down from the north his " army " of " twelve hundred men with cannon " to avenge the attack on Lawrence and release the prisoners. It was from Lecompton that orders to disperse the Topeka Free State assembly were sent. From Lecompton went urgent appeals to Colonel Sumner in Fort Leavenworth for aid to repress the bloody bushwhacking activities of " Border Ruffians," " Red Legs " and individuals like John Brown of Ossawattomie, who was to make his name in Kansas history as the murderer of five inoffensive men, and in national history as the hero of the abolitionists.

Meanwhile, as the great slavery contest deepened and widened throughout the nation then torn with a presidential election and the consideration of the Dred Scott case, the town of Lecompton rose to the height of its fame and power. Here were set up the territorial offices. Here were built hotels to accommodate officials, landseekers, leaders and followers of the pro-slavery cause. Among this group — as was natural in a community whose chief industry for the moment was the transfer of land — was the surveyor-general, John Calhoun. In his person, as it were, Lecompton came in touch with wider issues and with greater men. Appointed by the influence of his friend, Douglas, he reported to the commissioner-general of the Land Office in Washington, Thomas A. Hendricks, later vice-president of the United States. He came from Sangamon County, Illinois, where he had been surveyor and where he had as his assistant for a time one Abraham Lincoln. Finally, he was to preside over the body which ensured Lecompton's place in history.

For his use and that of the territorial administration, a building was erected, land-offices below and legislative hall above. A post-office was established; a stage-line put in operation and presently appeared a newspaper, the *Lecompton Union*. In its yellow pages we may still feel something of the thrill of that conflict on this remote frontier which was to sweep the land. Founded, as its fiery editor wrote, in that " hot-bed of Abolitionism," Douglas County, it avowed its purpose to " be ever found battling for the rights of the South and Southern institutions." " Believing the soil and climate of Kansas to be admirably adapted to the institution of Negro Slavery as it exists in the Southern States," it " proposed to zealously advocate all honorable measures designed to protect and sustain it in the territory and ultimately have it recognized in the constitution of the future state of Kansas." Its pages still echo the bitter phrases of the controversy; its denunciations of " Black Republicans," of " Abolition outlaws and hirelings of the New England Aid Society " in reply to Free State taunts of " Border Ruffians " and the " Demon of the Black Power."

In such fashion was Lecompton equipped for territorial business and the spread of pro-slavery propaganda. To crown the whole, Congress appropriated fifty thousand dollars for the erection of a capitol, whose stone foundations and rising walls presently appeared among the stumps and weeds of the ten-acre tract assigned to it. Thus the town flourished while the cause it represented became the chief issue of politics in the world outside. Its population grew, it is said, doubtless with exaggeration, to three or four thousand. Houses and stores were built; and it appeared that it was on the way to fortune and that " permanence " to which it had been dedicated.

As a focus of official life, as well as of political activity, it was visited by men whose names bulk large in national history. Most of that long list of governors who succeeded each other so rapidly in the ungrateful task of guiding the destinies of a land torn with contending factions, set up headquarters here. Reeder, Woodson, Shannon, Geary, Stanton, Walker, Denver, Walsh, Medary and Beebe — now names and less than names save to inquisitive historians — were in turn its residents. Not least among the many men associated with the place were the officers of that First Cavalry regiment at Fort Leavenworth which spent its time striving to keep order in this prologue to the Civil War in which so many of them played much greater parts. Captain McClellan had left the regiment, but there remained with it, or at the post, Hancock, Sumner and Sedgwick, who were to win their laurels on the Northern side, and Joseph Johnston and J. E. B. Stuart on that of the South.

Their task was far from pleasant, save, perhaps, to some whose strong political sympathies gave zest to putting down the partisans of the other side. For a time it seemed hopeless, but when Shannon was replaced by Geary as governor, they had what they and Kansas had needed, a man of courage and resolution at its head. He came in July, 1856, and it was none too soon. Two hundred lives and two millions of property had been destroyed. The Missourians, it was said, threatened another raid; Lane was prepared to fight; and the stage was set for even bloodier strife. In national affairs " bleeding Kansas " had become the chief issue. The House was eager to admit it under the Topeka constitution as a free state; the Senate refused; and the issue was thrown into the national election. Geary did what man could do. The threat from Missouri was headed off; Lane was checked; and, for the time being, Kansas ceased to bleed. With the new president, Buchanan, came another change. A great financial panic diverted attention for a moment even from politics; the Dred Scott decision which had hung fire for years was finally handed down; and though it favored the Southern claims that free soil did not make free men, though the great Fugitive Slave Law supported it, the North found in the Underground Railroad and like means the way to circumvent the law.

Buchanan came in avowedly as a peacemaker, but his first act was unfortunate, for he replaced Geary with Walker. He urged all Kansans to co-operate, and a day was set for electing delegates to a constitutional convention. But Free State men refused to take part in the election, fearing a trick and waiting to secure a majority in the legislature, which was to be chosen later in the year. In consequence pro-slavery men filled the convention, and with its meeting between September and November, 1857, Lecompton reached the height of its career. For there assembled then that body which, protected from its angry Free State enemies by a detachment of Federal troops, framed and adopted a constitution designed to perpetuate slavery in Kansas.

It was the last, desperate move of the pro-slavery men. The race for the control of Kansas had been virtually won by the section which had used its strength and resources to best purpose. The North had sent more men. They were now superior in numbers; they seemed about to gain control of the legislature which their opponents had thus far managed to dominate, the Free State men believed, by fraud not unconnected with officials friendly to the South. Though the Lecompton convention met in September, it adjourned to wait on the result of the elections for the legislature in the following month. In it the Free State party had a large majority, and the Lecompton convention thus became the last hope of the South.

Its programme was shrewdly conceived. It framed a constitution among whose articles was a provision legalizing slavery. That provision, and that alone, was to be submitted to the people of Kansas; and that provision was ingenuity itself. It declared that the right of property was above all constitutional sanction; that, in consequence, the right to slave property and its increase was inviolable; and that there was no power in the state to free slaves without consent of their owners, nor prevent their entrance. Even were this article rejected, the slaves then in the territory would not be freed — and time might bring a change. This they proposed to submit to a vote — " For the Constitution with Slavery," or " For the Constitution without Slavery " — a vote supervised by officials appointed by the convention itself. It was promptly repudiated by Governor Walker as a fraud; it was bitterly denounced throughout the North; but it was upheld by President Buchanan under the influence of his Southern advisers.

At this dramatic moment Douglas appeared again. To approve the constitution was, as he realized, political suicide; and he joined with his section in denouncing it. None the less, President Buchanan declared in his annual message that the Lecompton constitution was legal and called for an election. It was held; but Free State men abstained from voting and by a vote of more than six thousand — of which nearly half were later adjudged fraudulent — to less than six hundred, the constitution was approved with slavery. Meanwhile Walker had been succeeded by Stanton as governor. But he, like most of his predecessors and successors, was won to the Free State cause; and having convened the legislature which provided for a new election in which men might vote against the constitution, he was in turn removed.

The election was held, none the less, and more than ten thousand votes were cast against the constitution, with a few scattering ballots on the other side. In such form the case went again to Congress and the President. The latter sent the constitution to Congress recommending the admission of Kansas under its provisions as a slave state " as much," he added needlessly, " as Georgia or South Carolina." But Douglas, though attacked by all the strength of the administration and the South, was destined to triumph in the end. The Senate voted to admit Kansas under the constitution, the House to resubmit the question to the people. English of Indiana offered a compromise; and in the ensuing election, the voters of Kansas rejected the constitution by more than five to one. They preferred to remain a territory rather than to accept statehood with slavery. Thus the dramatic struggle came to an end; and three years later, on the eve of civil war, Kansas was admitted to the Union as a free state, and the whole episode was submerged in the larger conflict.

Again this is a part of history, the echo of dim, far-off, forgotten things. And again, what of Lecompton, which in a sense, was the focus of it all; and what of the people of Kansas in this period of furious political activity? What kind of people were they; how did they live; and what, if anything, did they do, save vote, hold conventions, frame constitutions and wage guerilla war? The answer to these questions is not far to seek, though it has managed to elude the curiosity of most historians. It is given in part, and perhaps most vividly, by a certain Albert Richardson, a newspaper man, who, at this moment, with the sure instinct of his kind for being where news is, left St. Louis on a journey through the West, and wrote a book about it. In his pages we may still catch something of the spirit and the atmosphere of those rude, early days; sense something of that people and its activities and, possibly, modify our conceptions of that tragic episode.

From St. Louis to that " dreariest and dismalest of State capitals," Jefferson City, he went by rail. There he embarked on the Missouri, that river whose muddy stream had been described by Benton " as a little too thick to swim in and not quite thick enough to walk on," and so made his way through the " vast wilderness," the steamboat " rubbing and scraping " on the sandbars and stopping abruptly a dozen times a day. It was crowded with passengers, every state-room filled, men sleeping all over the cabin floor, gamblers, missionaries, backwoodsmen, pioneers, both men and women, planters, speculators and business men. It took him two days and nights to reach Kansas City, and he thought it excellent time; for in low water it might well take nine.

There he came in touch with the two principal issues of the time and place — real estate and politics. In Kansas City his host preached slavery to him, with small success or none. The men of Wyandotte across the river, a town then four months old, with four hundred inhabitants and waiting settlers living outdoors or under tents till their homes were finished by the hurrying carpenters, talked real estate to him, until he took the stage for Lawrence through the Delaware reservation. That Free State headquarters, he tells us, had " two weekly newspapers, a Congregational and a Unitarian church, five or six religious societies, a large schoolroom and the ruins of the Free State Hotel." For a third of a mile on both sides of the principal thoroughfare, then, as now, Massachusetts Street, were " rows of frame trading-houses, with three or four brick and stone buildings, interspersed with a few pioneer log-cabins ", though he noted that " On the elegantly lithographed map of the town the other streets were systematic and regular." " Lots were selling at from two hundred to two thousand dollars each " as compared, he wrote, with Wyandotte " shares " of ten lots each at eighteen hundred. And, as he further notes of this as of the other towns he visited, " If the town succeeds, the original proprietors grow rich. If it fails, having risked little, they lose little." Lawrence, he observed, was already historic. " Yet no halo of romance clothed the miry streets and rude scattered buildings. All was prosaic and commonplace, from the soiled floors and little dingy sleeping-rooms of the public houses, to the horse-traders and town-lot speculators along the thoroughfares."

So he made his way again by stage to Topeka — Indian for potato — a hamlet of fifteen or twenty houses; and so back to " Quindaro," just founded by Robinson and his partners. There he met the third great characteristic of Kansas, a public meeting. " There were," he says, " always public meetings. The people were the victims of oratory." This was a temperance meeting, which resolved itself into a vigilance committee and proceeded to break up a bar. So, escaping from this atmosphere, he went on to Leavenworth, then two years and a half old and, with its four thousand inhabitants, the largest place in Kansas. Building lots, twenty-five by a hundred and twenty-five feet, on the river landing, were valued at ten thousand dollars; three or four blocks away at two thousand; half a mile distant at twelve hundred. Everyone was speculating. Lots which cost eight dollars six months before were sold for twenty-two hundred; some which had cost five were sold for a thousand. " Hotels were crowded with strangers, eager to invest. Almost anyone could borrow gold without security or even a written promise to pay; and the faith was universal that to-morrow should be as this day and yet more abundant."

Thence he made his way to Atchison, stopping at night with a hospitable family who announced that they were pro-slavery " Border Ruffians," gave him a drink of whiskey and a part of their mattress " between the twins," and refused pay for his entertainment. So presently he came to Atchison, " the most violent Pro-slavery settlement in Kansas " — yet in which " General " Pomeroy and other Free State men had recently bought heavily and had come to live. It had, wrote Richardson, with his strong anti-slavery bias, " the dull, thriftless air of Pro-slavery towns " ; yet he admits that property was already high, and new settlers had given it fresh impetus. And everywhere he found the burden of the song was town-site speculation. There was Sumner, three miles from Atchison, where shares sold for a hundred dollars; two weeks later they had doubled; three years later they were worthless. There was Doniphan, a pro-slavery settlement — but of which " General " Lane and other Free Soilers were now joint owners — with fifteen hundred acres laid out in building lots, a population of three hundred and shares selling at five hundred dollars. There was Geary City where shares had risen from two hundred and fifty to four hundred dollars in a week.

That great motif runs through his pages like a golden thread. Money was plentiful — at three to five per cent a month — but what was that in days when one might multiply his investment a hundred-fold in six months, a thousand-fold a year? Transactions were all in cash, and there were all the usual phenomena of a land-rush. Servant-girls speculated in town lots; a Minnesota wood-sawyer made half a million dollars. " Anything was marketable. Shares in interior towns of one or two shanties sold readily for a hundred dollars. Wags proposed an act of Congress reserving some land for farming purposes before the whole territory should be divided into city lots." " It was not a swindle but a mania. The speculators were quite as insane as the rest. . . . Any one of them could have turned his property into cash at enormous profits. But all thought the inflation would continue; and I do not remember a single person who sold out except to make new investments."

But of them all, the towns on the Missouri were the worst. " On paper they were magnificent. Their superbly lithographed maps adorned the walls of every place of resort. The stranger studying one of these, fancied the New Babylon surpassed only by its namesake of old. Its great parks, opera-houses, churches, universities, railway depots and steamboat-landings made New York and St. Louis insignificant in comparison. . . ." The reality was different. " The town might be composed of twenty buildings; or it might not contain a single human habitation. In most cases there might be one or two rough cabins, with perhaps a tent and an Indian canoe on the river in front of the ' levee.' " And, in spite of this, Richardson succumbed! In August he became a " squatter " and filed a claim; and, having done that, he went to the trial of Governor Robinson in Lecompton.

He was as little pleased with that place as with the other pro-slavery towns he visited. " The Border Ruffian capital," he tells us, " in a rough little hollow, was composed of a few dwelling-houses, many land-offices, and multitudinous whiskey saloons." " The United States district court . . . was held in a rude apartment, furnished with three tables, two chairs and half a dozen planks for seats, resting on blocks, stones and boxes. Judge Cato was an avowed disunionist of the South Carolina school. Tall and thin, with closely shaven face, and overgrown moustache, he wore the ermine carelessly, studied the *Charleston Mercury* intently through his heavy gold spectacles, and gave only an occasional glance at the business before him." Yet the judge seems to have been a fair man, and even more than fair. In due course of time, Robinson was acquitted of the charge of usurpation of office, on the ground of his defence that it was only " preparatory," which, Richardson, Northerner as he was and strongly biassed against the pro-slavery party, observes " was not quite true. Nearly all the Free State men had designed to set the Topeka government in motion and support it by force of arms, whenever the Border Ruffian Territorial authorities should drive them to the wall."

Such, if we except his presence at a city election in Leavenworth marked by force and fraud, was his introduction into Kansas politics. But once introduced, his progress was rapid. A few days later he attended a Free State convention at Grasshopper Falls, passing Hickory Point which had been besieged and captured by Free State men a year earlier, after some loss of life on both sides. There he heard debated the question of whether the Free State men should take part in the fall elections. It was carried by Lane who declared that " The Territorial legislature belongs to us, and we are going to have it — by the ballot, if we can, by the rifle if we must. If we elect only one member we intend to make him a good working majority."

Then came the Lecompton constitution and the meeting of the Free State legislature which, in an extra session, passed over the governor's veto an act enrolling the entire population capable of bearing arms. Besides this, it elected a military board, consisting of Lane as major-general, eight brigadiers, an adjutant, an inspector, a quarter-master, commissary and surgeon-general — and, among other things, Richardson himself as assistant adjutant-general and secretary of the board. With that he came into the heart of politics. The board, meeting over the Commercial Restaurant in Lawrence, entered " in slouched hats, top-boots and blue army overcoats, with enormous capes, crowded around the stove and canvassed the latest news or rumor or disturbance. No inferior rank was tolerated, every man was a general." Then, Lane having assumed his place, the board having been called to order, and its fifteen members having been provided with hot whiskies, punches, and a box of cigars, it went about its work, concerning which most of them, as Richardson admits of himself, " knew no more than of Sanskrit."

" Excitement," he observes at this point, somewhat superfluously, " now ran high. Force was almost the only law. Civil war seemed ready to blaze forth again at any moment. The fierce strife had lasted for three years and the end was not yet. According to Daniel Webster, our fathers fought seven years for a preamble; a later writer declares that the people of Kansas battled four years to veto an act of Congress." So the conflict went on, with Richardson a part of it. That winter President Buchanan replaced Walker with Denver as governor, and as his first experience the new executive was forced by the Lawrence men to surrender a hundred and fifty guns seized from a Free State emigrant train and stored in Lecompton. It was a typical exploit of the Free State men, whom Richardson records as having another hundred and fifty muskets from Delaware City and a brass twelve-pounder from Kickapoo, both pro-slavery towns.

The pro-slavery men retaliated by election frauds, as Richardson records. Kickapoo with a hundred registered voters cast over a thousand ballots; Delaware with thirty-five cast over five hundred; and, he declares, of seven thousand votes for the Lecompton constitution less than two thousand were legal. They copied names from an old Cincinnati directory; they voted Henry Ward

Beecher, President Buchanan, Horace Greeley and the actor Edwin Forrest. And if pro-slavery men had been agressive earlier, the Free Staters were now on the offensive. A Lawrence convention, debating whether its members should or should not take part in the election for state officers under the Lecompton constitution, was electrified by a statement from Lane's forces, then encamped near Fort Scott, that they would resist even the Federal troops rather than lay down their arms.

Nor were they far behind their rivals in town-site promotion. A year later, he observes, when the legislature for the first time was composed of Free State men, " They laid out a town twenty miles south of Lawrence, calling it Mineola; passed a charter enabling the company to hold two thousand acres of land; and then enacted a law making Mineola the territorial capital. The members owned the town, and by making it the seat of government hoped to make their fortunes likewise." "A large amount of Mineola stock had been set aside for members of the press." But Richardson, like his fellow newspaper men, was not amenable to a bribe. He, and perhaps others, accepted stock in the enterprise, but the press exposed the scheme. The thirty-nine members and the clerk of the legislature were nicknamed the " Forty Thieves." The governor refused to recognize the law; the project failed — and Richardson sold his eight shares for fifteen dollars!

But this legislature did not confine its energies entirely to real estate. It passed a series of resolutions, protesting the admission of Kansas under the Lecompton constitution; and " hurled back with scorn the libelous charge contained in the message of the president of the United States that the freemen of Kansas are a lawless people." With a certain fine inconsistency its members followed this by pledging their " fortunes and sacred honor " to resist the Lecompton constitution " by force of arms, if

necessary " ; appealed to the " friends of freedom everywhere " to assist them; and authorized a new constitutional convention to be held in Leavenworth. With its
meeting and activities, there were four governments in
Kansas — the territorial, and the three state organizations under the Topeka, the Lecompton, and the Leavenworth constitutions, each claiming the allegiance of its
citizens and each hoping for recognition by Congress.
Each had a full complement of officials, according to
Richardson; and, counting the ex-governors in the territory, it seems probable that few similar areas, if any, at
any time, were ever torn with such conflicting loyalties
or ever had so many empty titles within their borders.
And, as it happened, the state came in finally under
none of them, but under the so-called Wyandotte constitution.

Until that time the tragi-comedy went on. In May,
1858, the massacre of eleven Free State men at Marais
des Cygnes re-lighted the flames of civil war in south-
eastern Kansas — if they had ever been quenched. A
Free State guerilla leader, Montgomery, drove out the
pro-slavery settlers, and even attacked the county held
by Federal troops. In June, Governor Denver, who had
succeeded Stanton, with his suite and various newspaper
correspondents, of whom Richardson was one, endeav-
ored to make peace. They found the country armed and
sentinels everywhere. Their Ohio landlady voiced the
pious wish that if the governor tried to hurt Montgomery
she hoped he would be drowned. They even met that
hero who came riding a white horse which he had taken
from the leader of a party of Missourians who were sent to
arrest him. He proved himself, as Richardson records,
" a peculiarly entertaining conversationalist," who
amused the governor and his company with a description
of just how guerilla warfare should be carried on successfully.

Despite such episodes, little by little Kansas grew
quieter; though at its best it was none too quiet. The
territorial legislature of 1858–1859, to which Richardson
himself was nominated by the people of Sumner where he
had taken up land, was, he says, " a more reputable
body " than its predecessor; but it was, according to his
own account, lively enough. It repealed all " Border
Ruffian " laws and sent a copy of them to the governor of
Missouri, as no longer needed in Kansas. It passed an act
of general amnesty for all political offences. It passed
scores of divorce bills; and divorce became so easy that a
Boston friend of Richardson's wrote to discover whether
his wife had gone to Kansas to get a divorce — and
Richardson found that she had. She and many more; for
Kansas, like some other western states, became the Mecca
for those seeking release from matrimonial ties. True to
the tradition of Kansas legislatures — or establishing
that tradition — it exhibited the peculiar sense of
humor which from that time to our own has marked some
of their sessions. In view of the number of divorce bills,
one member introduced a bill abolishing marriage in
Kansas and establishing free love; another moved that
the legislative bachelors ballot for the divorced " wid-
ows " ; and another made a still more ribald oration on
that delicate subject.

Moreover, as Richardson noted, the spirit of mob vio-
lence was not dead. The day after the legislature adjourned, there was an outbreak, which Governor Medary
tried in vain to quell — so much in vain that he was
forced to listen to an attack upon himself from the " old
war horse," Lane, who, " emerging from the crowd,
threw off the shaggy bearskin overcoat which he always
wore " and " recited an appalling catalogue " of Medary's " political crimes; first in Ohio, and afterward as
Territorial governor of Minnesota." But Richardson's
stay was nearly over; and presently he left Leavenworth

on a stage, with Horace Greeley as his companion, for Denver and the new gold-fields of the Rocky Mountains. It was a sign that the scene of excitement was moving farther west. With the conclusion of his Kansas chronicle, and the resumption of his travels, Kansas began to lose the center of the stage; and its people, those of Lecompton among them, turned more and more from the excitement of politics and even real estate speculation to the more prosaic pursuits of farming and business.

It was not easy for the pro-slavery capital to adjust itself to its new situation. It did not disappear, like so many of the mushroom towns along the Missouri. But if its decline was slow, it was no less certain. Its fortunes were bound up with those of the constitution; and with the rejection of that document the town's prospects of greatness were shattered once for all. Though for the time being it remained the legal capital, the Free State men who controlled the legislature refused to hold their meetings in a place so intimately associated with the cause of their enemies — and in which, perhaps, they held no property, for it is difficult to dissociate that element from politics in those days. From session to session, in response to the governor's summons, they, or enough of them to form a quorum, met at Lecompton only to adjourn to Lawrence until the day when Topeka became the capital of a free state.

Lecompton's business, like its political importance, suffered proportionately. Its population rapidly declined as those who had been attracted to it by politics gradually withdrew. Constitution Hall was abandoned to the rough humors of a mock legislature with debates on " the (f)laws of Congress," " the (hand)organic act " which established the territorial government, and parodies of the governor's messages. The *Lecompton Union* was transformed into the *National Democrat*; and as the United States turned to civil war to settle the question which had come to a head within its borders, Lecompton sank into the status of a Kansas country town. Yet it was full of rude and vigorous life, aside from politics. In the very months of the constitutional convention, some of its inhabitants stirred by the news of gold discoveries in the Rocky Mountains formed an association which, within a year, sent a party to the edge of the Rocky Mountains to found a new outpost named for the then governor of Kansas, Denver. Thus were the boundaries of the nation stretched still farther — and more lots were sold. For such is the spirit of the pioneer.

So, when the great struggle was over, Lecompton did not suffer the fate of many of its kind once the impulse which founded them was lost. It was not like Jamestown or Old Sarum. When the frontiersman and adventurer, the politician and promoter had passed, there remained the sturdy original stock which had established the settlement, most of whom had never been in sympathy with the cause with which the name of their town had been identified. Nothing, perhaps, is stronger indication of this than the tradition that in this center of pro-slavery agitation there was never but one slave, a body-servant who had insisted on accompanying his master from their southern home. Moreover, what the village lost in the departure of government and politics, it regained in some measure as the years went on and the surrounding country was, in western phrase " settled up " by incoming families from both north and south.

Little by little it took on its present aspect. Many of the landmarks of its furious youth began to disappear. Some of its temporary " hotels " burned down or were transformed to other purposes; its too numerous barrooms disappeared. In place of temporary " shacks " rose more permanent and more attractive houses, with

gardens and orchards; and in a generation more the purpose of its original settlers was achieved.

Their descendants are still there, an intermingled
strain peculiarly American. Their village still lies well up
among the rolling bluffs which rise from the south bank
of the Kaw River, a little aside from the railroad which
runs close along the bank of that slow, muddy, but sometimes dangerous stream. It is a pretty place, half hidden
in spring and summer by the orchards which reach and
invade its boundaries. In three-quarters of a century the
population of the township has changed but little; and
though the village itself is smaller by a third than forty
years ago, it seems in no danger of extinction; it seems,
indeed, " permanent," though in a fashion not designed
by those who saw in it a means to wealth and power.
With half a dozen well-shaded streets, as many stores,
its cottages for the most part well-kept, and a few more pretentious houses, good walks and quick hill-drainage
carried off in stone gutters, it offers a pleasing contrast to
the picture one conjures up of an unkempt and muddy
western town. It recalls, in fact, not so much the memory
of a frontier post as that of a New England village or a
town of the Middle States, quiet, secure, with the wild
days of its boisterous youth well behind it and all but
forgotten, even by itself.

It has now been many years since I was in Lecompton,
yet, one fancies, the place has not greatly changed. Then
on every hand were evidences of larger population and of
wider boundaries. Half way up the hill were the heavy
foundations of two earlier hotels, long since destroyed by
fire. Nearly across from them stood the small " Federal "
prison, built of native stone. Its inside partitions were no
longer there, but the heavy oak door jambs were still in
place, its old nail-studded door leaned against the outer

wall, and some of the iron bars were still in the narrow slits that served for windows. About it an orchard had grown up — and the old prison was used to house some hens!

As one went through the town he saw the sites of old buildings, the pillars from Governor Woodson's " mansion "; the spot where stood the " great house " of Governor Shannon; and many more mementos of that vivid past. Here were the crumbling foundations of an Episcopal church; there what remained of a Catholic edifice, the priest's house and the outline of the church alone remaining. From the hill-top one looked toward Big Springs, just over the next ridge, where was held the first Free State convention; and, the other way, the traditional site of the first settlement, Stonehouse Creek, a trading-post established long before the Douglas bill had turned the land into a battlefield. There, the story went, among its traders was a son or grandson of the famous Daniel Boone. On every hand were relics of a past, not old as human history calculates, yet pregnant with great memories of a period as distant from our own in form and spirit as that of the Pilgrim Fathers.

Of these some were then still intact. At the very center of the town, there stood a large stone building, three stories high and notable by that fact. In the days when Lecompton became the capital, and it appeared that the pro-slavery propaganda might succeed, enterprising men united to erect a rival to the Free State Hotel in Lawrence. Here was the chief abiding-place not only of official Kansas but the headquarters of that powerful movement which sought to win the territory for the South. These rooms were once crowded with politicians, army officers, cadets of Southern families, home-seekers, land speculators, contractors, men of many kinds and many interests. For this was the largest, the most famous — and the most " permanent " — of Lecompton hotels; the only one surviving as it stood; the — shades of Scotti! —

— *The Rowena*! Its fate was typical of the whole. When the capital was moved, and the war fought, and the " cause " had failed, it was left among the aftermath of the wreckage. For many years it was used as a dormitory and recitation-hall of a so-called " university " established in the town; and when that moved away, it was turned to business purposes, a hardware store and a bank below and a dwelling above.

It was not alone in its memories of past greatness. Not far away there was a square stone building, two tall stories high, in the midst of a plot of ground some acres in extent. It is what remained of the old capitol. The fifty thousand dollars appropriated for that purpose by Congress sufficed to begin the work on what it was then reckoned would cost eight times that sum. Foundations were laid and walls begun, which, among other things, served as rude breastworks against Lane's " army of liberation." But the original appropriation was soon, perhaps too soon, exhausted. Congress refused to vote further sums in the disturbed condition of affairs, and the admission of the free state with Topeka as its capital brought with it the abandonment of the whole project. The place presently became the property of the state; and thus the matter stood till near the close of the great Civil War. Then, first of all ironical revenges of history, this monument of lost causes came into the hands of a religious denomination and there rose in time on the foundations of one wing of the old capitol a college styling itself, after the manner of its kind  a " university." Upon it was bestowed the name of the most violent opponent of pro-slavery, the man who had led the Free State men against it when it formed part of the defences of their enemies — James H. Lane! It took some twenty years to build; it was occupied some twenty more; then the institution merged its identity into that of another and so moved away. The town acquired it for school purposes; and the

halls which were to have resounded with legislative eloquence came at last to less sonorous but perhaps no less
useful pronouncements of the pedagogue.

But there was still another relic of the past; and not the
least impressive of the three. Down the main street, past
the butcher's, the barber's and the post-office, there stood,
well up from the roadway, a weather-beaten wreck of a
two-story frame structure. Unpainted, neglected, with
two decrepit chimneys on the side, it looked not unlike a
cross-roads country store far gone into decay. Half a
dozen steps led to a porch or platform whose unsafe floor
still stretched across its narrow front. Another flight of
steps on the side led to the second story. The single door
in front was still in place, but the windows had suffered
the fate of all their kind in abandoned buildings. The
shingles and sides were slowly yielding to time and weather
and the whole structure seemed to lean a little under
the weight of long neglect. Around it the long grass and
weeds emphasized the sense of desertion and futility.

" And this — ? " I asked my guide as he paused before
it. " This," he replied, " is where the Lecompton Constitution was drawn up. This is Constitution Hall."

Here in that busy autumn of 1857 men crowded into
the upper room of this building to plan the last move in
the effort to save Kansas for slavery. " The right of
property," they declared in words that sound strange to-
day, " is before and above any constitutional sanction."
They pushed that dictum to a conclusion suited to their
needs — " the right of the owner of a slave to that slave
and its increase is the same and as inviolable as the right
of the owner of any property whatever." In such words
they framed their creed and planned to secure its recognition by a hostile majority.

This was the end of all those dreams. It provokes reflection on that most prolific subject of all reflection, the
vanity of human wishes. Above all in this case, for,

crowning irony of fate, across the front of this abandoned wreck of disappointed hopes there stretched an old and faded sign. Accident surpassing all design and all the dreams of novelists' coincidence, decreed it should proclaim, in letters a foot high, the name of a business itself departed from this house of dead ambitions and long buried hopes — UNDERTAKING! That sign, no doubt, has long since disappeared; the building itself perhaps has followed it. Yet Lecompton has won a double immortality. It is still alive, its name is now a part of history. What more can towns desire?

SOME "NEW" HISTORY AND
HISTORIANS

# SOME "NEW" HISTORY AND
# HISTORIANS

IF WE admit, with the philosopher, that our judgment
of others is a measure of ourselves, there is no better
touchstone of any generation than the way it views the
past, that is to say, the history it writes. Whether or not
history is, or should be, philosophy teaching by example,
it reveals, consciously or unconsciously, the philosophy of
the historian and, measurably, that of his audience and of
the generation to which they both belong. Of this there
are innumerable examples, from the " patriotic " and
" national " historians of the nineteenth century through
mediaeval chroniclers to the most ancient masters of the
craft, each reflecting in some fashion the spirit of his
times with his own. That being true, what does the history and biography of our time tell us of the character,
the meaning, and the spirit of our age? It is a question
which, rightly viewed, is no mere " academic " speculation. It goes to the heart of things. It involves not merely
an evaluation of recent historians, their methods, manner, and materials, but the tastes, emotions, and mentality of those for whom they write and who make their
writings possible. What, then, is the peculiar character
of the " modern " school, or schools, of history; what, if
anything, marks us off from our historical predecessors;

when and how and in what hands did the present vogue arise, how has it developed and what does it tell us of ourselves, our tastes, and our intelligence?

To pass over its earlier and gradual development, in a sense its first great manifestations were perceived toward the close of the nineteenth century, when there broke out in many countries, especially in Germany, a vigorous controversy as to the proper method, content, and point of view in writing history. It was then strongly urged — though the contention was not new, since Voltaire had suggested it nearly two centuries earlier — that the range of history as then written was too narrow to explain the past, that it was necessary to take account at least of economic and what were then coming to be called " social " phenomena. That movement was in part a reaction against the current school of so-called " scientific " history of the last half of the nineteenth century, which, in turn, had been a reaction against the " picturesque " historians of the preceding generation. It was in part related to the enormous economic development and social changes of the period in which it took its rise; in part to the emergence of an interest in what was called " society," which was marked on the one side by the rise of sociology and on the other by the development of socialism. It was profoundly affected by the new science called psychology. It presaged the decline of what had been the chief motive of the old history, that is, political, institutional, military, and diplomatic development and activity; and it was not unrelated to the evolution of democracy.

If not much beyond its new and fearful pseudo-scientific terminology, which found long names for obvious and well-known qualities, was novel in this school, it was highly self-conscious, organized, and technical, and it had, like all such movements, the zeal of a crusade. As its great champion, Lamprecht, said, " the new, progressive, and therefore aggressive, point of view" in this struggle, which he defined as the conflict between the " social-psychic " and the " individual-psychic " factors, " is the socio-psychological, and for that reason it must be termed modern." Even in English the new terms were impressive; in German they were overpowering, at this " parting of the ways in historical science," with its insistence on " psychic processes," " psychic mechanism," and " psychic currents," its disregard of the personal and individual elements, and its treatment of human " mass reactions."

Among the followers and prophets of the new school not even Lamprecht himself was more eminent or more characteristic than another and far more widely read writer who, though he differed widely from Lamprecht, showed something of the same tendencies — Guglielmo Ferrero. Son of an Italian engineer, assistant and son-in-law of the criminologist Lombroso, just as the nineteenth century turned into the twentieth, he published two volumes on *The Age of Caesar*, as introduction to a larger work, *The Greatness and Decline of Rome*. In the fact that he was a well-educated man with an unusually broad outlook on life, he was prepared for writing history. In a narrower view he was less so. To that task he brought no special training or knowledge as historian, no new investigations, sources, or discoveries, but based his work on well-known general histories like Mommsen and Duruy and on less-known monographs. But with fresh points of view, hypotheses, and generalizations, simply, entertainingly, even at times brilliantly written, full of parallels between the ancient and modern worlds, it was a novelty in historical writing which for a generation had, with few exceptions, stressed the " scientific " side — that is to say, exactness of knowledge —- at the expense of literary quality. In one sense Ferrero was no historian at all. Psychologist, publicist, sociologist, journalist — almost any other definition would have seemed appropriate. He was unlike Froude or Taine, who, whatever their gifts of style, had seen the documents; he was still more unlike the men then reckoned in the first rank of historians, Gardiner and Henry Adams, Sorel and Aulard, who like Ranke and his fellows had devoted their lives to sources and archives.

Thus, since his work cut sheer across the then accepted canons of historical writing, the reaction of the profession he invaded was inevitable. It was summed up in current epigram. " He is no historian, that man Ferrero," observed a friendly critic, " but he will arrive." " He will," another agreed, " and where? " Historical scholars with one voice denounced him as " dilettante," " charlatan," " improviser," " novelist," his work as " pretentious ingenuity " " full of errors and declamation." Inevitably perhaps, the public verdict was the opposite. In Italy, where literature was a precarious profession and history a peculiarly unremunerative field, his book brought him an income and a reputation still more profitable. He was invited to lecture, to become a candidate for the Chamber of Deputies; he even became prominent enough to be exiled for his political opinions. Thus elevated to those heights which only publicity achieves, he was called to lecture in Paris and in South America and, under the patronage of President Roosevelt, was given his widest and most profitable vogue in the United States.

When he was on the threshold of that great adventure, an American scholar wrote that it was " unfortunate that there has been thrust upon him a journalistic notoriety which he must sincerely deprecate." It was kindly meant, but it reveals how remote that worthy scholar was from realities. For, his " publicity value " assured, Ferrero contributed to *Hearst's Magazine* a series of articles whose titles reveal his faith and his appeal, especially to America — " The Rockefellers of Ancient Rome," " The Collapse of Roman Tammany," and " Riding to a Roman Fall." These, presently gathered into a volume, *Ancient Rome and Modern America*, with a pseudo-romance, *Between the Old World and the New*, formed with his *History* what he called a " trilogy." With this he had arrived — and where?

There is no doubt that, whether as historian or prophet, he took himself seriously. Without some sense of personal infallibility no man could have written that last volume, much less have described a history of Rome, a volume of essays, and a novel as a " trilogy." There is equally no doubt that even his most superficial utterances were taken seriously by multitudes. His thesis was simple and easily understood. No country, he declared, " reflects more of the great political and social questions of every age," especially our own, than Rome. Since, as he says, its older histories were written in an age which still contended over forms of government, "which now have lost their interest," it has become necessary to " widen our point of view and adapt it to the moral and social needs of the day," to replace political with moral and psychological interest. Moreover, " human history," he observes, " like all other phenomena, is the unconscious product of an infinity of small and unnoticed efforts," like, presumably, a coral reef. So, with a certain inconsistency, he launches into an account of the great Roman politicians, statesmen, and generals, culminating in the career of Julius Caesar.

This is far from disparagement; were it so, his popularity would prove his critics wrong, for as we say to-day, " the customer is always right." If one can find in wise saws and modern instances a light to guide one's feet along the ways of ancient history; if even by stressing the likeness of modern America to Rome one can attract thousands of readers to whom otherwise the subject would have been Golgotha and anathema, who shall say him nay? He who can by any means interest the present in the past renders a great service to society, for he preserves that sense of continuity without which the present grows egotistic, self-centered, and largely meaningless.

If not a true historian in the older sense, Ferrero was a portent and an example as well as a potent influence. He drew popular attention to his subject; he revived even the interest of specialists by antagonizing them; and though his interpretations provoked much heat, they shed a certain light by that same process; and he became the forerunner, if not the model, of many like him since. Men like him act as liaison officers between scholars and public; but like all liaison officers they are apt to be misunderstood. They do not always render the truth's infinite shades of meaning quite in accordance with the taste of the specialists, and their words do not always bear precisely the significance to their audience that they mean them to convey. Among life's little ironies, one may trace Ferrero's influence on American publicists who perceived in his analogies that the great dangers which brought Rome to the ground and faced America were socialism and aliens — and Ferrero was an Italian Socialist!

The popularizers, or what the French more cynically call the " vulgarizers " — for, despite a too common belief to the contrary, *populus* and *vulgus* are not quite the same — have always reaped the greatest benefits in fame as well as money from the work of the investigators, whether as writers of " popular " histories or of textbooks for the schools. It is not surprising, therefore, that men have turned aside from scholarship, from teaching, from journalism, or even from fiction, to this profitable pursuit. And one may not leave the subject of the New History, as it has been described in possibly too grandiloquent capitals, without some mention of a leading American exponent of that phrase.

About the year 1912, Professor James Harvey Robinson, then of Columbia University, collected into one volume a series of essays and addresses under that title. Seventeen years later he read a paper before the American Historical Association under the title of " The Newer Ways of Historians " ; and some years before that he published a volume on what he called *The Mind in the Making*. He was pre-eminently what is sometimes called in the United States an " educator." Having followed the straight, paved road of academic life from undergraduate to professor, inspired by the movement toward social and psychological history, he compiled along its lines what has been in this generation probably the most widely used text-book of European history for rather elementary students, with many edited texts, documents, readings, extracts, and like educational aids. For this highly useful work he received consequent reward in money and reputation; and crowned his career by election to the presidency of the American Historical Association. Speculative, or as we say " suggestive," rather than scholarly, he turned philosopher, and there attained an eminence comparable to his position as a writer of text-books. So, judged by the standards of his country and his time, he must be reckoned the most typical and successful of his kind, a model for the young which has been widely and sedulously imitated. Even in this brief chronicle it is apparent how greatly the world has changed. For where, three-quarters of a century ago, men like Macaulay and Motley, Prescott and Parkman, made both money and reputation out of history which was at once scholarly and literary, those rewards are now confined to the authors of school text-books and popular manuals.

Possessed as he was of an engaging style, we can only guess what Professor Robinson might have accomplished had he written what we call " scholarly " history. If it be the business of a historian to contribute to our " factual " as well as " interpretative " knowledge of the past, Professor Robinson is, of course, not a historian at all; yet since history has become so large a factor in education, to omit him would be to disappoint those who regard him as our leading historian. To the so-called " new history " he contributed little but the adjective, which he made peculiarly his own. Doubtless he chose the better part — but one may be permitted to express regret.

Essentially a Lamprechtian, he summed up in his first essay the defects of current historiography — " the careless inclusion of mere names," the emphasis on political events to the exclusion of " other matters of greater moment," and the narration of " extraordinary episodes not because they illustrate the general tendencies of a particular time, but because they are conspicuous in the annals of the past." To such doctrines there can be little objection. They echo not only the principles of the German *Historisches Kulturkampf* but the practice of most great historians, who, however, are still influenced by the fact that contemporary events have a certain weight, if only in their influence on their own generation and so on its successors. What Professor Robinson has done has been to inject these principles into the text-book field; and if it has been urged that here he went too far; that, virtually, he eliminated chronology from history; and that, without some corrective, his followers would be as far in one direction from real knowledge of the past as those he denounced were in another — to this there is one answer, his popularity, for " royalties are an unanswerable argument."

His second doctrine, noted in his presidential address, is the recommendation that the work of " animal psychologists be frankly recognized as essential contributions to the historian's problems," since " the discoveries in animal psychology are by no means irrelevant to man's conduct in all times." To this, one of his followers, Mr. Barnes, has added that history or biography needs not only psychology but physiological chemistry and the study of glands; for all biography written before 1900 is only " rhetorical goose-eggs," since there was no " valid psychology " before that time. Again this is not wholly new, for various physicians at various times and in various places have interpreted literary genius by physiology; and not only has Napoleon's lack of success in some of his later enterprises been explained by acute indigestion and even less agreeable ailments, but Mr. Berman has proved that the great Emperor was merely the product of an enlarged pituitary gland.

To these may be added two corollaries. The school to which Professor Robinson and Mr. Barnes belong has, in general, aligned itself against the existing social and economic system, and its work has been done largely in that peculiarly profitable branch of effort, the writing of text-books for the schools and of " popular " pseudo-scholarly manuals for uncritical and ill-informed readers. It has revealed, as well, a strong tendency toward terminology from which history has hitherto been free; though both Professor Robinson and Mr. Barnes have categorically, and no doubt wisely, refused to be drawn into any attempt to define the words they use, as, apparently, an irrelevant and academic exercise tending to hamper thought. In consequence, they have not escaped criticism; and one of the most eminent and acute of American scholars, Professor Shorey, has gone so far as to say that we need look no farther than Professor Robinson's pages " to find illustrations of every form of sophistical, prejudiced, and unfair reasoning . . . and every fallacy for which the mediaeval Latinists found a name," and that, professing to speak as a historian of ideas and in the name of progressive science, Professor Robinson

has abused the authority and credit of both with the public to prostitute science in the service of propaganda and . . . misrepresents the facts and the lessons of history to readers who lack opportunity and time to control his statements. . . . He probably knows that in the judgment of those he once would have regarded as his peers he is fast forfeiting his claim to the title of historian.

Such controversial matters aside, this school has raised at least one great question. Pushed to their logical conclusions, such doctrines tend not only to eliminate chronology and personality and to reduce history to that so-called " historical sociology " of which Mr. Barnes was once professor, but to depress even mass history into a sort of anthropology or humanized zoölogy. In spite of their insistence on their own virtues and the shortcomings of their predecessors, especially on the scientific side, one may question whether they are quite as scientific as they profess to be. For even science admits that it is the exceptional, not the usual, which leads to differentiation of the higher from the lower organisms, and so produces that " progress " which is the great, if not the only, god to which such a philosophy bends the knee  Followed to its logical conclusion, this pseudo-scientific doctrine destroys the basis of its own belief, for, obviously, had all men remained " common," men would still be primitive savages — or worse. But, as Oscar Wilde once observed in another connection, " each man kills the thing he loves."

With all the vogue of Robinson and Barnes, so neatly uniting the Utilitarians, the Positivists, and the Sociologists, the great cause of science and society has found a champion even more conspicuous than these. Under the compelling influence of the Great War, which turned some souls to history as it did others to religion, and still others to far less worthy causes, the English novelist, Mr. H. G. Wells, for a brief time abandoned his chief profession to compile a history of the past, preparatory to his greater task of foreshadowing the history of the future of mankind. Deeply influenced by the doctrines, or the fallacies, of science and society which so permeated the early years of the twentieth century, inspired by his conceptions not only of what has been but what should be, like Ferrero he brought to history his skill and equipment from another field. Like Ferrero he depended on others for his facts; but unlike his Italian predecessor, he enlisted other elements. He called in experts to revise his work; and, equipped with their advice, a vivid if commonplace imagination, a gift of equally vivid and commonplace narrative style, a stenographer, a mass of reference-books, and a set of preconceptions, he became, as it were, a historical syndicate, to explore and exploit that most ancient, if not most honorable, field of universal history.

After the manner of all universal histories, he began his work with Creation; not with the Creation of his predecessors, not with classical gods or Biblical Genesis, but the Creation of the scientists — astronomers, geologists, and biologists; not, as it were, with First Causes, but with First Results. So he proceeded to that subject which has so interested this generation — primitive man — and continued his story to the present day, more sketchily in the latest periods, as his authorities gave out. Finally, as a last, modern touch, his work was filled with pictures and diagrams, and sold in sixpenny parts on news-stands prior to its publication as a book.

Inevitably it had a popular success; due partly to Mr. Wells's reputation in a kindred field; partly to his ingenious linking of astronomy, geology, paleontology, and anthropology with history; partly to the narrative; partly to its timeliness. Inevitably it was attacked by the historians; yet even some historians favored it — where it did not discuss what they knew most about. The eighteenth-century specialist approved of the Middle Ages; the mediaevalist of the modern part; both, of the earlier ages, especially the prehistoric eras; the scientists approved of the history, the historians of the science; and all agreed it was an excellent account of every field, except, of course, his own. None quite approved his claim that he had spent no less than three years and a half in its composition; for cynics pointed out that men had spent whole lifetimes on far briefer periods, and that, however valuable Mr. Wells's hours were, those of Mr. Edgar Wallace and Mr. Oppenheim were more valuable still.

Severer critics resented his claim of novelty, save in the pseudo-scientific parts; for universal histories were no novelty. The ancients knew them, and the Middle Ages; even modern times; and within the memory of men now living one John Clark Ridpath compiled one, which, though of very different character, might challenge even that of Mr. Wells in popularity. Nor was the novelist-historian unique; for Tobias Smollett wrote history, and Charles Dickens's *Child's History of England* had long been a best seller. Yet in comparison with his critics Mr. Wells had the best of it, as he soon pointed out. In an age when the multiplication table tends to be the final test, and God, as Napoleon said, is on the side of the heaviest battalions, Truth is no less obviously on the side of the largest circulation, for, in the advertiser's words, " two million readers *can't* be wrong."

But Mr. Wells scored more than by mere numbers. His critics pointed out his lack of perspective and pro-portion — three pages to the marital difficulties of Alexander the Great's parents, a triangular situation naturally appealing to a modern novelist, half a page to Mr. Kipling's worst story, " Stalky & Co.," and a sentence to Abraham Lincoln. They noted the confusion of his own prejudices with the verdict of history, in minimizing Napoleon to absurdity and in his comment on the American Constitution that its most notable characteristic to modern eyes was its omission of female suffrage. But they observed in vain that what men once described as the will of God, and later as the natural course of events, in his hands became the Wellsian concept of the future as the clue and standard of judgment of all human

history; that in his pages it seemed " primordial proto-
plasm in primeval slime lay dreaming of the League of
Nations and the Socialist Superstate." It was in vain, for
as one of his great admirers said, " I am not interested in
Mr. Wells's facts, but only in his conclusions." To that
there is, of course, no answer; and if the first step to truth
be error, right or wrong, he has done much for history.

For in the widest sense he represents one aspect of the
present age, and that a great one; the " public " whence
he sprung and for whose applause he writes. With no
great knowledge and still less real thought, but filled with
what are called " ideas " — that is to say, a certain contempt for the Christian religion and the old moralities,
vague aspirations toward an earthly millennium, expressed in universal suffrage, universal peace, and universal prosperity based on community of goods, with a
blind reliance on what are known as the " marvels of
science " and invention as the salvation of mankind —
his philosophy was essentially materialistic and humani-
tarian. For such there are few mysteries or none, save
those that science is now rapidly solving; while rights have
taken the place of obligations and self-expression that of
self-denial.

Their writing holds but little of heroic elements; it has
but little greatness of spirit superior to material concerns.
It tends to put all men upon a common plane; and even
its unconventionally colloquial language is essentially
commonplace. This is no mere fancy, still less exaggeration. There is no other history where we find that favorite
caption of Hollywood, " Came " ; as Mr. Wells says of
the Congress of Vienna, " came the vague humanitarian-
ism and dreamy vanity of the Tsar Alexander; came the
shaken Hapsburgs, the resentful Hohenzollerns. . . ." No
wonder Mr. Wells was popular; he reached an audience
inaccessible even to Ferrero, and a wider one.

That audience has, in a sense, become not merely the

spectators but the characters in the drama of the new history. It has now been some three-quarters of a century since Macaulay uttered his wish for more records of great events from the standpoint of insignificant individuals. Had he lived till now, he would have had his wish more than gratified, though not, perhaps, in precisely the way he intended. For in recent years the stone rejected by the earlier builders has become the head of the corner, and the " insignificant " man has become the most, if not the only, significant figure in history at the hands of that school of writers who have appropriated to themselves emphatically the word " new."

On every hand we have a multitude of books endeavoring to depict for us not the great figures and events and movements of the past, but the way the ordinary man lived, what he did for a living, what he ate and drank and wore, how much of various commodities he produced, what he did for his amusement, and what things attracted his attention as he went his daily round. Whether it calls itself " social," or is concerned with " civilization," it has chiefly to do with what it describes as the " common man," that heir of the ages once called the " average man," one of whose incarnations Ricardo christened the " economic man," the French revolutionaries " the man and citizen " ; he whom Sinclair Lewis called " Babbitt " and the author of the morality play called " Everyman." He now replaces Caesar and Alexander and Shakespeare and George Washington as the hero of the " new " history, and the effect upon historiography is of profound importance.

It is not necessary to insist, as some have insisted, that this is merely a sympton of lowering human values. It is a phenomenon to be observed rather than condemned. Naturally one of its leading characteristics is statistics, for common men are to be evaluated only in the mass, and figures are the sole means of discovering mass characteristics. Apart from that and the virtual elimination of politics, save to those who know little or nothing of the " old " history, there is little " new " in this but the enormous enlargement of description at the expense of narration and the consequent subordination of chronology. For " social history " was known to Herodotus, as to Tacitus; Voltaire revived it for the eighteenth century; Macaulay wrote what is still regarded as its greatest chapter — not omitting even the statistics; and Green, though he omitted the statistics, put in the food and clothes and daily round. Apart from their inclusion of great figures and events, and their insistence upon narrative as well as description, they were all as " new " as the latest " new historians." In defiance of the Lamprechtian formula, as of Professor Robinson, however, some of the most recent of these writers fill their pages not merely with statistics, but with lists of names which at times descend almost to a catalogue — though of a different character from those of Milton, Dante, and Homer. Some of them tend to reduce the chronicle of human striving to its lowest common denominator; and in at least one recent volume the most common individuals seem to be the inmates of public institutions, and even they are not so common as some might wish.

This phase of historical writing has unquestionably done something for historiography by its investigation of mass phenomena and consequent discovery of new " facts." But with that service it has raised questions of much importance to historiography. It is an obvious reaction against the " great man " theory of history; yet one wonders whether even in the history of civilization or society it is, let us say, the use of electricity and the cheap motor-car by the masses, or the achievements of Mr. Edison and Mr. Ford which were the determining factors in the case. Despite the recent assertion of a lady that " what interests us now is not what the Greeks thought or wrote or did, but how they lived," one wonders whether it was what the Periclean Athenians ate and wore and traded in that made that age immortal. If so, we should find out, and, instead of the various panaceas urged upon us, we should discover new greatness for ourselves by following that simple formula. Yet it is difficult to explain St. Francis of Assisi on the principle of externality; and whether in the long evolution of the human race it is the common or the uncommon man that makes for progress, whether it is what is outside of men or what is inside of them that makes them what they are, to these problems there seemed not long ago but one answer — and that answer still seems good.

It is neither a new nor a profound observation that man is a curious creature and human nature a paradox. There is an almost invariable rule that, given any particular tendency at any given time, you will find another and totally opposite tendency making head against it. Of that there is no more striking instance than the fact that at the precise moment of the apparent triumph of mass history there should appear an account of those individuals who, in all fields of thought and action, have somehow managed to escape the oblivion of the census-taker and raise themselves into individuals. For with history laying such stress upon the common qualities of common men, the *Dictionary of American Biography* appears to commemorate the uncommon qualities of uncommon men. It is a curious phenomenon, this contrast between the chronicles of the innumerable little men and the few great, near great, or at least exceptional, individuals. For what would seem more natural than to suppose that with the triumph of the common man the uncommon man would disappear not only from society but from its interest?

There was a time when gods were still a part of literature, when Homer and Virgil, Dante and Milton, took supernatural characters for their subjects, and ruder poets found superhuman creatures for their heroes. There was a time when painters and sculptors devoted their talents to saints and angels and the Deity Himself. That time has largely passed. There was a time when the activities of kings and conquerors, then of the aristocracy, were the chief subjects of literature; when from Shakespeare to Disraeli the doings of the highest society seemed the most fitting subjects for drama and fiction. That time, too, has largely passed. More modern artists whether of pen or brush have gone lower and still lower in the social scale; some now, descending farther, to the lowest of the low. What gods and kings and heroes and nobility were once, thieves, beggars, prostitutes, gangsters and scavengers have become. Whether mankind has gained or lost by the exchange, let each of us determine for himself. Yet if the old artists depicted life in tones too high for true reality, what of the extremes on the other side? History has not, as yet, descended from the palace to the gutter for the mass of its material; it has stopped, as it were, on the sidewalk; yet even here there is a paradox again. With all its passion for the common man and his statistics, it still loves a hero and a heroine; and it still recognizes difference in quality — as the *Dictionary* proves.

Moreover, with all its interest, much of this new " social " history is merely informative rather than intellectual. Its too frequent lack of wide reading and perspective, to say nothing of a certain thoughtful and reflective quality we see in the great masters, finds small compensation in statistics, in terminology, or in occasional pontifical pronouncements of its " new," " progressive " quality. It seems to lack height and depth; it certainly lacks any sense of the great mystery of life; and too often it proves by irrefutable and irritating figures what even a little thought would render obvious. With all of its virtues, it has not learned how to handle its materials. If and when, in the fullness of time, a New Historian of the calibre of Thucydides shall arise to chronicle the triumphs and defeats of peaceful evolution, we shall have a history which, like his, may immortalize " the greatest movement that ever stirred the Hellenes, extending also to some of the barbarians, one might say even to a very large part of mankind."

But there is another problem which confuses one — that of chronology. It is voiced in the ingenuous remark of a young reader, " It is fine to read if you know some history to start with." As Heine said of the Romans, " they had time to conquer the world, for they knew their declensions to start with," so these authors doubtless know the sequence of political events which still remains the A B C and the multiplication table of historiography. But many of their readers may not be so fortunate. As another youth inelegantly remarked: " If the ' old ' history was only a skeleton, this ' new ' history seems to me only a mess of meat."

It is related to the problem of the New Fiction with its interminable "chronicles" and "sagas" and "trilogies," which, the critic observes, "any one can write, the trick is to make the ordinary lives of ordinary people interesting." For in history as in fiction there are two things to reckon with; the first is that ordinary people and ordinary events are not so interesting as extraordinary people and extraordinary events; the second is that stories need action and a plot. History is, after all, a kind of story, as its name implies; and a story demands not merely description but narration, it must have some action and some continuity; and it must have some characters.

That problem, at least, the Old History solved. It appealed to human nature. It had characters and continuity and action. It stimulated the imagination by describing struggles of force or of intelligence. Thus far

the New History has not learned that art. It is, unquestionably, an addition to our knowledge and perspective.
It has contributed to the opening of fresh fields of investigation, especially to the graduate students, avid for subjects for theses. But to tell the truth, it is not as yet very
interesting reading. Some of it, as was once said of some
of Emerson's poetry, might as well be read backward as
forward; and at least one intelligent critic has recently
complained that it is, after all, not so much history as
journalism. It may be true, as Ferrero has observed, that
our generation has lost interest in politics, that political
has been replaced by social interest. Even so, it is incum-
bent even on social historians not only to tell the story of
that conflict with characters, action, plot, and continuity,
but to recognize that politics is a social activity at least
as important as the care of the criminal and the feeble-
minded.

It is no doubt important — to take a recent volume —
for us to realize that " in Tennessee and Georgia the
value of the annual lumber output reached nearly $500,-
000," and that "North Carolina boasted of no fewer than
118 tobacco establishments with a product valued at
$2,215,000." But, put in that way, it smacks too much of
the annual surveys of the past year in the daily press,
rather than of what we once called history, assuming that
Clio is still one of the Muses and not the offspring of an
adding machine and a typewriter, whose grandparents
were census tables and statistical abstracts.

So one wonders whether, after all, there is not something to be said for chronology, and whether tables of
figures supply the lack of characters or even of institutions. One wonders, too, whether it is possible to ignore
the fact that man is not merely a social but a political
animal; whether the body social can stand upright without a constitutional skeleton or move without political
nerves or muscles. Still more, one wonders whether with-

out passion or emotion, or what some still call a soul, this body could conceivably seem alive.

To be a social historian it is not enough to have a fluent style and a prejudice against society as it is organized. It is not enough even to have an interest in " social service," statistics of production, immorality, insane asylums, sex problems, and political corruption, and a speaking acquaintance with the more obvious examples of literature, art, music, and religious expressionism. It is necessary to know some economics, as well as " sociology " ; to know something of science and invention, of industry, commerce, and finance, of mathematics and of medicine; to know something of how the world of affairs is run; to be able to explain as well as catalogue the various phenomena which produce " society." It is not easy; but until there arise " social " historians who know as much of these things as the " old " historians knew of war, politics, diplomacy, law, constitutional development, and human nature, we shall have no social history worth the paper it is written on. And since the invention of sulphite paper — itself a social phenomenon — that is not much.

These problems another school of writers have answered on the principle which is as active in human affairs as in physics, that to every action there is an equal and consequent reaction. At the very moment that " psychic " and " social " and mass history was making its way into the world, Mr. Hilaire Belloc, half French, half English, and wholly Catholic, began to turn his talents to a study of the French Revolution which took the form of biographies of Danton, Robespierre, and Marie Antoinette, with other, if lesser, contributions to that great subject. In them he both avowed and exemplified a creed or method which, as he said,

consists in an attempt to reproduce as a living thing the action of the past. It depends on a special insistence upon physical details — dress, weather, gestures, facial expression, light, colour, landscape — and a corresponding lack of emphasis on mere chronicle . . . a method of literary presentation which shall aim at vividness . . . and an elimination of reference.

If other schools aspired to rival the newspapers, his more appealing method was a challenge to fiction, adapting many of its devices to the service of history, among them character-study, suspense, and even plot. If they sought to make it news, he aspired to make it a romance. Moreover, his work has another element still more at variance from theirs. Even where it has not been strictly biographical, it has centered its interest on personality.

Again his method was not wholly new. It owed something to his predecessors, especially in France. It was indebted to the Romanticists; at times it seems to have a vague echo of the historical passages in Hugo's *Ninety-Three* — though that is doubtless a heretical remark. But in English it established what is virtually a new school. His history — or biography — had much more than scenery, costume, and atmosphere; it was psychological, philosophical, even poetical. If it seems to echo something of the influence of Carlyle — whom Mr. Belloc so frankly dislikes — it has as well no little of that painstaking investigation of historical scholarship which he so sharply criticizes. It has a certain quality of epigram, a gift of style, the blessing of imagination, and a sense of brooding mystery and tragedy of life, at total variance with the cheerful commonplaces of most " social " history. Above all, it is full of what that lacks the most — emotion. Through its pages move real men and women and events; and if he chooses to call them Danton and Robespierre and Marie Antoinette, Wattignies, and the Reign of Terror, that lies between him and his readers.

It probably would please neither man to say that the first reincarnation of his method was the work of another son of Balliol, Mr. Philip Guedalla, who, some years ago, found in the ironic tragi-comedy set on the gas-lit stage of the mid-nineteenth century the subject for a study in Bonapartism which he called *The Second Empire*. Following the Bellocian formula, even to exaggeration, allusive to the last degree, familiar, even confidential, intimate, impertinent, full of "close-ups," "cut-backs," "atmosphere," with far horizons and high adventure in the best moving-picture manner, it was not ill-adapted to its incredible subject. And, apart from its cleverness of style, it injected a new element into history, the element of wit. "The fountain of honour" of the Second Empire, he observes, "played in a steady drizzle of decorations over the public services"; "There was an agreeable spontaneity about the Revolution of 1848 which it shares with the best earthquakes"; "The appearances of Prussia in history have something of the suddenness, if not all the agility, of the bad fairy." His entertaining volume was not, of course, in any proper sense a history of the Second Empire at all; but that very statement seems somehow out of place in speaking of such a brilliant *tour de force*, and to say of it, *c'est magnifique, mais ce n'est pas l'histoire* will, naturally, have no effect on any one.

Among the many smart sayings which glitter in his pages, Mr. Guedalla once remarked that " since the war the market in personalia bounded like the rate of exchange when one has trodden on the tail of a foreign minister." As one of its numerous phenomena he might have included, though he courteously refrained, that chatty, amusing excursus erroneously called a " Life " of Queen Victoria with which, as with his preceding studies of *Eminent Victorians*, Mr. Strachey brightened his readers' lives some ten years since; following it more recently with another popular success in his *Elizabeth and Essex*. With them he introduced still other elements into historical composition. Of these the first was something of that spirit of " Now it can be told " and " Better left unsaid " so evident since the war, the calculated indiscretion meant to shock — or at least to attract the attention of book-buyers.

It was bound up with what may be called, for want of better phrase, the patronage of the past and its great figures, the adroit reduction of greatness to a normal or even sub-normal size by the enumeration of its weaknesses rather than its strength. Perhaps the best comment ever made on his technique was that of the young girl who had just read his books as part of her work in history. " I should not like to have Mr. Strachey write my biography," she wrote, " for, even if I had been a great person, I would not have seemed so when he wrote about me." It finds expression in the portrait of Florence Nightingale, not in her prime but as a crotchety, domineering women of seventy in bad health. It even makes play with that " sure-fire laugh " of vaudeville — the proximity of a Bible and a bottle of whiskey before General Gordon as he sat in Khartoum waiting for certain, imminent, and horrible death at the hands of Moslem fanatics. One hopes that Mr. Strachey may be more fortunate in his biographer's choice of period in his life in which to describe him to another generation; one even wonders to what, in Gordon's situation, he would have turned for spiritual consolation.

It was, no doubt, inevitable that we should have had a reaction against the hero-worshipping Victorians such as this. It was, perhaps, no less inevitable that it should take the form of faint — or not so faint — condescension toward those various " old gentlemen " and ladies who once determined the world's fortunes, quite wrongly for the most part as we now perceive, and without that vatic gift vouchsafed to those who know how things came out. Yet, peopled by such curious figures in old-fashioned clothes, inspired by quaint ideas, now obviously absurd, infused with odd enthusiasms, duties, and loyalties now outdated, the past has none the less one eminent quality. It enables us to appreciate more fully, if possible, our own superiority. It occupies the place in the minds of our cleverest intelligentsia which their activities will presently occupy in the minds of their successors; for the great tragedy of all youth movements is that they grow old.

But if Mr. Strachey has made it difficult to understand how the past he describes was able to accomplish such great results with such feeble tools, in his *Elizabeth and Essex* he introduced another and still more important element into history, once called " love interest," more recently " sex appeal " — a difference in phrase which marks a world of change. For such a theme what better subject than the Virgin Queen; what better foil than a noble admirer; what better motive than the way of a man with a maid which, with the way of a ship in the sea and a bird in the air and a serpent on a rock, since the prophet's time has been reckoned one of the four great mysteries of life. It has what we call " human interest," that realm of emotion which includes hate, greed, love, fear, revenge, and sentiment, all the great melodramatic qualities, but especially sex.

Combining, as they do, so many of these elements in their work, strayed revellers from the field of letters like Guedalla and Strachey have done much service to the cause of history. Their formula is simple. It consists in choosing a notable personality, reading up some history, gossip, and letters, creating " atmosphere," a " character," and " situations," with costume and scenery appropriate to the times, and clothing it with clever writing more or less relating to the theme. They have their uses. They have attracted readers incapable, naturally, of distinguishing between clever writing and good history. They have lent a gayety of coloring to Clio's formal garden; and though some still prefer old-fashioned flowers of Truth, many more who had formerly but looked over the garden wall — if even that — were tempted inside by the newer and showier blossoms.

For these historical writers have one great virtue — they are unafraid. Unlike the " scholarly " historians who write for well-informed and critical professional audiences, they do not live in fear of being detected in deviation from the provable " facts " of history; for in so far as possible they avoid those " facts." They have no scholarly reputation at stake; they have all to gain and little to lose by brilliant writing; they can afford to plunge in generalizations and speculate in epigrams; they can afford to be amusing at whatever cost. Moreover, they descend to meet their audience; they are not hampered by uncomfortable doubts. It is not fair to break these butterflies on a wheel, and it is good for even old-fashioned historians to read their books — only not as history.

That this is no harsh judgment of their entertaining work, two circumstances prove. The first is that one need only compare Sir Sidney Lee's *Victoria* with Strachey's, or Simpson's *Second Empire* with Guedalla's to perceive the difference. And the second is that when Mr. Guedalla and Mr. Strachey lost that first fine careless rapture and tried to write real history, were it not subject to the penalties of *lèse majesté*, one might observe that knowledge of the facts but served to cramp their style.

Of the great trinity which some one has observed describes the charms of Paris — *antiquité, nouveauté*, and *frivolité* — one must admit that in a day when it is possible to compile from the Book of Books the numerous examples of ancient Hebrew backsliding from a state of grace and publish them as *The Truth about the Bible*, conceptions of the past have been profoundly influenced by both novelty and frivolity. Descending from the Stracheyan formula we find a school which occupies a place in the field of biography now too often hailed as the great

" historical " writers of our time. One need but to mention the name of Emil Ludwig — whose family name was apparently Cohn — and of him who writes under the name of André Maurois, or even that of F. Hackett or E. Barrington, to say nothing of Zweig, to touch the very heart of popular appeal. Even Mr. Gamaliel Bradford in his engaging studies of souls in various stages of *déshabille* and disrepair has been identified by less critical souls, however wrongly, with this group. To that school no longer is truth merely naked — though not unadorned — but in the latest fashion of undress, the all too transparent garb of biography. There is now no longer the decent obscurity of a dead language to conceal her charms, for apt translation lends her artful aid. Nor is there safety in obscurity for what the absence of materials might conceal, the penetrating imagination of the author supplies. Clio has waited long, but never before was it so evident that the muse of history was feminine.

This sex obsession may be due, as some believe, to Freud and his pseudo-scientific preoccupation with the sex complex. It may be due, as one cynic observes, to the emergence of the eternal feminine, for whom or by whom these biographies, like the sex novels, are said to be chiefly written. It may be due to what unscientific people call " the advance of science " ; or the decline of what old-fashioned folk called " decency " or reticence. It may be due to a reaction against " Victorianism," as Restoration drama and more recent phenomena have been attributed to reaction against that villain of the modern piece, " Puritanism." It may even be due, as some have ventured to whisper, merely to the fact that a certain type of publisher finds profit in pornography, and that certain authors and readers have naturally nasty minds, which they endeavor, unsuccessfully, to conceal under agreeable adjectives like " frank " and " daring " and " realistic." Whatever the cause, the thing is with us; and since it is improbable that the kind of biography described by an irreverent youth as "an account of Talleyrand and his girl friends" will permanently satisfy the demand for truthful or even entertaining pictures of the past, before the revulsion toward decency sets in, let us consider this phenomenon.

Its most appealing quality is sex; and one might think that these authors, reversing Pope's dictum, had determined that the proper study of mankind was woman. They remind one of Oscar Wilde's once famous epigram about the Bible, which, as he said, like all books of life, begins with a man and a woman in a garden and ends in Revelations. But that is not their only quality. There are two others of even more importance. The first is that which, for politeness' sake, we call " historical imagination," a debased species of the Bellocian genus which takes the form of describing the mental, and especially the emotional, processes of any given character at a given time. It is not unlike that Sunday-school question, " What do you suppose Melchizedek thought on this occasion? " It is not limited by the lack of evidence; for what Victor Hugo called " the penetration of genius," and others call by harsher names, more than supplies that lack.

It may, of course, be true. But, to take one instance, the most hardened historical imagination balks at Ludwig's picture of Napoleon sitting in his tent after the all but disastrous day of Aspern-Essling, reflecting on how pleasant it would be to have the soothing presence of the Countess Walewska at his side. Severely checked for the first time in his life, five hundred miles from Paris, all but cut off from his supports, with a powerful and victorious Austrian army before him, in the bitterness of defeat he may have spent his time in dreams of the attractive Polish lady, yet one cannot suppress the suspicion that his real thoughts were otherwise. It scarce beseems a mere student of history to question such a master of this variety of biography as Ludwig, but those who saw Napoleon on that evening at Ebersdorf reported him as overwhelmed by the disaster, and the letters which he wrote at that crisis are not to the Countess but to Marshal Davout and General Daru, and so far from being about love are acutely concerned with the collapse of a bridge and the necessity for reinforcements and supplies.

But the real problem raised by this method is not the mere truth or falsehood of the pictures thus conjured from the fervid imaginations of biographers. It is, in fact, two-fold. It is, in the first place, what was once called the " personal equation," that former bugbear of the scientists. Before the days of relativity, the " subjective " attitude was the villain, the " objective " the hero of the piece. Now we toy with the theory that truth is only relative. That may be true, but, if we push even relativity to its logical conclusion, only relatively true.

Unquestionably the most recent school of history finds excuse or defence in this convenient doctrine of the relative. It is a comforting thought to one who knows no dates and no geography to read in the pages of one of these books that " time and space fade into subjective conceptions." That is, as any teacher knows, the commonest phenomenon on examination papers. Their writers often hope, as well, that in the words of an American historical author of the newer school, their " work is to be judged . . . not by mere accuracy in detail but by the excellence of the general structure and by the pleasure it gives to the reader to whom it is directed." That is also true of the prospectuses of worthless mining shares. For however true in metaphysics, in the practical affairs of practical human life there seems what our youth calls " a catch " in this. One may say, to paraphrase the poet, " If it be not true to me, What care I how true it be? " But 1492, however relative it may be, and however arbitrary, is, after all, as little subjective, let us say, as the location of Paris in France instead of, as one subjective student once conceived, in mid-Siberia. As the satirist says:

> Nature and Nature's Laws lay veiled in night,
> God said " let Newton be," and all was light.
> It could not last.   The devil shouting " Ho!
> Let Einstein be! " restored the status quo.

But that does not eliminate chronology from history, nor statistics from financial operations, as yet; and when it does, we shall no longer care for either finance or history.

It is a familiar saying [Professor Dewey has written recently] that the great intellectual work of the nineteenth century was the discovery of history. The idea of evolution was an extension of its discovery of history, evolution but stretching history to its limit of elasticity. As we notice the shift of emphasis and interest which is now going on, we may question whether the familiar saying is more than a half-truth. Would it not be nearer to the truth to say that the nineteenth century discovered *past* history? Since what is characteristic of the present time is speculation about the future, perhaps it will be the task of the twentieth century to discover *future* history.

To such a pass have the great talents of Einstein brought us, that not only has history been " stretched to the limit of its elasticity " — in its definition at least — but, if Professor Dewey's prophetic definition finds favor, and men capable of meeting it are found, we shall have to develop a new technique of reading. We shall, perhaps, be forced to emulate the New Woman, of whom the poet has told us:

> There was a young woman named Bright,
> Who could travel much faster than light.
>     She went walking one day
>     In a relative way
> And came back on the previous night.

It was said long ago by a cynical reviewer in another field, " This volume, however entertaining, adds little that is new to our ignorance of God." Yet even as we write, our relative faith in relativity is shaken to the core not only by the alleged discovery of a new planet outside of the solar system which had begun to revolve around Einstein instead of Newton, but by the rapid revolutions reported in Einstein's opinions themselves. If relativity is not even relatively true, and if eager souls like the young lady who abandoned history for " social sciences " because, as she declared, she " couldn't bear to be bound down by facts " have their last hope that nothing is true destroyed, it may be, conceivably, that we shall have to go back to objective facts again.

Yet there remains another element. Let us accept, for purposes of the argument, the subjectivity of the new school; let us admit that, like the French critic, they write not of the great but of themselves as affected by it. Accepting that, we have a right to ask that they be great enough to gauge the greatness of those of whom they write. If biography should not be hero-worship, still less should it be merely the revenge of lesser upon greater minds. We have a right to ask that biographers shall not reduce their subjects to their own levels of intelligence or morality. What made Thucydides and Gibbon great historians, what made Plutarch and Morley great biographers, is that they had ability to comprehend the qualities of their subjects. The lack of this is what makes so many of these modern biographies so poor. Apart from all their sex nonsense and their ridiculous reconstruction of their characters' psychology, granted that they know no history, that they have even no ideas of any consequence, many of them, with all their literary cleverness and their great acclaim, raise serious question as to whether these authors quite realized who and what their heroes really were. It is quite possible to read M. Maurois's *Ariel* without discovering from it that Shelley was a great poet. It is hard to find from his volume on Pepys

that its subject was more than the author of a lively diary
with improper passages, who had some amorous adventures — that he was, in fact, the greatest Secretary
of the Admiralty England ever knew, who happened for
some years to keep a diary. If we are to have subjective
history and biography — and without a certain quality of
subjectivity there is no work of art — we have a right to
ask that the result bear more resemblance to its subject
than to the artist himself; we have a right to ask that the
author do not put on a mask and play that he is Napoleon
or Washington or Lincoln. It is not enough to don the
lion's skin; as Aesop pointed out some centuries ago, it is
essential at least to make a noise like a lion.

How is it, then, the public is deceived into believing
these are real lions? There are a score of answers all more
or less depressing. Some say it lies in the decline of morals
and intelligence; some that it is a passing fashion of the
times; some that it is innate natural depravity now evident through the collapse of decent inhibitions; some that
it is a phase of mass psychology influenced by ingenious
methods of what is called " the breaking down of sales
resistance " through book-clubs and similar devices in
the advertising field. Part of the answer undoubtedly lies
in the fact that these are entertaining books, far more
amusing than any that scholars write; they are good
journalism in the current vein. Part of it lies, as has often
been said, in the fact that though there are fully as many
intelligent individuals to-day as ever, and probably far
more, the spread of elementary education and the pressure of life have combined to produce a reading public
of almost incredible superficiality. Part of it lies, no
doubt, in that there are so few lions nowadays we have
forgotten what real ones should be like.

The enormous popularity of this sort of writing is, in
fact, some clue to ourselves. It was imagined by those
who sponsored universal education — it is still believed

— that merely by teaching men and women to read and write there would be released a mass of latent ability and intelligence previously concealed by illiteracy; that a development in taste and thought would follow of itself and the whole level of mentality would rise. It was of the same nature as the earlier belief that the mere gift of the franchise would automatically produce intelligent and conscientious citizens. In some measure that took place in each case; but as we know from our experience, too often it merely got those masses what they wanted instead of making them want something better. It did not make them, of necessity, desirous of reading the great works of literature or choosing better and still better men in government. What happened in a multitude of instances was that the publishers, like the producers of plays and politicians, gave the public what it seemed to want; and though there was, perhaps, an increase in printing literary classics, especially for the schools whose pupils could not easily help themselves, there was a vastly greater increase in that which by no stretch of the imagination could be regarded as either classical or literary. Letters were adapted to a new audience; and, however much the masses were elevated, it was inevitable that the average of literary production was depressed. It is true, of course, as our friends of the press declare, that newspapers have contributed enormously to the elevation of the mass. But there is something appalling in the thought that yellow journalism and the tabloid press have actually levelled up their readers.

It may be, as some deep-despairing souls maintain, that we perceive the triumph of the moron in affairs, and that with that triumph civilization must go down. It may be, as an exultant sports-writer says, that, after all, whatever else concerns men, " the heavy-weight championship of the world is the chief object of human interest from New York to Shanghai." It may be that in letters, as in politics, universal education and suffrage have merely levelled down, and that the low average governs in both fields. But it may be, as well, that it is too soon to tell; that not until these millions have been trained for generations, as the old reading public was, can the result of this greatest of all social experiments be known.

For there is hope. It was the ambition of both Gibbon and Macaulay — and doubtless many other historians — that their volumes should compete for popularity with fiction. That, they and others like J. R. Green achieved; and even now we have " epics " and histories of " civilization " which in their more immediate — and even in their almost equally ephemeral — popularity attain that great result. But in comparison with their great predecessors these newer historians reveal one quality which makes one hesitate. It is, to put it bluntly, their relative superficiality. " Language," as Talleyrand observed, " was invented to conceal thought," but it serves other no less useful economies — among them that of historical research. It is not enough to have an acquaintance with secondary books and a general idea of how in the main things went, to write sound popular history, which is so greatly needed, and so rare. Not even fluent style, nor impressive sales, nor new " ideas," nor even " points of view," quite " bridge the gap which only knowledge fills." Yet their success — however ephemeral — reveals a great demand for history; and that, at least, offers encouragement to those who now despair of the future of sound learning and sound style.

They have, indeed, one striking quality — they require a minimum of intellectual effort on the part of the reader. One may turn from the newspaper to them with no sense of transition, such as he has in exchanging the news columns for the writings of the great historians. He is in the same world, he finds familiar words and still more familiar ideas, he feels no sense of strain. So he reads them. As Emerson observed, "We descend to meet" — and this may be another index of the progress of society toward its unknown goal.

There is one aspect of the great problem which may give some cheer to even these sad souls, though it lies beyond their usual horizon. It might seem that, having passed from the realms of intelligence to those of the " intelligentsia," from scholarship to scandal, from books of the month to text-books for the schools, the market for history and its by-products was exhausted. But this is far from true; for history has a wider audience than any of these; and if " social " history is " new " and *chroniques scandaleuses* newer, this may be reckoned the newest history. It is expressed not in books but in our periodical literature.

Two generations since, no " popular " magazine but had historical articles, well-written, well-informed. That great tradition still maintains itself in European journals like the *Revue des Deux Mondes* and the English quarterlies; elsewhere, especially in America, it is extinct. No editor now would print them; he would say that public taste for all that sort of thing was gone, and it is highly improbable that Macaulay's essays, let us say, could find a place in an American periodical — if for no other reason, because they are too long. For, among its other interesting results, the " progress of civilization " has reduced what psychologists call the " limit of attention " almost to zero. As folios and quartos have declined to octavos and duodecimos, as sermons have shrunk from hours to minutes, articles have shrunk to paragraphs, and paragraphs to sentences, and sentences to slogans as we lose time either to read or think.

Yet if the interest in history of editors and readers of those magazines has declined, or gone into the " popular " biographies, historical work has found another and a greater audience. In the most characteristic and widely read of American periodicals, amid its wealth of fiction and its still more costly advertising may be found successors of those once popular historical articles. They deal, indeed, with reminiscence rather than with earlier periods; but they are often much more than reminiscence. In those same pages, too, the accomplished pen and imagination of Mr. Austin have restored for us, under the thin disguise of fiction, pictures of the past from caveman to Lenin more nearly accurate in spirit and in fact than much that passes as " true " history or biography in the form of books.

Nor is this all; for history in the sense of representation of the past to the present has found even wider audience than this, in the illimitable pages of the daily press. Amid its hints for health and beauty, cooking, sports, and crime, from week to week, or even from day to day, often on that editorial page which is itself a relic of past greatness, beside the labors of the humorous columnist and letters from readers, there is often a bit of history. Sometimes as a " column," not seldom as an editorial; sometimes by question and answer, sometimes by " picture story " of a character, an event, or a building of historic interest, the history debarred from popular magazines here finds revenge.

But this is not the end. More recently still it has taken another form appealing to an audience all but impervious to the printed word; for it finds place among the " comic strips." There, in a series of little sketches with explanatory text, it spreads the knowledge of the past in fashions inconceivable even a generation since. And more; the story goes that when the author of one of these serials proposed — or had proposed to him — that they should be abandoned, such protest arose that it was necessary to go on with them.

Nor is even this the end of Clio's wanderings which now take her into stranger places than Ulysses ever knew.

For on the packages of one of America's most characteristic and most widely used products, a "breakfast food" there now appears a series of pictures and descriptive text, "cut outs" of the adventurers who pushed forward the frontiers of America, Coronado, de Soto, Daniel Boone and the rest, together with pictures of animals and scenes appropriate to their adventures, and an account of their exploits. It would seem that the force of print could no farther go, yet even this may not be the end.

Finally, keeping touch with science and invention, history has taken its place in the moving-picture industry; not merely in the form most natural to that art — historical romance. An American university has set itself to reproduce the past and bring by what is called " visual education " some knowledge of that past in truer form than it reveals itself to the fancy of moving-picture magnates. More recently it has penetrated the intelligence of those directors of taste that "there may be something in this history people talk about " — to quote a remark attributed to one of them. The results have been distinctly encouraging to the historical profession. For not only has it been entertained by some admirable pictures, but there has been opened a new field for ambitious scholars, that of historical advisers to the moving-picture industry, with consequent rewards beyond the dreams, of simple scholarship. As yet, despite its efforts, history has not found an adequate technique to cope with competition from jazz orchestras and bedtime stories to the radio audiences; but that will doubtless come in time — it is, in fact, coming, and with it talking pictures of historical lectures. When these are all combined, as doubtless they will be, by television in the humblest home, the chain of scholar to consumer will be finally complete. All these, contemptuous scholars will declare, are not " history " at all; yet if " history " is the chronicle of the past, however expressed, they must be reckoned with in our evaluation of its present aspects fully as much as the work of Ludwig or of Wells.

This development, indeed, raises a great question; for this "history" is not in form or content that which now appeals to the great "reading public" of the canalized book-clubs and their devoted guides. What, then, is happening? Are the "plain people" of the newspaper getting out of touch with those who "keep abreast of the great intellectual movement of our time," expressed in sex novels and biographies? Is there — *absit omen* — such a gulf between newspaper readers and intelligentsia; can it be possible that the editors and publishers are wrong; or that the authors of the feature stories and the strips are truer devotees of real history than those who write the "human interest" histories? Has the childish desire for *nouveauté* and *frivolité* overpowered the natural human interest in *antiquité* among our intellectuals, and driven the rest of us to the newspapers for our history, as men have turned from the welter of sex novels and the eternal boring triangle of feminized fiction to the detective story for relief? Or have these various phenomena merely revealed what has always been true, that many men have many minds, and women most of all?

What, then, is the great moral of it all; and what may we expect of the next age of history? It is apparent that, for the time being, at least, the public has substituted for its earlier interest in politics an interest in what it calls "society" ; that its chief concern for the moment seems to be with prehistory and so-called "contemporary" history, so that the ages between the sabre-toothed tiger and Clemenceau are relatively neglected, save for their more romantic aspects. Despite its interest in the common man, it still retains its curiosity in personality, too often in the less eminent qualities of humanity. Believing in equality, it is none the less enormously concerned in both super- and sub-normal individuals.

With little interest in chronology and less in thoughtful processes, it desires what it calls " ideas," too often vague speculations without factual premises, logical processes, or rational conclusions. Not unlike the men of Athens, as described by Paul, who " spent their time in nothing else, but to tell or to hear some new thing," it is too often hypnotized by the mere sound of the word " new " which has become an adjective of quality, rather than of time. It is avid for information, however miscellaneous; but it tends to shrink from depth of thought and elevation of spirit, preferring that cheerful and entertaining commonplace described by publishers and reviewers as a " brilliant style." It loves statistics, especially of that larger sort which seem to provide some inner consolation to so many minds, and serve as a substitute for thought. It dislikes definitions; and it is essentially uncritical. Its limit of attention, without the use of the stimulating devices of fiction or journalism, is brief and growing briefer as the pressure of time and labor-saving devices grows heavier year by year. Finally, it tends to shun all questions of difference in race, religion, degree of civilization, intelligence, character, and color, all save those of sex. None the less, if we may judge by the output of the publishers, it is interested in what it is assured is history, and more especially in biography. And when — and if — the world works through the influence of the more romantic characteristics of a journalistic age, it holds out great hopes for a real " historically minded " public.

This is, of course, an optimistic or a pessimistic view, depending on one's conception of what history and our future civilization should be like. It has been said of the now popular histories that, admitting they disregard the old canons, that they are neither objective, judicial, nor well-documented, they " will be *read* when the standard histories will only be *referred to*." That dictum one may question, however timidly; for already some of the vogue of the most recent historical journalists is passing or already past. Though the " standard " histories can, of course, never attain such great, if evanescent, popularity as these " best sellers," the chances seem to be that they will not only be referred to but even read when these clever books are forgotten — for even Herodotus and Thucydides are still printed, and presumably read, though apparently not by the newer historians, who no longer have the time.

What, then, of the next step in history? In view of the developments of the past quarter of a century what may we expect of the new Thucydides when — and if — he arises? He must, of course, know sociology first of all — whatever form that shifting science takes by then. He should know economics and even politics, with all the sciences. He should be chiefly concerned with the masses, yet be able to infuse his chronicle of those masses with vivid personalities, though with no hint of their possible superiority to their fellow-men, in character or ability. He must have wit, humor, and a lively style; though whether it shall be the clear intelligence of Sorel, or the muddy vulgarisms of too many so-called " brilliant " writers nowadays, must be, as old New England used to say, " according to conscience." He must be able to appeal to almost any one who can read; and his book must obviously be crowded with pictures for those who by that time, through long and intensive study of the illustrated press and the moving pictures, will be trained to receive knowledge through visual rather than mental images. His story, however entertaining, must be in simple form, and make as little tax as possible on the continuous attention of his audience.

It must, of course, be " true." It must combine mass interest with dramatic quality. For wide success his book must be adaptable to school use, whether as " text-book " or " collateral reading " ; and it would be better if it

could be " filmed," perhaps still better if it could be
" put on the air." It must, of course, be international,
non-sectarian and non-controversial, with nothing to
offend the tenderest sensibilities of any race, color, belief,
sex, or previous condition of servitude. Finally, it must
be widely and continuously advertised, so that the public
may have before it constantly the fact that it is a great
and permanent necessity in every home.

To this end the great foundations and book-clubs
should combine to produce and to distribute this great
history and keep it up to date. And, as we have advanced
beyond the individual capacity to do anything on a large
scale, the new historian must, of course, be not a single
person but a carefully organized corporation. It must,
equally of course, have its divisions or departments of
scholarship, style, wit and humor, statistics, an art department, educational, sociological, and scientific bu-
reaus, and a " publicity " division.

Given such qualities and such agencies, it is obvious
that the historical problem will be settled once for all.
The rest may well be " scrapped," and this great work,
continued year by year, become the single, " standard "
account of human history, with spare parts obtainable at
any service station and fixed rates of exchange for new
models year by year. Thus standardized and serviced,
with a corps of editorial engineers, a great production
plant and an army of distributors and service men, this
history for all will naturally contribute to a bigger and
better world in ways as yet scarcely conceivable to us now
on the threshold of this great development.

Yet this — though this is all the present can endure —
is not half the tale. Despite all the phenomena of new,
newer, and newest history, never before were there so
many scholars of the old-fashioned sort at work; never
such breadth and depth of investigation; never such
masses of publication; never so many and such active

organizations enlisted in the cause. The field has widened and the crops have been diversified; but "old-fashioned" history goes on comparatively undisturbed. While it is apparent that another " movement " is on the way and that we may expect from it a new " interpretation " of the past, that this will supersede the historiography based on principles as old as the Greeks is too much to expect. Too much emphasis must not be placed on it as a sign that the ancient tradition will be overthrown, or that our general view of the past will be revolutionized. There will be much rediscovery and much restatement, much of what has been called " the startling discovery of the perfectly obvious." Our knowledge may be broadened if not much deepened. But history, like the life which it portrays, is a dynamic, not a static force, which means that it will not stop and begin again, but go on. For one may find new facts; one may alter one's opinion of the facts; but one can not make new facts, or distort the old ones, or ignore them, and remain a true historian.

One of the younger school, bringing his volume of " new history " to a close, remarks almost pathetically that, despite its wealth of statistics, its conclusions are " strangely like that of very old-fashioned history indeed." The reason is obvious. It is that there were heroes before Agamemnon. The oration which Thucydides puts in the mouth of Pericles still gives the most vivid picture of Athens in its social aspects, despite its lack of statistics. The best chapter on social history yet written is in Macaulay; and in his work, as in that of some men of still older fashion, you may find all the qualities, even humor, but excluding sex and columns of figures, of the most recent history — and some of us could get along with much less of either.

And you may find in them, as well, what is so sadly lacking in so many of these later works — thought and style. Moreover, there is hope. From time to time

# INDEX

# INDEX